HERBERT LOCKYER'S
MAJOR THEMES OF
THE NEW TESTAMENT

HERBERT LOCKYER'S

MAJOR THEMES OF THE NEW TESTAMENT

WHITAKER
HOUSE

Publisher's Note:

Certain words and phrases in Scripture have been printed in boldface type for emphasis by the author. However, the content of the verses remains unchanged.

Unless otherwise indicated, all Scripture quotations are taken from the King James Version of the Holy Bible. Scripture quotations marked (ASV) are taken from the American Standard Edition of the Revised Version of the Holy Bible. Scripture quotation marked (MOFFATT) is taken from *The Bible: James Moffatt Translation*, © 1922, 1924, 1925, 1926, 1935 by HarperCollins San Francisco; © 1950, 1952, 1953, 1954 by James A. R. Moffatt. Scripture quotations marked (PHILLIPS) are taken from *The New Testament in Modern English*, © 1958, 1959, 1960, 1972 by J. B. Phillips, and © 1947, 1952, 1955, 1957, by The Macmillan Company. Scripture quotations marked (RSV) are taken from the *Revised Standard Version of the Bible*, © 1946, 1952, 1971 by the Division of Christian Education of the National Council of Churches of Christ in the U.S.A. Used by permission. All rights reserved. Scripture quotation marked (WEY) is taken from *The New Testament in Modern Speech: An Idiomatic Translation into Everyday English from the Text of "The Resultant Greek Testament"* by R. F. (Richard Francis) Weymouth.

HERBERT LOCKYER'S MAJOR THEMES OF THE NEW TESTAMENT

(Previously published as part of *41 Major Bible Themes Simply Explained* and as *Selected Scripture Summaries: From the New Testament*, volume 2)

ISBN: 978-1-60374-967-1
eBook ISBN: 978-1-60374-251-1
Printed in the United States of America
© 1975, 1997, 2014 by Ardis A. Lockyer

Whitaker House
1030 Hunt Valley Circle
New Kensington, PA 15068
www.whitakerhouse.com

Library of Congress Cataloging-in-Publication Data (Pending)

1 2 3 4 5 6 7 8 9 10 11   ᦜ   21 20 19 18 17 16 15 14

CONTENTS

THEME 1

THE REPUTATION OF CHRIST

The Bible is a book of questions, some of which are asked but not answered, like the solemn one that should be asked in more sermons: *"How shall we escape, if we neglect so great salvation"* (Hebrews 2:3)? The majority of the questions asked are answered in some part or other of the sacred Volume.

The First Question in the Bible Is from Satan to Man About God

"Yea, hath God said, Ye shall not eat of every tree of the garden?" (Genesis 3:1). Satan became Satan by questioning the authority of God, and since the creation of man, he has sought to sow the seed of doubt in the human mind. But this question is answered in the declaration of the character of God, who *"cannot lie"* (Titus 1:2). What God said in the garden to Adam and Eve, He meant, and, true to His word, condemnation overtook those who listened to Satan's word of doubt.

The Second Question Is from God to Man About Sin

Conscious that they had treated God as one capable of lying, our first parents tried to hide from Him. Doubt led to desertion, and so there came the question, *"Adam...where art thou?"* (Genesis 3:9). Now a sinner, Adam required a Savior, and so *"Where art thou?"* leads to *"Where is the lamb...?"* (Genesis 22:7). When made conscious of his guilt before a thrice holy God, the sinner hears the voice calling, "Where art thou?" and, upon finding out where he is, he cries, "Where is He—the Lamb who is able to bear away my sin?" (See Matthew 2:2; John 1:29.)

The Third Question Is from God to Man About His Fellow Man

The firstborn of the world's sinners became the world's first murderer. This brings us to God's question to Cain, *"Where is Abel thy brother?"* (Genesis 4:9). Conscience-stricken, Cain shirked the divine question by asking, *"Am I my brother's keeper?"* (Genesis 4:9). Our Lord answered this question when He said, *"Thou shalt love thy neighbor as thyself"* (Matthew 22:39).

The Fourth (and Most Pertinent) Question Is from Christ to Man About Himself

The Pharisees had asked Christ, *"What thinkest thou?"* (Matthew 22:17), and He played their game by asking, *"What think ye of Christ?"* (Matthew 22:42). It is no wonder we read that, from that day forth, they asked no more questions! (See Matthew 22:46.)

We are all agreed on the point that it is easier to ask questions than to answer them, but the question we are to consider has been fully answered. We learn much in life by asking questions, and this greatest of all questions has much to teach us. All the pressing questions and problems of today are secondary to the pointed question, *"What think ye of Christ?"* Answer this, and you will find the answers to other questions. It will be noted that Jesus asked, *"What **think** ye of Christ?"* He respects the power of the mind He gave people to face and answer questions. His appeal is not merely to people's emotions. This is why His reputation stands the closest scrutiny and minutest inspection of the clearest and cleverest mind. Let us discover how the New Testament faces this question.

THE ANSWER OF HEAVEN

The best way to arrive at a right estimation of the character of a person is to approach it from every angle, discovering what that person's family, friends, and foes think, and comparing those answers with our own personal observations of the one in question. This saves us from the one-sided opinion, or bias, we sometimes are guilty of using in assessing character. In our consideration of Christ, therefore, let us ask both those who loved Him and those who hated Him what they thought of His character and claims.

God the Father

Reverently, we want to ask what the Father thought of His Son. Usually in a family, the father's thought of his child is the highest and best. Further, a father sees what the outside world rarely discerns, namely, the real person within his offspring. Parents may be somewhat biased and overlook their child's faults, for as they say, "love is blind." But with God the Father, it is different, for He has perfect justice as well as perfect love. Had there been any flaw in the character of His Son in a past eternity, He would have deposed Him as He did Lucifer, who perhaps was next to Christ in honor and dignity before he was cast out of heaven and became Satan.

Shall we ask the Father, then, "What think ye of Christ?" Such a question was answered when Jesus commenced His public ministry after living for thirty years as Mary's firstborn Son: "This is my beloved Son, in whom I am well pleased" (Matthew 3:17). Could an answer be more explicit than that?

Before time commenced, Christ was His Father's constant delight (see Proverbs 8:30), and throughout His earthly sojourn, His Father found perfect satisfaction in the Son's ways, works, and words. He always sought to do those things that pleased His Father, and thus He gave His Father pleasure. This is why we must hear Him, seeing as He was God's perfect Man and man's perfect God.

God the Spirit

God the Spirit is the author of Scripture, and, therefore, He is ultimately responsible for everything holy, including that which men recorded of the Lord Jesus Christ. He was also closely identified with Him in the days of His flesh. What did the Holy Spirit think of Christ? At Pentecost, *"the Spirit gave* [the disciples] *utterance"* (Acts 2:4), and what they uttered about Christ was divinely inspired: *"Hear these words; Jesus of Nazareth, a man approved of God among you by miracles and wonders and signs"* (Acts 2:22). Then came the Spirit-prompted declaration, *"God hath made this same Jesus, whom ye have crucified, both Lord and Christ"* (Acts 2:36). From Jesus' own teaching, we learn how the Holy Spirit loves to glorify the Lord, testify of Him, and unfold to saints the truth concerning Him. (See John 14–16.)

Can we say that we have made Him our *"Lord and Christ"*? When He has the lordship of every part of our lives, all questioning about Him ceases. Love obeys and does not ask questions. Once questions regarding His lordship were answered, we read that *"no man was able to answer him a word, neither durst any man from that day forth ask him any more questions"* (Matthew 22:46).

God the Son

To ask an ordinary person what he thinks of himself might produce an answer of self-adulation and reservation of any faults in his character. Christ asked others what they thought of Him, but in all humility, we can ask the question, "What did You think of Yourself, O Christ?" The answer is given in His august claims. He never thought of Himself more highly than He ought; neither was there any trace of self-assumption in His estimation of Himself, as there may be in us when we tell others what we think about ourselves. When a man thinks himself to be something when he is nothing, he is a fool, deceiving himself.

But with God's beloved Son, it was totally different, for He was all He claimed to be. David Strauss said of Him that He had "a conscience unclouded by the memory of any sins," and this was His own estimation of His character: *"The prince of this world cometh, and hath nothing in me"* (John 14:30) and, *"Which of you convinceth me of sin?"* (John 8:46). It was because He was holy, harmless, undefiled, and separate from sinners that His death *for* sinners is so efficacious. Had there been the least stain upon His character, He would have forfeited the right to die as the Savior from sin. Utterly devoted to the will and work of His Father, He could declare without fear of contradiction, *"I do always those things that please him"* (John 8:29). He, more than the best man who ever breathed, is the "selfless man and stainless gentleman."[1] Thomas Dekker, of the sixteenth century, said of Him,

> The best of men
> That e'er wore earth about him, was a sufferer,
> A soft, meek, patient, humble, tranquil spirit,
> The first true gentleman that ever breath'd.[2]

The Angelic Host

Having beheld the glory of their Lord from the eternal past, the angels surely knew how to value Him rightly, and thus we are right to ask them what they think of Him who, for our redemption, was made a little lower than the angels. The Scriptures abound with angelic praises for the one who laid aside His robe of eternal glory and was made in the likeness of sinful flesh. It was an angel who said, *"Thou shalt call his name Jesus: for he shall save his people from their sins"* (Matthew 1:21). It was an angel who announced, *"Unto you is born…a Saviour which is Christ the Lord"* (Luke 2:11). It was an angel who cried to another, *"Holy, holy, holy, is the LORD of hosts: the whole earth is full of his glory"* (Isaiah 6:3). It was an angel who proclaimed with a loud voice, *"Worthy is the Lamb that was slain to receive power, and riches, and wisdom, and strength, and honour, and glory, and blessing"* (Revelation 5:12).

> Angels, help us to adore Him;
> Ye behold Him face to face.[3]

---

1. Tennyson, *Idylls of the King.*
2. Thomas Dekker, *The Honest Whore, Part 1*, in collaboration with Thomas Middleton (1604), act 1, scene 2.
3. Henry F. Lyte, "Praise, My Soul, the King of Heaven," 1834.

Among the angels, the Lamb has all the glory, for they are ceaseless in their praise of Him who is in heaven as the glorified Son of Man and who is now higher than the angels. Having never sinned, the angelic hosts require no redemption. Therefore, although they magnify Him for all He accomplished as the Lamb for our salvation, they cannot praise Him in the same way sinners can—who were emancipated from the thralldom of sin by His sacrifice.

The Glorified

By this vast host we mean those who, while on earth, repented of their sin and received Jesus as their Savior, and who are now, according to His desire, with Him in glory. (See John 17:24.) If they could come back to earth, what a testimony they would give as to the wonders of their glorified Lord! Having seen the King in His beauty, they would confess that, while on earth, they were not told the half of all His might and majesty.

Yet John tells us what the ravished hearts of all those who form the triumphant church in glory think of Christ: *"Thou art worthy, O Lord, to receive glory and honour and power"* (Revelation 4:11). *"Thou wast slain, and hast redeemed us to God"* (Revelation 5:9). *"Blessing, and honour, and glory, and power, be unto him that sitteth upon the throne"* (Revelation 5:13).

Thus, all heaven is emphatic in its answer to the question, *"What think ye of Christ?"* They see His face and gaze upon His wounds and behold Him as the Father's constant joy. He is the center of all attraction, the constant admiration of seraphim and cherubim, and the object of the ceaseless adoration of angels. Not until we see Him as He is will we be able to praise Him as we ought. We can, however, prepare for such a glorious sphere by living for His honor as we await our transition.

> 'Tis the Church triumphant singing
> Worthy the Lamb;
> Heav'n throughout with praises ringing,
> Worthy the Lamb.
> Thrones and pow'rs before Him bending,
> Odors sweet with voice ascending

Swell the chorus never ending,
Worthy the Lamb.[4]

THE ANSWER OF HELL

Very often our foes can give as true a verdict of our reputation as our friends. Because of all He was as the One who had no sin and who hated all that was alien to His holy mind and will, Jesus had many foes. Shall we ask, then, all the dark and devilish inhabitants of hell the same question, *"What think ye of Christ?"*

Ask the Devil

It has been suggested that it was the devil's jealousy of Christ in the past eternity that made Lucifer, as he was then known, the devil he became. Doubtless he knew all about the plan of redemption, conceived by the Father and His Son, and gave himself to the destruction of such a plan. Because he was close to Christ before time began, the devil witnessed His perfect rectitude and knew Him to be the well-beloved Son in whom the Father was pleased. After his fall, the fall of man that he was responsible for, and the announcement of the coming of Christ as the seed of the woman, the devil set about in every possible way to thwart the appearance of Christ as the Savior of the world. When his plans failed, the devil sought in many ways to destroy Christ before His death on the cross, which was to be God's remedy for sin.

Cognizant of our Lord's inherent holiness, the devil strove to make Him sin, hence the temptations in the wilderness. Had you asked him what he thought of Christ after that fierce conflict, he would have said, "He is different from sinners. He does not yield to temptation. He is the spotless Lord." When Peter tried to dissuade the Master from going to the cross, He said to him, *"Get thee behind me, Satan"* (Matthew 16:23). He did not reply directly to Peter, but spoke to the subtle one who had prompted Peter to urge his Lord to take an easier way than the way of His cross. Reluctantly, the devil must have recognized that Christ was beyond his power to destroy His character and purpose.

---

4. John Kent, "'Tis the Church Triumphant Singing," 1803.

Ask the Demons

The myriads of demons, who had once been angels but rebelled with the devil and left their first estate, know all about Christ's preexistence. They possess full knowledge of all that He was and all that He became at His incarnation, and the Gospels recall His encounters with these denizens of hell. Dare we ask them the question, *"What think ye of Christ?"* The Master, we read, *"suffered not the demons to speak, because they knew him"* (Mark 1:34). But one demon did speak when dealt with by the Lord, *"I know Thee who thou art, the Holy One of God"* (Mark 1:24). Some professed theologians cannot acknowledge His deity as that demon did! James had in mind the demoniac estimation of the authority and power of Christ when he wrote, *"The devils also believe, and tremble"* (James 2:19). But while the satanic host may tremble at the thought of Him, because they know all about Him, very few among men tremble as they remember Him. Can it be that sinners do not fear God as they should because the pulpit has failed to present Him in all His justice and hatred of sin, as well as in all His love and mercy?

Ask the Pharisees

We put these constant foes of Christ under this section because He called them children of the devil. (See John 8:37–44.) In their antagonism of His claims, these religious hypocrites were inspired by the devil, hence our Lord's scathing denunciation of them as his puppets. Yet, strange as it seems, these Pharisees gave utterance to some of the sweetest truths concerning His grace, love, and wisdom. What did they think of Christ? They uttered a blessed truth about Him when they said, *"This man receiveth sinners"* (Luke 15:2). How hopeless we would have been had He not! Then was given this Pharisaic estimation, *"Master, we know that thou art true, and teachest the way of God in truth, neither carest thou for any man: for thou regardest not the person of men"* (Matthew 22:16). What a remarkable confession this was! Those wily Pharisees certainly knew that Jesus did not care a hoot for their opinion of Him. Confounded by His wisdom, we read that *"when they had heard these words, they marvelled, and left him, and went their way"* (Matthew 22:22).

Ask the Lost in Hell

It might be deemed impossible to glean what the doomed in perdition think of Christ. Yet He gives us a glimpse of their attitude toward Him. In answer to the questions of the Pharisees, He related the episode of the rich man and Lazarus and indicated, in this dramatic portrayal of life beyond the grave, that those who are in hell are now conscious, not only of their eternal loss, but also of the saving power of Jesus that they heard all about while on earth. (See Luke 16:19–31.) Tormented in the flame of the remembrance of slighted opportunities, they recognize Christ's power as the risen One. *"If one went unto them from the dead, they will repent"* (Luke 16:30). But Jesus knew that sin-blinded souls on earth are not so easily persuaded, hence His reply to the request from hell, *"If they hear not Moses and the prophets, neither will they be persuaded, though one rose from the dead"* (Luke 16:31).

There is no doubt about the reality of Jesus and His saving gospel among those who are eternally restless in the caverns of hell. Some who reside there can tell others the plan of salvation, but for them there is no relief from their perpetual misery! On earth, they were surrounded with Christian influences. Perhaps they were born in Christian homes, were in and out of church all their days, and were familiar with the saving truths of the gospel. They said prayers, read the Bible, and engaged in religious activities, yet they lived and died without Christ as their personal Savior. Such glorious truth, never to be realized by the lost, only accentuates their misery in hell. In their lifetimes on earth, they received many good things from God, but they failed to acknowledge the Giver.

THE ANSWER OF EARTH

Countless volumes have already been written about the greatest Figure of all ages, but as John puts it at the conclusion of his gospel regarding the life and works of Jesus, *"If they should be written every one, I suppose that even the world itself could not contain the books that should be written"* (John 21:25). There is much food for faith in the meditation upon all that saintly minds have written about Him. The more we read works about His magnificent person and mighty influence, the more we feel like saying with dear old Samuel Rutherford, who was deeply in love with Christ, "My ever-running over, Lord Jesus."

But great testimonies as to His worth and work have come also from those who were not His committed followers. The testimony of opponents is often the best evidence we can obtain of the reality of a man or a movement. Napoleon the Great, for instance, said that Alexander, Caesar, Charlemagne, and himself founded empires upon force, while Jesus founded one on love, with the result that millions would die for Him. Here is another reputed witness that Napoleon gave to the transcendent majesty of our blessed Lord—

> Everything in Christ astonishes me. His spirit overawes me, and His will confounds me. His ideas and His sentiments, the truths He announces, His manner of convincing, are not explained either by human observation or the nature of things. His birth and the history of His life, the profundity of His doctrine, which grapples the mightiest difficulties, and which ask of those difficulties, the most admirable solution. His gospel, His apparition, His empire, His march across the ages and the realm—everything for me a prodigy, a mystery insoluble, which plunges me into a reverie which I cannot escape—a mystery which is there before my eyes, a mystery which I can neither deny nor explain. Here I see nothing human. The nearer I approach, the more carefully I examine everything that is above me. Everything remains grand, of a grandeur which overpowers. His religion is a revelation from an intelligence which certainly is not that of a man.[5]

Then what did Renan, the renowned French skeptic, think of Christ? Why, he declared Him to be the greatest genius who ever lived or will live; he said that His beauty is eternal and His reign endless. "Jesus is in every respect unique, and nothing can be compared with Him. Be the unlooked phenomena of the future what they may, Jesus

---

5. Napoleon Bonaparte, "Napoleon's Testimony to Christ at St. Helena," *Bible Treasury*, Vol. 17.

will never be surpassed."[6] Further, testifying to His early influence upon Rome, Renan said, "Jesus Christ created a paradise out of the hell of Rome."[7] We could go on, *ad infinitum*, quoting the admiration of both friends and foes for Him who is the "fairest of all the earth beside."[8] But let us confine ourselves to what various Bible characters had to say about the Son of God, who became the Son of Man so that He might make the sons of men the sons of God.

What Did the Prophets Think of Christ?

It was to Him that all the prophets gave witness—and what sublime truths they prophesied concerning Him! (See Acts 10:43.) The Holy Spirit revealed to these holy men much of the grief and glory of the Messiah who was to appear. (See 1 Peter 1:11.)

Abraham had a preview of His redemption and reign; Jesus confirmed that the patriarch rejoiced to see His day, and he saw it and was glad. (See John 8:56.)

Moses, too, was given a glimpse of Christ, whom he would see in the flesh on the Mount of Transfiguration. Scripture tells us that Moses esteemed *"the reproach of Christ greater riches than the treasures in Egypt"* (Hebrews 11:26).

Isaiah, more than any other prophet, received divine insight into all that the coming Messiah was to accomplish, earning himself the title of the "Evangelical Prophet." What did he think of Christ? He said, "[Christ's] *name shall be called Wonderful, Counsellor, the mighty God, the everlasting Father, the Prince of Peace"* (Isaiah 9:6).

What Did the Kings Think of Christ?

Among the kings who testified beforehand about the glories of Him who was born a King and will yet reign as the King of Kings, there was David, of whom Jesus said called Him Lord in spirit. (See Matthew 22:43.) To the psalmist, the one who would be born of his house and

6. Renan, quoted in W. H. Griffith Thomas, *Christianity Is Christ* (London: Longmans, Green and Co., 1916), 89.
7. Ibid., 90.
8. Manie P. Ferguson, "That Man of Calvary."

lineage was "*fairer than the children of men*" (Psalm 45:2). King Solomon, who knew all about the Calvary Psalm that his father wrote (see Psalm 22) likewise believed that Christ would come as the perfect expression of the wisdom of God (see Proverbs 8:30–32). Whether he had the Messiah in the back of his mind when he wrote his renowned Song of Solomon, we cannot say. Anyhow, much of what he wrote of the beloved is symbolic of the beauty and worth of Christ: "*My beloved is white and ruddy, the chiefest among ten thousand...His mouth is most sweet: yea, he is altogether lovely*" (Song of Solomon 5:10, 16).

What Did Christ's Contemporaries Think of Him?

We can divide those who lived at the same time as Christ into two classes—those who knew Him from within and those who knew Him from without. What impression did Christ make upon those who surrounded Him in the days of His flesh?

First, let us take the testimony of those within, those who were more closely associated with Him than others who knew Him. It is most profitable to gather together all their written tributes to Him who came as the Lord of glory. This fact is evident—the influence He had upon the lives of many around Him enabled them to go out and do exploits for Him.

Take Mary

The privileged mother who bore Him surely knew Him as no other did. As He was her child, Mary gave Him love, thought, and tenderness; and if He bore the facial resemblance of any, it would have been that of His mother, seeing as He had her flesh. What did she think of the Christ she had brought into the world? "*My spirit hath rejoiced in God my Saviour*" (Luke 1:47). Then she knew Him to be not only the one who came as the promised Redeemer, but as the One worthy of implicit obedience: "*Whatsoever he saith unto you, do it*" (John 2:5).

Take the Disciples

Jesus could say of those He chose to follow Him, "*They which have continued with me in my temptations*" (Luke 22:28). They walked, talked, slept, ate, and wept together. They had countless opportunities to watch Him under all circumstances, and they knew Him more intimately than the common people who heard Him gladly. They looked at Him from different angles, yet their testimonies concerning Him concur.

John the Baptist was His cousin, and they must have played together as lads. But John knew that he was to prepare the way for Jesus as the coming King, and he confessed that he was unworthy to unloose His sandals. (See Luke 3:16.) After John's initiation of Christ into His public ministry, he exclaimed, *"Behold the Lamb of God, which taketh away the sin of the world"* (John 1:29).

Peter was another who had close and intimate contact with Christ, but who, every time he heard a cock crow, remembered how shamefully he had deserted Him in a time of trial. If this rugged disciple was asked *"What think ye of Christ?"* what answers would he have? By divine inspiration, he said of Him, *"Thou art the Christ, the Son of the living God"* (Matthew 16:16). In later years, when Peter came to write his epistles, looking back on those three years he spent with Christ when he watched Him under all circumstances, he wrote, *"Who did no sin, neither was guile found in his mouth"* (1 Peter 2:22).

John was also one of the chosen twelve who knew the Master. In fact, whenever he is mentioned, it is always as "the disciple whom Jesus loved." (See, for example, John 13:23.) It was John who leaned on the bosom of Jesus and knew His secrets as no other disciple did. This is why his gospel, his epistles, and the book of Revelation tell us so much of Him who came as God's beloved Son to die for a lost world. What did John think of Christ? *"We beheld his glory, the glory as of the only begotten of the Father...full of grace and truth"* (John 1:14). *"The blood of Jesus Christ his Son cleanseth us from all sin"* (1 John 1:7).

Thomas was the disciple who wanted tangible proof that his Master had risen from the dead and who, when he finally saw the wound-prints in His hands, cried, *"My Lord and my God"* (John 20:28).

James, one of the pillars in the early church, who insisted that faith must produce works of mercy and who proclaimed himself to be *"a servant of God and of the Lord Jesus Christ"* (James 1:1), tells us in no uncertain terms what he thought of his Master: *"Our Lord Jesus Christ, the Lord of glory"* (James 2:1).

Paul never hesitated to tell men wherever he traveled what he thought of Christ. To him, *"to live is Christ, and to die is gain"* (Philippians 1:21), because if he died, he would be *"with Christ"* (verse 23). No disciple has ever surpassed the apostle in his superb estimation of Christ, whom he lived to preach and teach about. *"I count all things...but dung, that I may win Christ"* (Philippians 3:8). *"God also hath highly exalted him"* (Philippians 2:9)—so did Paul highly exalt the Savior he suffered so much for in his life and labors.

Having considered the opinions of some of those who belonged to the inner circle of Christ's contemporaries, let us now select a few from others in the wider circle of those who knew Him, allowing them to give us their answer to the question *"What think ye of Christ?"* It may surprise us to learn that some of the greatest evidences of our Lord's unique character and sinlessness came from those who were brought into contact with His sublime personality.

Judas, the betrayer, was called a "friend" by the One he sold for thirty pieces of silver, and he was among those chosen as Christ's disciples, yet he was never Christ's at heart, and he proved to be a traitor to his solemn trust. Ask this man of whom Jesus said it would have been better for him had he never been born, "What think ye of the one you betrayed?" Here is his answer, *"I have sinned in that I have betrayed the innocent blood"* (Matthew 27:4).

Pilate, who had Christ before him as a prisoner, had the opportunity of studying Him firsthand. Impressed with His air of sincerity and courageous demeanor, he asked Christ, *"What is truth?"* (John 18:38), not knowing that the Truth stood before him. What did he actually think of Christ? After examining the charges brought against Christ, Pilate repeated, *"I find no fault in this man"* (Luke 23:4). When forced to yield to the mob demanding the death of Christ, his protest was, *"I am innocent of the blood of this just person"* (Matthew 27:24).

Lady Pilate had a troubled night after that unjust trial and could not get the sight of that suffering man out of her mind. Going off to sleep, her conscience was stirred while dreaming, and in the morning, she said to her husband, *"Have thou nothing to do with that just man: for I have suffered many things this day in a dream because of him"* (Matthew 27:19). Pilate had Christ on his hands, and Pilate's wife had Him on her conscience, and both testified to the innocence of Christ. At His trial, no two witnesses agreed together. Each found something about which to praise Him.

Herod, who had heard all about the reputation of Christ, was a man of keen intellect. He requested to see the prisoner, because he thought Him to be a kind of magician able to produce miracles at will, but Christ did not oblige. Herod was *"exceeding glad"* (Luke 23:8) when he saw Him, but his gladness was not of faith, only of curiosity. Pilate and Herod had been at enmity, but they became friends again through their meeting with Christ. Well, Herod, *"What think ye of Christ?"* After his cross-examination, he could only confirm Pilate's verdict. Herod said, *"Nothing deserving death has been done by him"* (Luke 23:15 RSV).

The dying thief, Christ's fellow sufferer and companion in death, knew that although he was dying for the sins he had committed, the man on the middle cross was dying for sins that were not His own. He said, *"This man hath done nothing amiss. And he said unto Jesus, Lord, remember me when thou comest into thy kingdom"* (Luke 23:41–42).

The centurion responsible for the details of the crucifixion had the grim task of seeing that the cruel sentence was carried out. It was his responsibility to stay to the bitter end and pronounce the victim dead. He watched Jesus die and was overwhelmed by His manner and by the messages He uttered. What was his verdict on Christ? *"Certainly this was a righteous man"* (Luke 23:47).

What has history to say in reply to the self-addressed question, *"What think ye of Christ?"* Testimony to His worth is not less real among us than it was in the past. In *Christianity Is Christ*, William Thomas says,

In the case of all the other great names of the world's history, the inevitable and invariable experience has been that the particular man is first a power, then only a name, and last of all a memory. Of Jesus Christ the exact opposite is true. He died on a cross of shame, His name gradually became more and more powerful, and He is the greatest influence in the world to-day. There is, as it has been well said, a fifth Gospel being written—the work of Jesus Christ in the hearts and lives of men and nations.[9]

It is most fascinating to follow succeeding generations and select those from every walk of life, whether sympathetic or hostile to the claims of Christ. Ask and discover from them their estimation of Jesus of Nazareth.[10]

The question before us, however, resolves itself into a personal testimony, What do we think of Christ? It is not about what others above, around, and below think of Him, although their tributes, as we have seen, are valuable. The only Christ worth anything to you is the one you know for yourself. So, what do *you* think of Christ? Can you confess with Peter His preciousness? (See 1 Peter 2:7.) Or is He not much more than a name to you? You can evade or ignore the question *"What think ye of Christ?"* You alone can decide what to do with Him who is called Christ. Even an attempt to avoid Him is in reality a confession of an opinion about Him.

If you want to be certain of His reality, then you must answer the fourfold call He uttered while among men:

"Come to me"; He is the Redeemer (See Acts 4:12; Hebrews 9:25.)

"Learn from me"; He is the Teacher (See John 7:46.)

"Follow me"; He is the Master (See John 13:13.)

"Abide in me"; He is the Life (See John 14:6.)

We must abide in Him for peace (see John 16:33; Ephesians 2:14); for direction (see Mark 7:37); and for friendship (see Proverbs 18:24).

9. W. H. Griffith Thomas, *Christianity Is Christ*, 91.
10. For more on this subject, read Herbert Lockyer's *The Man Who Changed the World*.

The personal question is, What is Jesus worth to me? Do I consider His price to be above rubies? Can I apply to Him what a multitude of Israelites thought of David?—*"Thou art worth ten thousand of us"* (2 Samuel 18:3). Is He not worth ten thousand times ten thousand of us? Who can we liken unto Him who is incomparable? He is holier than the holiest, mightier than the mightiest, kinder than the kindest. A remarkable fact is that the more we think about Him, the closer our resemblance to Him becomes. By every act of trust and self-surrender to His claims, we receive ever larger measures of His life, so that all the while we are being changed into His image from glory to glory, as by His Spirit. Do you ask *me* what I think of Christ? I have only one answer— He is the center and circumstance of my being, the one I cannot live without and dare not die without. He is my all, and He is in all!

> Infinite excellence is thine,
> Thou lovely Prince of grace!
> Thy uncreated beauties shine
> With never-fading rays.[11]

---

11. John Fawcett, "Infinite Excellence Is Thine," 1782.

THEME 2

THE GIFTS AND GLORY IN JOHN 17

The atmosphere of prayer pervades Scripture. God made men capable of accessing Him by prayer, and thus we are provided with an abundance of saints and sinners who seek Him in this way. Scripture also confirms the privilege and power of waiting upon God; likewise, it sets forth the conditions upon which God answers prayer.

Among all the recorded prayers, none is as sublime and sacred as the one complete prayer Jesus offered and preserved for our enlightenment and edification by John in chapter 17 of his gospel. We read in Hebrews that *"in the days of [Christ's] flesh...he had offered up prayers and supplications with strong crying and tears...and was heard in that he feared"* (Hebrews 5:7). What a remarkable spiritual classic it would be if all of those tear-saturated prayers could have been recorded in a volume! The one we do have, however, is without doubt the most remarkable prayer ever prayed—the prayer perfect! As we approach a meditation of it, we bow in reverence, for the place whereon we stand is holy ground. This intense intercessory prayer has been described as "the noblest and purest pearl of devotion in the New Testament." Looking at it in the light of its context, we see that after having spoken to His disciples about the Father, Jesus turns to speak to the Father about His disciples.

Without doubt, John 17 is a simple, filial prayer, containing the outpouring of the Son's heart in the presence of His Father. In fact, Christ uses the filial term *"Father"* six times in the prayer. It was His favorite expression, and this speaks of a holy intimacy between Father and Son. Once He calls God *"Holy Father"* (John 17:11)—the only time in Scripture He is so named. This term is used in the section of the prayer where Jesus prays for the sanctification of His own. Then we have the phrase *"righteous Father"* (verse 25), implying that the basis of any appeal to God is His righteousness.

We look upon this priceless intercession of Christ as a model prayer in that it reveals a methodical presentation of accomplishments and pleas. Too often, our prayer lives are ineffective because we lack a plan. When we come before God, we ramble, give utterance to any thought that troops into our minds, and wander all over the world without arriving anywhere. When the disciples saw Jesus at prayer, they came to Him and asked, *"Lord, teach us to pray"* (Luke 11:1). Then He gave them a truly model prayer, the one we call "The Lord's Prayer." We ought, however, to describe it as "The prayer Jesus taught His disciples to pray," because it was not a prayer He could use since He is the sinless One.

The plan of this favorite prayer is clearly evident, being made up of invocation, supplication, and adoration—a division we should always have before us as we come to commune with God. Too often, we come before Him as beggars, beseeching Him to give us this, that, and the other thing. Jesus taught His own to come, first of all, as worshipers, blessing God for all that He is in Himself, then to present their needs, and last of all, to magnify God for His power to answer their petitions.

A similar method can be traced in the marvelous prayer before us in John 17, in the twenty-six verses that fall into three clearly defined areas.

1. *The first section is personal.* (See John 17:1–8.) Lifting up His eyes to heaven, Jesus talks to the Father about His aspirations and accomplishments.

2. *The second section is particular.* (See John 17:9–19.) Here Jesus concentrates upon His own—those given Him of the Father. The exclusion will be noted, *"I pray for them: **I pray not for the world**"* (verse 9).

3. *The third section is general.* (See John 17:20–26.) This part of the prayer is focused on all who throughout the ages will receive Christ through the witness of His disciples. The divine Word they believed (see John 17:8, 14) in turn became *"their word"* (verse 20)—so effective is their testimony.

Further, this is the great High Priestly Prayer, a forecast of Christ's entry into His perpetual ministry as the great High Priest, to make intercession for His redeemed ones. (See Hebrews 7:25.) Four times over we have the term *pray,* which indicates intercessory prayer. (See verses 9, 15, 20.) Enthroned in glory, the Redeemer is our Advocate, pleading the efficacy of His shed blood on our behalf—

> There for sinners Thou art pleading:
> Then Thou dost our place prepare;
> Thou for saints are interceding
> Till in glory they appear.[12]

Among the fascinating features of this true Lord's Prayer (see John 17)—the prayer He uttered with eyes uplifted—mention can be made of the following three:

"I HAVE" IN THE HIGH PRIESTLY PRAYER

The phrase *"I have"* occurs ten times and represents the authoritative assertion of accomplishment. The fourfold declarations in the first part of the prayer is full of spiritual significance: *"I have glorified thee on the earth: I have finished the work which thou gavest me to do"* (John 17:4); *"I have manifested thy name"* (verse 6); *"I have given unto them the words which thou gavest me"* (verse 8).

---

12. John Bakewell, "Hail, Thou Once Despised Jesus," 1757.

GIFTS IN THE HIGH PRIESTLY PRAYER

Gifts are prominent in the prayer. The word *give* and its cognates occur fifteen times in the chapter. Christ refers to several gifts the Father had bestowed upon Him, which, in turn, He gave to His own. Christ Himself was the love gift of the Father to the world (see John 3:16), and believers are the Father's love gift to Christ. Some seven gifts appear in the prayer:

The Gift of Saints

Seven times over they are represented as being given to the Son by the Father. (See John 17:2, 6, 9, 11–12, 24.)

The Gift of His Name

The life of Christ manifested God's name. As *name* means "nature" or "being," this assertion implies that Christ, by His character and works, revealed what God is like—and He continues to do so: *"I have"* (verse 6) and *"I will"* (verse 24).

The Gift of Power

What an arresting phrase this is about the Father having given His Son *"power over all flesh"* (John 17:2), so that authority could be His to *"give eternal life"* (verse 2) to believing sinners. After His resurrection, Jesus assured His disciples that all power was His in heaven and on earth, and that this all-embracing power was at their disposal as they went forth preaching eternal life to all who would repent and believe. (See Matthew 28:18–20.)

The Gift of Service

At the outset of His ministry, Jesus made it clear what He came into the world for. *"My meat is to do the will of him that sent me, and to finish his work"* (John 4:34). Here in His High Priestly Prayer, which anticipates the cry of the cross—*"It is finished"* (John 19:30)—He says to the Father, *"I have finished the work which thou gavest me to do"* (John 17:4). Work, then, for Him was a gift, not a grind, for He delighted in the accomplishment of a God-given task.

The Gift of a Message

How striking is the phrase *"The words which thou gavest me"* (John 17:8). Jesus did not originate the truth He taught. The message He expounded was not conceived in His own mind but received from God, as the repetition affirms: *"I have given unto them the words which thou gavest me"* (verse 8). *"I have given them thy word"* (verse 14). Our Lord was God's Messenger in God's message. (See Haggai 1:13.)

The Gift of Joy

This bequest was realized by His disciples after Pentecost, when they experienced what it was to be filled with the Holy Spirit and with joy. What do we know about the possession and fulfillment of His joy? (See John 17:13.)

The Gift of Glory

An old promise reads, *"The LORD will give grace and glory"* (Psalm 84:11). Here Christ prays that the glory that was given to Him by the Father might be shared by His disciples. (See John 17:22.) Such glory reveals the unity of the Godhead and the unity of the church as a body. *Glory* as well as *gifts* dominate this most precious prayer. The word *glory* and its cognates occur eight times in it. Paul reminds us that God-given glory could be seen in the face of Jesus Christ (see 2 Corinthians 4:6), and the Master prayed that this glory might be given to His followers.

1. *The Glory of Sonship.* John could declare about His relationship to the Father, *"We beheld his glory"* (John 1:14), and He glorified the Father by His works, ways, and words. Read to His assertion, *"I have glorified thee on the earth"* (John 17:4). Now He asks the Father to glorify Him, which He did when He highly exalted Him at the time of the ascension. (See John 17:1; Philippians 2:9–10.)

2. *The Glory of Union.* One purpose of God-given glory is to authenticate the unity of the Godhead and the spiritual unity of believers. (See John 17:11, 22.) We are not able to add anything to this divine attribute.

3. *The Glory of Identification.* Because we belong to the Father and the Son, Christ is glorified in us. (See John 17:10, 22.) He is no longer here in the flesh to manifest His glory, yet in and through His followers, Jesus continues to be glorified. Every child of His is—or should be—a cabinet displaying His glory. Paul could say of the saints in Judaea, *"They glorified God in me"* (Galatians 1:24). Peter would have us so live and act that *"God in all things may be glorified through Jesus Christ"* (1 Peter 4:11). The Scottish Catechism states that "man's chief end is to glorify God, and to enjoy Him forever."[13]

PETITIONS IN THE HIGH PRIESTLY PRAYER

There is yet another way of expounding our Lord's intercessory prayer, namely, by dealing with its seven distinct petitions. *Petition,* which means "asking," is an aspect of prayer. Jesus said, *"Ask and ye shall receive"* (John 16:24). He, too, asked petitions of His Father, like the following seven petitions:

First Petition (See John 17:1.)

He asked the Father to glorify Him, which He did at His entrance into heaven. (See Philippians 2:9–10.) There was the glory that Jesus won by being the Son who was obedient to the Father. But He asks for the return of a past eternal glory that the limitations of His humanity withheld. His has now a special glory through the security of redemption for us.

Second Petition (See John 17:5.)

Here we have an emphatic plea for the restoration of His ancient glory *"before the world was."* Having glorified the Father here on earth,

---

13. *Westminster Shorter Catechism,* 1648.

the Son besought Him with His own self to continue the glory He'd had with Him in the past and that He now has with added glory.

Third Petition (See John 17:11.)

Jesus goes on to ask the Father for the security and safety of those who are given to Him. While He was here below, He kept His own (see verse 12); now He commits them into His Father's hands (see John 10:28–29) for a double grip. Jesus never lost Judas. This son of perdition lost himself. Our eternal security rests upon the Father's faithfulness to His Son.

Fourth Petition (See John 17:15–17.)

Although Jesus was about to leave the world, He asked that His own might remain *in* it, but not *of* it. *"Keep them from the evil"* (verse 15), He said. He sought for the sanctification of His own through the sanctifying Word. He clearly states the identification of those He prayed for when He interceded for them, that they might be holy as God is holy. (See John 17:6–7, 11.)

Fifth Petition (See John 17:11, 21.)

Twice Jesus asks that the unity of the Godhead might be reflected in the body of believers: *"That they may be one, as we are"* (verse 11) and, *"That they all may be one"* (verse 21). Such an organic spiritual unity is a testimony to the world of the reality of our Lord's incarnation. It is the outworking of this unity that we so sadly need. We may know much about the Bible, its doctrines, and prophecies, but we do not know how to get along among ourselves.

Sixth Petition (See John 17:20.)

Our Lord interceded not only for those God had given Him while here among men; He looked down the vista of the ages and thought of all who would believe in Him through the life and witness of His own, asking for security and unity for them. In heaven, He continues to intercede for them.

Seventh Petition (See John 17:22, 24.)

The glory God gave His Son has been given to us. Now Jesus expresses the wish that we might share heaven with Him and behold His glory. Note that He says, *"I will"* (verse 24), not "I pray." He does not request the Father to have us with Him, but asserts His authority: *"I will that they also, whom thou hast given me, be with me where I am"* (verse 24). Because they are redeemed by His blood, it is His right to have them with Him. As the shadows lengthen, let us cling to the double desire of the Master: *"I will that they also, whom thou hast given me, be with me where I am; that they may behold my glory"* (verse 24).

> O Jesus, Thou hast promised
> To all who follow Thee,
> That where Thou art in glory
> There shall Thy servant be;
> And, Jesus, I have promised
> To serve Thee to the end;
> Oh, give me grace to follow
> My Master and my Friend.[14]

---

14. John E. Bode, "O Jesus, I Have Promised," 1869.

THEME 3

ACTS: THE ATMOSPHERE OF PRAYER

The dictum "An army marches on its stomach" is attributed to Napoleon. A contemporary writer, Robert J. Yeatman, says, "Napoleon's armies always used to march on their stomachs, shouting: 'Vive l'Intérieur!'" Plentiful food not only made the soldiers think well of their leader but also enabled them to follow him in his military adventures. One cannot read the fifth book of the New Testament, sometimes called "The Fifth Gospel," without realizing how it shows us the church marching to glorious victories, not on her stomach, but on her knees. Prayer, importunate prayer, pervades the book of Acts, and it is the secret of the church's power to turn the world upside down. Being wrong side up as it was, it was the dynamic intercession and witness of the apostles that reversed it to its right position.

Used as an acronym, the term ACTS suggests the different aspects of prayer, all of which the book illustrates—

Adoration
Confession
Thanksgiving
Supplication

The opening words of Acts, like those of the gospel of Luke, are addressed to Theophilus. This proves the identity of the author, namely,

Luke, the beloved physician. He deemed his historical account of the church's activities as the result of the promised Pentecostal effusion of the Holy Spirit to be a natural sequel to the human gospel he had penned. Rev. E. H. Plumptre writes,

> The natural sequel to such a Gospel was a record of the work of the Holy Ghost, the Sanctifier. Looking to the prominence given to the work of the Spirit, from the Day of Pentecost onwards, as guiding both the Church collectively and its individual members, it would hardly be over-bold to say that the book might well be called "the Gospel of the Holy Spirit."[15]

There are, of course, various approaches one could make to this most dramatic book of the Bible. Concentrating upon its references to the Holy Spirit, we could show how, at every stage of the church's mighty advance, the Spirit's action is emphatically recognized—a fact that prompted A. T. Pierson to suggest that the title of the book should be "the Acts of the Holy Spirit Through the Apostles."

Because Acts is a record of the history of the growth of the church of Christ among Jews and Gentiles—from the church's inception at Jerusalem and ending at Rome—the book is most valuable as a guide to the organization, mission work, and worship of the church that Jesus said He would build. All of the apostles believed that it was their solemn responsibility to work with the divine Builder in the introduction of a new society, which, built of *living stones* (1 Peter 2:5 RSV), was to be the temple of the living God.

What presently interests us about Acts is its prayer emphasis, and how prayer was a potent factor in the remarkable evangelistic activities of the apostles, as well as in their lives as individuals. A careful study of this prayer element convinces reader that "more things are wrought by prayer than this world dreams of."[16]

Whenever or wherever those saints in the early church prayed, something happened, for their prayers were no vain repetitions, but

---

15. Charles John Ellicott, ed., *A New Testament Commentary for English Readers by Various Writers*, vol. 2 (London: Cassell & Company, 1884), viii.
16. Alfred Lord Tennyson, "Morte D'Arthur," lines 247–248.

heart expressions inspired by the Holy Spirit, who was very closely related to those who are found praying. The following analysis proves this.

PRAYER OF PREPARATION

These all continued with one accord in prayer and supplication.

(Acts 1:14)

Several thoughts emerge from a consideration of this first reference to prayer in Acts. It was a daily, united prayer meeting. The word *accord* is akin to *symphony*, suggesting the harmony of differing instruments in an orchestra. Those disciples were not only in one place, but also in one mind, and actuated by one purpose. Prayer and unity are vitally connected. As to those who formed that first prayer meeting of the church, in addition to the eleven apostles, there were the "*devout and honourable women*" (Acts 13:50) that Luke mentions as having ministered to Jesus (see Luke 8:1–3; 23:49), in addition to "*Mary the mother of Jesus*" (Acts 1:14). As to "*his brethren,*" these were our Lord's brothers according to the flesh, who, although unbelieving while their brother was alive (see John 7:5), were doubtless converted through the raising of Lazarus and through the death and resurrection of their mother's firstborn Son. As about 120 formed that communal prayer meeting, which probably included the seventy Jesus had sent forth (see Luke 10:1), a mighty volume of earnest prayer must have gone up from that upper chamber.

The prayer group had not been told how long those daily gatherings for prayer were to go on. "*Not many days hence*" (Acts 1:5) was the indefinite amount of time the Master had spoken of. They were told that the fulfillment of the promise would not be long, lest faith and patience should fail. The uncertainty as to the exact period they were to wait was a discipline to their faith and patience. Whereas the King James Version combines *prayer* with *supplication*, ancient versions mention only *prayer*. How they prayed, whether publicly or silently, we are not told, but pray they did in respect to "*the promise of the Father*" (Acts 1:4). What must be borne in mind is that they did not focus prayer on the coming of the Holy Spirit. To ask God to do something He has already promised to do is a travesty of the true function of prayer. Faith accepts the promise, and prayer prepares the heart for the fulfillment of that promise. Those 120 or so disciples waited for God to redeem His promise, which He did on the day of Pentecost; but the daily prayers of those saints prepared a fitting atmosphere within their hearts for the reception of the promised gift.

Regretfully, in our modern times, church prayer meetings are passing out of fashion. The church no longer lives on her knees, but on her schemes and wits, for survival. And, with her efficient business-like methods of raising money to keep her machinery running, she has little need of communal prayer for support. Deny it as we may, the fact remains that the church was born in a prayer meeting, and her life can only exist in the same atmosphere. Any church, believing that prayer changes both things and persons, and giving prayer priority in its program, is an irresistible spiritual force in the community it represents. This is the witness of Acts, where we read startling results from the church at prayer. As those disciples commenced, they continued (see Acts 2:42), and mighty things happened: *"When they had prayed, the place was shaken where they were assembled together; and they were all filled with the Holy Ghost, and they spake the word of God with boldness"* (Acts 4:31). What a distance the church has traveled from this form of Spirit-inspired intercession with its wonderful spiritual accompaniments! It was only when Zion travailed that she brought forth children.

PRAYER FOR A SUCCESSOR

And they prayed and said, Thou, Lord, which knowest the hearts of all men, show whether of these two thou hast chosen. (Acts 1:24)

Through his dark betrayal, Judas Iscariot had lost his position among the apostles. Thus, at a church meeting, prayer was offered for a successor who was qualified to fill the gap. Two disciples, who had followed the Lord Jesus throughout His earthly ministry, namely, Barnabas and Matthias, were brought before the church. Although heaven's choice was sought, the successor was chosen by lot, or by casting votes for each presented candidate. Thus the question arises, Was

Matthias the Lord's man or were the voters biased in his favor? While Luke included him in the recognized twelve when it came to the election of the first deacons (see Acts 6:2), and the appointment of Matthias was an honest transaction, there is not sufficient reason to believe that Peter and the rest were divinely directed in their action, which, perhaps, was somewhat premature.

Did not Jesus constantly affirm that disciples were His choice, and His alone—*"I have chosen you"* (John 15:16)? Did those in the upper chamber, then, undertake to do what their Lord had kept in His own power? Knowing of David's prediction of another filling the place of Judas, and desiring to have an apostolate of twelve in place before Pentecost, the resolve to appoint a successor was taken. As Peter was spokesman for the church, he took it for granted that God would approve of the choice made, without asking whether His choice was between two. Are we not guilty of this same fault of going to God not *before* a course of action but *after* we have decided upon it? As if to say, "Well, Lord, here's our plan; approve it, please!"

After his election by lot, Matthias does not appear again in sacred history. Doubtless he proved to be a most loyal follower of the Lord. Tradition has it that like Stephen he was stoned, and then he was beheaded because of his allegiance to his Lord. Our conviction is that the vacant place in the apostolate was filled by the Lord Himself when He personally chose Saul of Tarsus (see Acts 9:15), who could later write that he was an apostle *"not of men, neither by man, but by Jesus Christ"* (Galatians 1:1). Although at the time of the election of Matthias, Paul was a fierce persecutor of the church, through grace he became an *"apostle of Jesus Christ through the will of God"* (1 Corinthians 1:1), and not by human lot.[17]

When vacancies occur in church circles, it is necessary for united prayer to be focused on evident divine tokens of successors. Too often, a pastorless church knows what kind of a man it wants, and although formal prayers are offered for guidance, behind the scenes a good deal of wire-pulling and influence secures the preacher they desire. Spirit-inspired, united intercession, without human bias, never fails to produce

---

17. For more information, read Lockyer's book *All the Apostles of the Bible.*

the man after God's own heart, whether for the vacant pulpit or for any office in a church's ministry. Somehow in church circles it has been forgotten that when God's work is done in God's way for God's glory, it never lacks God's vindication.

PRAYER IN THE TEMPLE

Now Peter and John went up together into the temple at the hour of prayer, being the ninth hour. (Acts 3:1)

It is interesting to observe how Luke combines these two co-apostles, Peter and John, for theirs was a striking mutual relationship. In spite of the marked difference in character and conduct, after their joint mission to prepare for the last Passover, they seem to have been inseparable. (See Luke 22:8.) Peter alone denied his Master; John alone continued with Him to the end. (See John 18:15; 19:26.) Yet such was John's magnanimity that although he witnessed Peter's denial, he says nothing about it in his gospel. You find the two of them together at the sepulcher and in Galilee after the resurrection. (See John 20:2; 21:7.) Here we have them together in the hour of prayer. The word *together* implies not a mere coincidence of place, but a unity of purpose. The hour of prayer Peter and John observed together was the third stated hour of prayer according to Jewish custom. Corresponding to our 3 o'clock in the afternoon, this was probably the hour of evening sacrifice. (See Psalm 55:17.) For a while after Pentecost, the disciples "*continu*[ed] *daily with one accord in the temple*" (Acts 2:46), and on this day, which was to witness a miracle of intrinsic magnitude, Peter and John visited the temple not only for private devotions but also to participate in the ceremonial service of the sanctuary.

It seems, however, that the joint purpose of the two apostles to pray and worship was not fulfilled that day, for as they were about to go into the temple, a beggar, lame from birth, was stretched out at the gate pleading for money. These two partners as fishermen, sharers in looking for the consolation of Israel, companions at the gate of prayer, were now to become joint channels of miracle power, with Peter preaching a most remarkable sermon that resulted in their imprisonment. On that never-to-be-forgotten day, when these two came to the temple to pray, God took the will for the deed and magnified His power through them.

The temple, then, had its *daily* hour for prayer, but there are many churches today without a *weekly* hour for prayer. Prayer meetings, once a mighty factor in church life, are gradually being abandoned. The Peters and Johns going together to the church *just* to pray are becoming scarcer. Prayerless churches have no power to say to our poor, lame world, *"In the name of Jesus Christ of Nazareth rise up and walk"* (Acts 3:6). A church may have no silver and gold to give, but if she lives on her knees, she has far greater wealth to distribute to a bankrupt world.

PRAYER AND MINISTRY

But we will give ourselves continually to prayer, and to the ministry of the word.   (Acts 6:4)

Because of the dynamic witness of the early church, there was an almost daily increase of men and women becoming disciples. This resulted in an ever-increasing burden of responsibility on the part of the leaders. The charitable side of the church's life, namely, the care of widows and their children out of an organized administration of a common fund for relief, was consuming more and more of the time of those who felt called to preach and teach. So the Twelve brought the church together and explained that the serving of tables was taking up too much of their time, and they suggested that seven deacons be appointed to deal with all matters related to almsgiving. Such men had to have an *"honest report"* and be *"full of the Holy Ghost and wisdom"* (Acts 6:3) for a service just as spiritual as preaching the Word.

As for the apostles, such an appointment would set them free for continual prayer and the ministry of the Word. We understand *"prayer"* (Acts 6:4) to mean all the public worship of the church in all its various developments, as well as private prayer and intercession. *"Ministry of the word"* (verse 4) implies all forms of preaching and teaching. The promise was given that they would give themselves continually to this dual ministry—the word *continually* meaning "to persevere in, or adhere to with single purpose." This plan pleased the church; the seven were appointed, and the apostles commended them to God and laid hands on them. (See Acts 6:6.) Mentioned here first in the New Testament, the ritual of laying on of the hands did not imply the transmission of the gifts the chosen seven were to exercise as deacons, but the recognition that they already possessed, the requisite qualification for the office—namely, the testimony of others as to their character, the fullness of the Spirit, and wisdom, the latter implying not only practical skill, but also a heavenly prudence that taught them how to act in all emergencies. That God set His seal upon this arrangement is seen in what followed. (See Acts 6:7–8.)

Apostolic recognition of the preeminence of prayer is seen in that the apostles named it first. The effective ministry of the Word is dependent upon prayer, as the history of Acts proves. If churches could be persuaded to give more time to intercession than to the preaching and teaching of the Word, greater things would happen through the presentation of truth. The Grecian Jews *were not able to resist the wisdom and the spirit by which he* [Stephen] *spake* (Acts 6:10), because of the deep prayer life behind his public utterance.

Later on, when it came to the setting apart of Barnabas and Paul for their God-given tasks, prayer of ordination is again seen. This time, however, the leaders not only prayed and laid hands on the two being separated, but they fasted, as they likewise did at the ordination of elders. (See Acts 13:3; 14:23.) In each case, the fasting indicated that the new command called for that intensity of spiritual life of which fasting was more or less the normal condition. Paul, a mighty intercessor, made a practice of fasting. (See 2 Corinthians 6:5; 11:27.) The mind is more alert to and aware of the divine presence, and one prays more effectively when the stomach is not overloaded with food. Prayer warriors are those who have learned to spend more time on their knees than sitting at a table.

PRAYER OF RESIGNATION AND FOR FORGIVENESS

As they stoned Stephen, [he called] upon God…saying, Lord Jesus, receive my spirit. And he kneeled down, and cried with a loud voice,

Lord, lay not this sin to their charge. And when he had said this, he
fell asleep.   (Acts 7:59–60)

Here we see a noble martyr at prayer. What a wonderful way to die,
whether brutally or naturally! Rev. E. H. Plumptre reminds us,

[These] words are memorable as an instance of direct prayer
addressed, to use the words of Pliny in reporting what he had
learned of the worship of Christians, "to Christ as God".…
Stephen could not think of Him whom he saw at the right hand
of God, but as of One sharing the glory of the Father, hearing
and answering prayer.[18]

Perhaps Stephen had been present at Calvary, and his dying prayer
echoed the one he heard Jesus use: *"Father, into thy hands I commend*
my spirit" (Luke 23:46). We read in Acts, *"They stoned Stephen, calling*
upon God, and saying, Lord Jesus, receive my spirit" (Acts 7:59). It will be
noted that the term *"God"* in the sentence is in italics, and it was only
inserted to complete the sense. The phrase *"upon God"* was introduced
by the King James Version. Tyndale has it, *"Calling on and saying."* The
designation *"Lord Jesus"* involves a recognition of Him in the twofold
character of both a Sovereign and a Savior. Stephen addressed Him as
a divine Person, asking of the Son precisely what the Son on the cross
asked of His Father. Elijah and Jonah petitioned that the Lord would
take away their lives or suffer them to die, but the church's first martyr
prayed that Christ would receive him when separated from his battered,
blood-stained body.

Prostrate on the ground because of the cruel stoning he suffered,
Stephen, although exhausted, lifted himself to a kneeling posture and
reechoed another Calvary prayer. As the dying Savior prayed for divine
forgiveness for those who had crucified Him (see Luke 23:34), Stephen
prayed for his murderers: *"Lord, lay not this sin to their charge"* (Acts
7:60). Certainly he had the mind of Christ.

Augustine in one of his sermons suggested that we owe the conversion of Saul to the prayers of Stephen, which we can accept as the

18. *A New Testament Commentary for English Readers by Various Writers*, vol. 2, 46.

expression of a great spiritual fact. John Wesley said that his "preachers died well." Stephen the martyred deacon died well, for he died praying. No wonder "he fell asleep" (Acts 7:60). While "sleep" is used as a figure of speech in connection with the death of a believer (see 1 Corinthians 15:18; 1 Thessalonians 4:14), it can also imply that Stephen died a peaceful death in spite of the fury of his murderers and the brutal, violent means by which he lost his life (see Psalm 37:37). "When good men die, it is not death, but sleep."[19]

> Prayer is the Christian's vital breath,
> The Christian's native air,
> His watchword at the gates of death;
> He enters heaven with prayer.[20]

PRAYER FOR THE HOLY SPIRIT

When [Peter and John] *were come down,* [they] *prayed for them, that* [the Samaritans] *might receive the Holy Spirit.* (Acts 8:15)

In this chapter, we have Philip the Evangelist fulfilling the part of the Great Commission about witnessing in Samaria—the bridge between Jerusalem and the world. Hearing and seeing the miracles Philip performed, the people eagerly listened to his message, and there was great joy in the city over his presence and ministry in it. While in Jerusalem, Peter and John heard of the fruitful evangelistic efforts of Philip, and they visited Samaria as representatives of the church. Meeting a group of the Samaritans who had believed, the apostles prayed for them, that they might receive the Holy Spirit.

As these converts had been baptized in the name of the Lord Jesus, this presupposes that they had received the "renewing of the Holy Ghost" (Titus 3:5; see 1 Corinthians 12:13). Thus regenerated, they already had the Spirit within them: "If any man have not the Spirit of Christ, he is none of his" (Romans 8:9). But "as yet he was fallen upon none of them" (Acts 8:16), meaning that they had not yet experienced their share of

19. Callimachus.
20. James Montgomery, "Prayer Is the Soul's Sincere Desire," 1818.

the Pentecostal gift. When, therefore, the apostles prayed for those saved Samaritans, they received a super addition of the Spirit's unction, manifesting itself in His extraordinary influences, either in inspiration or miraculous endowments or both combined, as in the case of the apostles themselves. (See Acts 10:14; 19:1–7.)

Doubtless Philip had prayed that his converts might have the installment of Pentecost, for his prayers were no less effectual than those of Peter and John; but as the latter were in Samaria to inspect and report the mission of Philip to the church and to instruct the converts, being there as the divinely appointed founders of the church, they prayed for them, and their prayers were answered. The Holy Spirit's power was not bestowed through the imposition of the laying on of hands. Such an act simply testified to the fact that the Spirit had fallen upon the believing, baptized Samaritans.

It is vain to pray for a blessing to be emptied out on other believers, blessings we ourselves have not experienced. How certain, then, we must be that we have entered into the fullness of the blessing of the gospel of Christ. But if we have discovered the secret of spiritual wealth, then we dare not hold our peace, but must pray that others may come to share the secret. At Pentecost, the Holy Spirit fell upon Peter and John; thus it was with deep feeling that they prayed for the Samaritans that they might be mantled with His power for service.

PRAYER FOR PRESERVATION

Simon…said, Pray ye to the Lord for me, that none of these things which ye have spoken come upon me.   (Acts 8:24)

Simon the sorcerer, witnessing the effect of the prayers and the laying on of hands on the Samaritans, offered Peter money to bestow on him the same authority. The key to this wretched man's character was spiritual ambition, and so Peter said, *"Thy money perish with thee"* (Acts 8:20). The sin of Simon is seen in the term *simony*, which denotes trafficking of sacred things, chiefly in the purchase of ecclesiastical offices and preferments. Peter impressed upon Simon the greatness of his sin and urged him to repent, lest he became a captive of iniquitous ambition. Alarmed at the thought of such dread punishment, he begged Peter to pray for him, not that his wickedness might be forgiven him, but only that the evils threatened might be averted.

Peter had told Simon to pray for himself, *"Pray God, if perhaps the thought of thine heart may be forgiven thee"* (Acts 8:22), but he asked the apostles to pray for him. Evidently, he had no confidence in the prayer of faith, but thought that the disciples possessed some peculiar power with heaven. He turned, not to the Lord, who was ready to forgive, but to a human mediator. Peter must pray for him who has not faith to pray for himself. Whether Peter did accede to such a request we are not told. Simon disappears from the history of Acts. Tradition says that he became "the hero of the romance of heresy." Among the many legends attached to his name is the one of how he tried to prove his unusual power by flying in the air, trusting that the demons whom he employed would support him, but, through the power of the prayers of Peter, he fell down, and his bones were broken; then he committed suicide.

PRAYER OF A CONVERT

Saul, of Tarsus...behold, he prayeth.   (Acts 9:11)

Ananias, who had been instructed by the Lord where to find the remarkable trophy of His grace, was a little afraid to go to a man who had so severely persecuted the saints. However, when the Lord assured him that he had nothing to fear because he would find Saul on his knees praying, Ananias went on his mission in a different frame of mind. The persecutor was no longer *"breathing out threatenings and slaughter"* (Acts 9:1) but pouring out his heart to the One he had persecuted. What a change Jesus had wrought in the heart of Saul! Instead of persecuting, he is found praying. Rev. E. H. Plumptre comments on the verse *"Behold, he prayeth"*:

Estimating that prayer by that which came as the answer to it, we may think of it as including pardon for the past, light and wisdom for the future, strength to do the work to which he was now called, intercession for those whom he had before persecuted unto the death.[21]

Saul, who became Paul the apostle, started his Christian career in prayer, went on to become mighty in prayer, and wrote much on this holy exercise and privilege. Young converts should be encouraged to give themselves to prayer. At first, their prayers may be short, simple, and perhaps not altogether correct as to scriptural conditions of prayer; but the more they pray, the better they pray, discovering that prayer is a gift that increases with its use. As they journey on, the newly saved come to realize that

> Prayer is the Christian's vital breath,
> The Christian's native air.[22]

PRAYER FOR RESURRECTION

Peter...kneeled down, and prayed; and turning...said, Tabitha, arise.   (Acts 9:40)

The power of the prayer of faith calls for the silence and solitude of communion with God. Therefore, Peter asked all the people gathered in the death chamber to retire and leave him alone to stand between the living God and the dead girl. No doubt Peter recalled how Jesus acted in the case of the raising of the daughter of Jairus. (See Matthew 9:23–24.) We are told that Peter *"kneeled down, and prayed"* (Acts 9:40). Such "kneeling became the lowly servant, but not the Lord Himself, of whom it is never once recorded that He knelt in the performance of a miracle." Peter was only the instrument in the miracle of the resurrection of Tabitha, but Jesus was the miracle worker Himself in the raising of Jairus's daughter.

How graphic, yet how simple and natural, is the narrative! Peter had the inward assurance that his prayer would be answered, so he said, *"Tabitha, arise"* (Acts 9:40).The girl opened her eyes and sat up, and Peter presented her alive—evidence of the completeness of the miracle.

---

21. *A New Testament Commentary for English Readers by Various Writers*, vol. 2, 59.
22. "Prayer Is the Soul's Sincere Desire."

There is about this incident an air of charming reality. Power to raise the dead was an apostolic gift, which has been in abeyance since the end of the apostolic age. What the church calls "prayers for the dead" are not related to their present physical resurrection from the grave. As for praying for them after they are dead, they remain dead as far as their bodies are concerned, and are beyond the realm of prayer. Our prayers can only be for the living. For those sick unto death, we may pray that if it is the divine will, they may not die but live to declare the glory of God. We can, however, intercede with tears for those who are *spiritually* dead, that they will arise from their grave of sin and lust into the newness of life forevermore.

PRAYER OF A SOLDIER

Cornelius...one that feared God...and prayed to God alway.

(Acts 10:1–2)

This devout soldier must have been conspicuous among the Roman officers in Nero's legions. With this chapter, we enter on an entirely new phase of the Christian church, in that it describes "the opening of the door of faith to the Gentiles." Peter, the Apostle of the Circumcision, and very much a Jew, received the honor of initiating the entrance of Gentiles into the church without circumcision. Cornelius was the first Gentile to be received by baptism without the rite of circumcision. Peter, of course, required a vision from God to persuade him to take this critical step. Even afterward, he was not very consistent in his conduct about this matter. (See Galatians 2:11–12.)

Cornelius, the man chosen by God to be the first Gentile to be received into Christian fellowship, was held in high repute for his virtues. But with all his admirable qualities, he needed to be saved and to receive the salvation Christ alone can give. (See Acts 4:12; 11:14.) Famous and good though he was, Cornelius was not exempted from the use of what the *Westminster Shorter Catechism* calls those "outward and ordinary means, the Word, sacraments, and prayer, whereby Christ communicates to us the benefits of salvation." Perhaps we can briefly summarize the recorded facts of this renowned praying soldier in this way—

He lived in Caesarea, a Roman town and the residence of the Roman governor. It was the most markedly Gentile town in all Judaea.

He held the rank of centurion, an officer who had command of a legion, which was made up of one hundred soldiers. A centurion could not rise to a higher rank, save through exceptional circumstances.

He was wealthy, as his large household of servants and slaves, his liberal almsgiving, and his love for the Jews indicates. The size of his household marks him out as a man of superior social position. This name connects him with the *gens Cornelia*, one of Rome's old aristocratic families.

His high personal character is presented to us in seven features. He was "*devout*" (Acts 10:2), meaning he was sincerely religious and had the special type of devotion belonging to a Gentile convert to Judaism. He "*feared God*" (verse 2), which implies that he had forsaken his native paganism as a Roman and had come to believe in and serve with reverence and godly fear the God of Israel. The phrase "*with all his house*" (verse 2) is interesting to consider. He was not content with having found the living and true God for himself, but sought to impart the knowledge of his new faith to those near and dear to him, as well as to his soldiers and slaves, all of whom loved to serve such a master. (See verse 7.)

> When Jesus has found you,
> Tell others the story.[23]

He was kind to the Jewish people, giving them "*much alms*" (Acts 10:2). By "*the people*" (verse 2), we are to understand the Jews of Caesarea as distinct from Gentiles. (See Acts 26:17, 23; 28:17.) With Paul, the centurion felt he was a debtor to the Jews. This almsgiving was seen by the eye of God. (See Romans 1:16; Acts 10:31.)

He was a man given to prayer. He looked beyond the people of God to the God of the people. He "*prayed to God alway*" (Acts 10:2), and, as

---

23. Samuel O. Cluff, "I Am Praying for You," 1860.

Peter assured him, his prayer was heard. (See Acts 10:31.) On the day of his momentous vision, Cornelius continued in prayer until the tenth hour—about 3 p.m.

He was visited by an angel and an apostle. In response to his prayers and alms, God sent an angel to Cornelius, one of those blessed spirits sent forth to minister to the heirs of salvation. Angels are usually invisible, but this one came in visible form, and the soldier was frightened. But the angel reassured him. Then Cornelius replied, *"What is it, Lord?"* (Acts 10:4). He was told to send to Joppa for an apostle who would tell him all about God's comprehensive redemptive purpose. Thus Peter, and not an angel, was the appointed preacher of the good news of salvation for Gentiles, and of their union with saved Jews in the church of the living God. As Peter proclaimed the message of Christian liberty, a second Pentecost was experienced by those first Gentile believers. Cornelius was not required to be circumcised, but he was obliged to be baptized.

Prayer is prominent in the record of Cornelius, for it was as Peter was praying that he received the vision of God's purpose to be no respecter of persons, and to welcome Jews and Gentiles alike into Christ's kingdom. (See Acts 11:5; 22:16.) Cornelius is presented as a man of unceasing prayer. Although a soldier in the Roman army, he was not ashamed to be seen praying. He saw no contradiction between serving his emperor and the God he had come to fear. He was a devout soldier, and down the ages, there have been many like him in the fighting forces.

One of the most notable among British soldiers was General C. Gordon, who was not only a brave and fearless officer, but a sincere Christian. When in a campaign, his fellow officers knew that when they saw a white handkerchief outside Gordon's tent, he was praying and was not to be disturbed.

Sir William Dobbie, the gallant soldier associated with the siege of Malta in World War II, wrote of prayer,

It is the means by which we establish living contact with Almighty God, our Heavenly Father, a contact through which

His Spirit and His vitalizing power flow from Him to us, and by which His strength is imparted to us and our life is renewed. As we read the Gospels we cannot but be struck by the immensely important part prayer played in our Lord's life. He was constantly in touch with His Father through prayer, and devoted long periods to its exercise.

PRAYER FOR DELIVERANCE

Peter therefore was kept in prison: but prayer was made without ceasing of the church unto God for him.   (Acts 12:5)

What a fervent church prayer meeting that must have been! It was held in the home of *"Mary the mother of John, whose surname was Mark; where many were gathered together praying"* (Acts 12:12). This was an emergency calling for instant and earnest intercession, not only for Peter's liberation, but for a happy outcome of his trial, both for the sake of the apostle and of the cause for which he was suffering. This was a crisis prayer meeting, such as we find in the book of Nehemiah.

Those heartfelt petitions were heard, and God sent an angel to deliver Peter from prison and to safely conduct him till he was out on the street. Conscious of what the angel had done, Peter made his way to the home where he knew the saints were praying and knocked on the door, and the young maid Rhoda came and asked who was there. (See Acts 10:9, 11.) When Peter answered, the girl immediately recognized his voice and became so excited she left Peter standing outside and ran back to tell the prayer partners that their prayer had been answered and that Peter was outside the door.

What was the reaction of those who were unceasing in their intercession for Peter's release? This fact is evident: Those dear saints did not mix faith with their prayers. They failed to remember the word of the Lord Jesus, *"Whatsoever ye shall ask in prayer, **believing**, ye shall receive"* (Matthew 21:22). Think of their exclamations when the maid said Peter was at the door. They said, *"Thou art mad"* (Acts 12:15). This is a reaction a person can scarcely resist when he hears news that seems far too good to be true. *"It is his angel"* (Acts 12:15). No, it can't be Peter himself. Perhaps it is his disembodied spirit. How exquisite is the touch of nature here! Though Peter's release had been the burden of their fervent prayers during the time they spent together in communal intercession, they, despite themselves, thought of the answer to their prayers as a thing incredible. Theirs was the same unbelief displayed by the disciples who *"believed not for joy, and wondered"* (Luke 24:41) at the tidings of their Lord's resurrection.

How true to pattern was their unbelief! Often, when we receive an answer to prayer, we can hardly credit it to our devotion. "This, however, argues not so much hard belief as that kind of it incident to the best, in the land of shadows, which perceives not so clearly as it might, how very near heaven and earth, the Lord and his praying people are to each other."[24] Doubtful though the praying saints were when Rhoda asserted that it was Peter knocking at the door, she kept steadfastly affirming that it was he. How shamefaced the rest must have been when finally they discovered that Rhoda's testimony was true!

> Faith is a living pow'r from heav'n
> Which grasps the promise God has giv'n;
>
> ———
>
> Such faith in us, O God, implant,
> And to our prayers Thy favor grant.
> In Jesus Christ, Thy saving Son,
> Who is our fount of health alone.[25]

PRAYER AT A RIVERSIDE

A river side, where prayer was wont to be made.   (Acts 16:13)

In this stirring, momentous chapter, we have three wonderful conversions associated with prayer. The bank of a river became a house of prayer for godly women who had no synagogue to gather in. How

24. *A Commentary, Critical, Practical and Explanatory, on the Old and New Testaments* (Jerome B. Names & Co., 1882), 509.
25. Petrus Herbert, "Faith Is a Living Power," 1874.

grateful they must have been when Paul and Silas joined them for prayer and to minister the Word. Gathered at this prayer meeting alongside a small stream were the first fruits of Europe unto Christ, and they were of the females, of whose accession and services honorable mention is made. (See Acts 16:14.) Lydia, the prominent businesswoman of Thyatira, attended the open-air Bible conference that Paul conducted, and her heart became responsive to the deep, spiritual teaching the apostle presented. No earthquake was necessary to save her, as in the case of the jailer later on. Her heart opened to the Lord as silently as a bud opening to the morning sun. "The scene is one which might call for the master touches of a great painter. The river flowing calmly by, the preacher sitting and talking familiarly, quietly, but earnestly to the group of women, one, at least, among them listening with looks and tears that told of deep emotions, and the consciousness of a new life."

A day or two after Paul and Silas had rested up in the hospitable home of Lydia, they made their way to the usual place of prayer by the riverside, and another female came under the sound and spell of the gospel. Demon-possessed, this damsel was totally different in character from Lydia. The one was at the top of the social ladder, the other at the bottom; but the God who saved the one was able to save the other. They *"went to prayer"* (Acts 16:16), but it would seem that they never reached the prayer meeting. There came an interruption, which resulted in a marvelous trophy of God's saving grace. How would we react if, on the way to the weekly prayer meeting in our church, God thrust a lost, degraded sinner in our pathway?

It is more than likely that this slave girl had found her way to the riverside sanctuary, and she had heard Paul expound the Scripture, for she said of Silas and him, *"These men are the servants of the most high God, which show unto us the way of salvation"* (Acts 16:17). Through Paul's exorcism of the evil spirit possessing her, she came to experience the power of that salvation in her own life. Her continued cries for deliverance from her thralldom were heard. Grace restored her to her true self, and in all likelihood, she became one of the women who labored with the apostle, repaying them to some degree for the suffering she had unwillingly brought upon both Paul and Silas. For as the result of her conversion, the apostles were beaten with many stripes and cast into prison through the instigation of those men who had controlled the girl and made money on her supposed fortune-telling.

PRAYER IN A PRISON

At midnight Paul and Silas prayed, and sang praises unto God.
(Acts 16:25)

These faithful evangelists, wonderfully used of God, entered into the fellowship of their Master's suffering. Taken prisoners, they first endured punishment of unusual severity, for the many stripes would leave their backs lacerated and bleeding. Paul wrote afterward of being *"shamefully entreated"* (1 Thessalonians 2:2) at Philippi. Then they were cast *"into the inner prison"* (Acts 16:24), a dark cavernlike cell below the ground, dark and damp and foul, where the vilest outcasts were imprisoned. To add to their torture and indignity, their feet were made fast in stocks. Further, the jailor was commanded to exercise more than usual fidelity and strictness in the execution of his treatment of these two prisoners.

But tribulation could not silence Paul and Silas—*"at midnight* [they] *prayed, and sang praises unto God"* (Acts 16:25). Habitually they had prayed and sung hymns, and they were not going to let a dirty dungeon close their mouths, even though they could not kneel, fastened as their feet were in the stocks. Their prayerful psalmody revealed their confidence in God and their superiority to human spite and violence. How apt are the words of Tertullian to the martyrs of his time, "The leg feels not the stocks when the mind is in heaven. Though the body is held fast, all things lie open to the spirit." From the sufferers came *"songs in the night"* (Job 35:10). *"[They] prayed, and sang…praises"* (Acts 16:25).

Prayer and praises go in pairs,
He hath praises who hath prayers.

What a delightful touch Luke gives us when he wrote, *"And the prisoners heard them"* (Acts 16:25). It was midnight, but they could not sleep. Instead, they listened eagerly to the two unusual prisoners in the filthy den. Ordinarily, the vile vaults echoed with wild curses and foul jests. Never before had the outcasts and criminals heard prayers and praises in such a place. Perhaps some of those prisoners were won over to Christ as the result of the joyous and victorious example of the two men who were suffering unjustly.

Suddenly, as Paul and Silas prayed and praised at that midnight hour, there was a great earthquake. Was there any connection between the indifferent attitude of the apostles to their suffering and the convulsion of nature? As a young believer, I had the privilege of hearing the late General William Booth, founder of the Salvation Army, preach on the conversion of the jailor, and this sentence has remained with me for well over sixty years: "God was so well pleased with the prayers and praises of Paul and Silas that He said 'Amen!' with a mighty earthquake."

Well, it took an earthquake to save a coarse, brutal, hardhearted man like that jailor. When he saw the supernatural calmness and courage of these evangelists, and realized how they had saved him from suicide, trembling and conscience-stricken, he cried, *"Sirs, what must I do to be saved?"* (Acts 16:30). Immediately, his question was answered, and he believed, as did all his family and servants.

That restitution is one evidence of conversion is seen in the striking action of the saved jailor: *"He took* [Paul and Silas] *the same hour of the night, and washed their stripes"* (Acts 16:33)—the cruel stripes he himself had inflicted on those innocent men. He sought to alleviate the suffering he had caused. There were the two washings. The jailor washed their stripes, as a sign of repentance toward God and his reverence for the godly prisoners; then he yielded to baptism, a symbol of the washing of regeneration. He washed the blood off the backs of Paul and Silas. Now through the blood of the Lord Jesus Christ, the jailor was cleansed from wounds worse than those he had inflicted on others. What a happy ending to that apostolic prayer-and-praise session in a prison cell! The saved, rejoicing jailor could sing, "Jesus' blood can make the vilest sinner clean."[26] Like Lydia and the demon-possessed girl, the prison keeper came to know *"the way of salvation"* (Acts 16:17) these men declared.

---

26. Anna W. Waterman, "Yes, I Know!" circa 1920.

PRAYER OF FAREWELL

When [Paul] had thus spoken, he kneeled down, and prayed with them all.   (Acts 20:36)

There is no recorded speech in the entire realm of literature comparable to Paul's farewell. This moving message to the elders of Ephesus, which Luke the historian recorded word for word, is full of living personal interest. Rev. E. H. Plumptre's comment of the address of Paul, bearing as it does the internal marks of genuineness, offers a most fitting summary—

No writer of a history adorned with fictitious speeches could have written a discourse so essentially Pauline in all its turns and touches of thought and phraseology, in its tenderness and sympathy, its tremulous anxieties, its frank assertions of the fulness of his teaching and the self-denying labours of his life, its sense of the infinite responsibility of the ministerial office for himself and others, its apprehension of coming dangers from without and from within the Church. The words present a striking parallel to the appeal of Samuel to the people in 1 Sam. xii. 3.[27]

The parting scene at Miletus is most heartmoving. Those elders, feeling they would never again see the much-loved face of Paul, kissed it in the last embrace before he embarked. Nothing can be more touching than the three last verses in the chapter containing Paul's farewell message. They leave an indelible impression of rare ministerial fidelity and affection on Paul's part, and of warm admiration and attachment on the part of those Ephesian elders. A passing reference to another parting scene of perhaps even tenderer emotion can be found in Paul's second letter to young Timothy. (See 2 Timothy 1:4.) Would that such scenes were frequent in the church today! Prayers, tears, and kisses were associated with that sad farewell.

The next chapter records another farewell not as sorrowful as this one. Before Paul took ship to Ptolemais, he kneeled down on the shore

---

27. *A New Testament Commentary for English Readers by Various Writers*, vol. 2, 140.

and prayed for and with the disciples, their wives, and their children, who had assembled to bid the apostle bon voyage. (See Acts 21:5.) The preacher will find a good deal of sermonic material in the farewells or partings in the Bible record. Alas, not all of them are associated with sincere, heartfelt prayer.

PRAYER OF GRATITUDE

When [Paul] had thus spoken, he took bread, and gave thanks to God in presence of them all.   (Acts 27:35)

Luke's account of Paul's voyage to Italy and all the perils of the sea that all the prisoners endured is surely a literary classic. J. S. Alexander, in *The Acts of the Apostles Explained*, says that this chapter, containing Paul's last recorded voyage with its shipwreck, "is chiefly remarkable for the fulness and exactness of its nautical details, which the latest and most critical investigations have only served to render more surprising in themselves, and more conclusive as internal proofs of authenticity and genuineness."[28]

The divine word of encouragement *"Fear not, Paul"* (Acts 27:24) may have been an answer to his prayer "prompted by the fear, not of death or danger in itself, but lest the cherished purpose of his heart should be frustrated when it seemed on the very verge of attainment."[29] Although the narrative carries no actual prayer that the apostle prayed during that disastrous storm, we can be certain that if he had not prayed, the visit of the angel of God would probably not have occurred. The angel assured him that while the ship would be lost, there would be no loss of life, all being saved. (See Acts 27:22–25.) Believing this message of divine protection, Paul became the source of calm strength to the crew and prisoners, and he had the presence of mind to act aright in such a state of emergency.

Too often in times of physical danger, people panic, become terror-stricken, and desperately cry out to God for deliverance. Misery and dejection grip their hearts. But here was one man whose looks and tone,

---

28. Joseph Addison Alexander, *The Acts of the Apostles Explained*, vol. 2 (London: James Nisbet and Co., 1857), 432.
29. Ibid., 415.

suggesting a brave, calm confidence in the God to whom he belonged and whom he served, steadied the nerves of the rest on that doomed ship. Soldiers and sailors under such adverse circumstances might have become sullen and unwilling to help. They were, in fact, prepared to seek self-preservation and to let the ship sink, but the prompt vigor, clear discernment, and declared faith in God that Paul manifested kept all on board together until the worst was past and *"they escaped all safe to land"* (Acts 27:44).

Paul urged the hungry men, who had battled with the elements for so long without food, to eat what rations they had to keep soul and body together until they landed at Melita. The apostle's practical insight and human sympathy must have endeared him to the rest on board. He assured them that not a hair on their heads would fall. As they all sat down to eat, Paul prayed and *"gave thanks to God in presence of them all"* (Acts 27:35), not only for the food before them, but for the way He had preserved them from death. No wonder those 276 souls were all of good cheer! The faith and influence of one brave and godly man had banished their despair. "The hearty cheerfulness…of the Apostle had communicated itself, as by a kind of electric sympathy, to his companions. They looked to him as their friend and leader, and had spirits to eat once more."[30] (See Acts 27:25, 36.)

Paul's prayer of gratitude was a most impressive act in such circumstances, and it planted a testimony for the God he so faithfully served in the hearts of all who sailed with him. Do we display the faith and courage that sustains us in the adverse circumstances of life? And do we by word and action recommend the God we serve to those similarly tossed about by the billows of trial and suffering, but who do not yet know Him as "the Master of ocean, and earth, and skies"?[31]

PRAYER FOR HEALING

Paul…prayed, and laid his hands on him, and healed him.

(Acts 28:8)

---

30. Ibid., 419.
31. Mary A. Baker, "Master, the Tempest Is Raging," 1874.

The shipwrecked voyagers found hospitable people on the island of Melita. By the word *"barbarians"* (Acts 28:4) Paul uses for inhabitants of Melita, we are not to understand that they were a savage people. The term was used to describe all races that did not speak Greek. (See, for example, Romans 1:14; 1 Corinthians 14:11.) The travelers to Italy found the natives to be considerate people, who *"showed no little kindness"* (Acts 28:2). Because of the rain and cold, shelter was provided, and as warmth was necessary, the ever-practical Paul gathered a bundle of sticks. Out of this bundle, a viper fastened onto his hand, and the natives judged this an omen that Paul was a murderer and that, although he had escaped the storm, a terrible death would now overtake him: *"Though he hath escaped the sea, yet vengeance suffereth not to live"* (Acts 28:4).

Paul, however, thought nothing of it. He simply shook off the beast into the fire. The people waited to see his hand inflame and the quick poison bring almost sudden death. But Paul felt no harm. We are not to gather from this that the viper was not poisonous and was, therefore, unable to produce a terrible death. Believing that God would continue to preserve him, the apostle rested in the promise of his Master, *"They shall take up serpents and...[they] shall not hurt them"* (Mark 16:18). The natives changed their minds when nothing happened to Paul; they called him a *"god"* (Acts 26:8) instead of a *"murderer"* (verse 4).

Publius, the chief, or governor of the island, kindly extended to Paul and one or two of his companions the hospitality of his home for three days. The father of Publius *"lay sick of a fever and of a bloody flux"* (Acts 28:8)—language Luke the physician uses with professional precision. Paul entered the sick room, prayed for the stricken man, and laid his hands on him, and he recovered. Other diseased people around came to the apostle, and he healed them in accordance with the same promise in Mark 16:18—healing of the sick by the laying on of hands. Thus, as Jesus rewarded Peter for the use of his boat (see Luke 5:3–4), so Paul richly repaid Publius for his gracious hospitality. Laden with many gifts, and also with necessary provisions for the voyage on the ship, *Castor and Pollux*, the whole company, now greatly refreshed by the stay on the island, set sail for Rome. While nothing is said of their three-month stay at Melita, we can be assured that Paul took every opportunity to preach Christ to the islanders. An accredited tradition affirms that the beginning of the Christian church at Malta, the modern term for Melita, sprang out of Paul's memorable visit.

James has some pertinent things to say about intercession for the sick. (See James 5:13–20.) Prayer, even though accompanied by faith, does not always heal the sick. Paul himself had a most troublesome physical disability that he prayed to the Lord about three times; but his thorn in the flesh remained, and he received the promise that he would have sufficient grace to live with his "thorn," which would thus magnify divine strength in his weakness. Sometimes, prayer seems to prevail and the sick are healed. But there are other times when prayer is just as earnest and sincere, but sickness in those prayed for remains. *"The will of the Lord be done"* (Acts 21:14).

Concluding our coverage of prayer in Acts, we find Paul ultimately settled in his own hired house, where seekers came from far and near to hear him preach and teach the things concerning the Lord Jesus Christ. (See Acts 28:30–31.) What a house of prayer that must have been! As a prisoner, the apostle was not allowed to go out and preach in synagogues or "churches" in the homes of disciples, but all were allowed free access to him, which turned out to be more favorable for the furtherance of the gospel. (See Philippians 1:12.) The periods of intercession as well as of spiritual instruction in that hired house must have exercised a tremendous influence over those who visited it. Paul wrote of prayer as being an all-sufficient resource for saints in their warfare: *"Praying always with all prayer and supplication in the Spirit, and watching thereunto with all perseverance and supplication for all saints"* (Ephesians 6:18).

> All earthly things with earth shall fade away;
> Prayer grasps eternity; pray, always pray.[32]

---

32. "Master, the Tempest Is Raging."

THEME 4

ROMANS: THE TEACHING OF SALVATION

The apostle Paul is preeminent among New Testament writers as the exponent of the many facets of God's salvation from the penalty and power of sin. His matchless epistles are saturated with all that is involved when sinners are saved from sin's guilt and government. He is, indeed, "the evangelist extraordinary." Terms such as *save, saved, salvation*, and *Savior* occur almost fifty times in his writings, and the kindred term *deliver*, used in connection with the emancipation of the soul from satanic dominion, is employed some twenty times. The apostle's undying passion was to preach salvation by grace (*grace* is one of his favorite terms) and lead sinners to the Savior, who had delivered him from so great a death.

Doubtless such particular emphasis sprang from his own remarkable experience of God's power to suddenly apprehend a sinner, convict him of his sin, and then just as suddenly snatch him as a brand from the burning. Nothing could be more dramatic than what happened to Paul, when, as Saul of Tarsus on the way to Damascus, he was found breathing out threatening and slaughter against the disciples of the Lord. He had given his consent to the murder of a truly saved soul, Stephen, and waited to witness the brutal slaying of this first martyr of the Christian church. Such a magnificent, victorious, Calvary-like death, with the murdered one praying for the forgiveness of his slayers, must have blistered his conscience; and to drown its voice, he redoubled his efforts to hunt down all who claimed to follow the Savior. While Philip the evangelist was strenuously saving souls in Samaria, Paul was tireless in his persecution of the saints.

> *And Saul, yet breathing out threatenings and slaughter against the disciples of the Lord, went unto the high priest, and desired of him letters to Damascus to the synagogues, that if he found any of this way, whether they were men or women, he might bring them bound unto Jerusalem.* (Acts 9:1–2)

The term *"breathing out"* (verse 1) implies that Paul was living in an atmosphere of rage and murder. Possibly there is an allusion here to the panting or snorting of a wild beast. But in a moment of time, the miracle happened—his chains fell off, and he rose up and followed the One he had persecuted. The illumination from heaven, which enlightened Saul, who became Paul, was not a flash of lightning, but a supernatural light into which he was translated. (See Acts 9:1–9.) Almost immediately after that transforming vision, Paul preached that Jesus was the Son of God, and wherever he went, he *"spake boldly in the name of the Lord Jesus"* (verse 29). This unique trophy of God's saving grace and power had sought to slay those who followed Christ as "the Way." Now that he was a conspicuous follower himself, the Grecians—against whom Paul, the new convert, disputed—went about to slay him. (See Acts 9:29.)

From the moment of his deliverance from the shackles of sin and religious bigotry, Paul had no doubt about the reality and depth of his salvation. *"I know whom I have believed, and am persuaded that he is able to keep that which I have committed unto him against that day"* (2 Timothy 1:12). Further, with his dynamic conversion, there came a divine, direct call to serve the One who had saved him, and he went forth to proclaim unceasingly, as a chosen vessel, the amazing grace of God to the Gentiles, to kings, to the children of Israel. Through his instrumentality, multitudes were brought to the Savior, and down through the ages, myriads more have come to experience the gospel as the power of God unto salvation through the apostle's Spirit-inspired and grace-saturated writings. The apostolic apologia will never be superseded: "*This is a faithful saying, and worthy of **all** acceptation, that Christ Jesus came into the world to save sinners; of whom I am chief*" (1 Timothy 1:15).

It would be a most profitable exercise to go through the fourteen epistles (if we include Hebrews), among Paul's masterly works, which we have no hesitation in doing, and classify his teaching on the doctrine of salvation. But let us confine ourselves to Romans, which Frédéric Godet, the French theologian, described as "the Cathedral of the Christian Faith." At the outset of our pursuit, do we fully understand what is meant by the glorious, evangelical, biblical term, *salvation?* Too often, we limit its implication to initial deliverance from all just guilt as we receive by the faith the Lord Jesus as our personal Savior. Going out to testify, we thank God that we are saved—saved on a certain day in a stated place.

But if someone should stop you one day and kindly ask you, "Are you saved, my friend?" you would be right to reply, "Do you mean have I *been* saved, or am I *being* saved, or have I yet *to be* saved?" In Romans, Paul emphasizes these three aspects of salvation—past, present, future—and his teaching on the subject cannot be understood unless the distinction between these tenses is recognized.

+ Our *past* salvation became ours the moment we received Jesus as the only One able to save us from all our former sins.

+ Our *present* salvation concerns our daily deliverance from sin's government and dominion by the power of the indwelling Spirit.

+ Our *future* salvation is yet to be experienced, and will be ours when Jesus returns, as He said He would, to completely deliver us from sin within our hearts and sin around us in the world.

I HAVE BEEN SAVED

Ever conscious of that instantaneous salvation that came to him on that Damascus road, Paul, who as we know from Acts related the miracle of his conversion three times over, could write to the Romans, *"I am not ashamed of the gospel of Christ: for it is the power of God unto salvation to every one that believeth"* (Romans 1:16).

Salvation, then, from an evil past is a gift we receive as soon as we open the avenues of our beings to the One who died to save us. *"If thou…shalt believe in thine heart that God hath raised* [the Lord Jesus] *from the dead, thou shalt be saved"* (Romans 10:9). We are continually being saved, *"with the mouth confession is made unto salvation"* (verse 10). Then comes the message God has used for the salvation of countless numbers since Paul penned it: *"For whosoever shall call upon the name of the Lord shall be saved"* (verse 13).

Writing to the Ephesians, Paul could say, *"By grace ye **are** saved"* (Ephesians 2:5). The apostle also wanted Titus to remember that *"according to his mercy* [God] *saved us"* (Titus 3:5). All of these, and many other passages, emphasize a finished, irrevocable transaction, for what God accomplishes by His Spirit on the basis of Christ's death and resurrection is forever. Regeneration is a divine act in the life of the repentant, believing sinner, and it can never be repeated. Thus, in this sense, it is true to say, "Once saved, always saved" and, "I am His, and He is mine—forever!"

God sent His Son into the world so that the world might be saved through Him. (See John 3:17.) Then comes the authoritative word of the Son Himself: *"He that believeth on the Son hath everlasting life"* (John 3:36). *"Hath"* means "has it at the present time, never to lose it." If, therefore, we are asked the question, "Are you saved?" and we reply, "I hope so," or "I think so," we reveal a lack of assurance in the positive declaration of both our Lord and Paul. The moment we accept the Savior, we pass from death into life, and we become new creations in Him.

A fact we are apt to forget, however, is that salvation is not *something* but *Someone*, namely, the Savior Himself. *"Behold, God is my salvation"* (Isaiah 12:2). True, salvation is a gift, but the gift is in the Giver Himself. John makes this clear when he says, *"This is the record, that God hath given to us eternal life, and this life is in his Son. He that hath the Son hath life"* (1 John 5:11–12). This life, then, that we receive when we accept the Savior is not only *in* Him but *is* the Savior Himself. Jesus says, "*I am...the life*" (John 11:25; see also 14:6). Therefore, when He enters the heart as Savior, it is to abide there. (See Revelation 3:20.) I know whom I have believed,

Paul could not explain the miracle of all that happened on that spiritual birthday of his, but he did "*know whom he had believed*" (2 Timothy 1:12), and he ceaselessly witnessed to the certainty of his salvation from past sin. When some of us look back to the days of our former lusts, we cannot tell how the red blood of Jesus made the black heart of the sinner whiter than snow (see Psalm 57:7; Isaiah 1:18); but we know that when He entered our sin-cursed, sin-stained lives, transformation of life and character became evident. How grateful we should be, then, if out of redeemed hearts we can sing,

'Tis done, the great transaction's done;
I am my Lord's, and He is mine.[33]

I AM BEING SAVED

While it may appear to contradict the point just considered (past completed salvation), the statement "I am *being* saved" is really complementary to it. In writing to the Philippians, Paul urged them, "*Work out your own salvation with fear and trembling*" (Philippians 2:12), but he was careful to add, "*It is God which worketh in you*" (verse 13). If salvation is not within, then it cannot be worked out. The present aspect of salvation is but the outworking of the inwrought work of grace. Having received Jesus as the Savior, we set out to walk in Him as such. This brings us to the practical side of our position in Christ, for, as His, we are to show forth His salvation from day to day. Or, because *He* is our salvation, we must allow Him to manifest His life through our victorious living. It is this present tense that brings us to a consideration of Paul's repeated "*much more*" phrases: "*Christ died for us.* **Much more** *then, being now justified by his blood* [present assurance of a past transaction], *we **shall be*** [future experience] *saved from* [coming] *wrath through him. For if, when*

---

33. Philip Doddridge, "O Happy Day That Fixed My Choice."

*we were enemies, we were reconciled to God by the death of his Son, **much more**, being reconciled, we shall be saved by his life"* (Romans 5:8–10).

To have passed through the wicket gate of salvation is indeed something to be eternally grateful for. Bless God we have been saved, or reconciled, to God! But let us guard against making the starting place the stopping place, for Paul says there is *"much more"* for us than being saved when we first believed. Our salvation from coming wrath is assured, for *"there is therefore now no condemnation to them which are in Christ Jesus"* (Romans 8:1). The question is, Are we being daily saved from the enticements and dominion of sin? It will be noted that Paul speaks of a double salvation, namely,

+ A salvation by the death of Christ
+ A salvation by the life of Christ

The first aspect takes us back to that happy day that fixed our choice on Christ as Savior. We saw Him hanging on a tree for our sins, and, receiving Him into our lives, we became saved sinners because of His death.

The second aspect is concerned with the present. When we were saved, our sins were dealt with: *"I, even I…will not remember thy sins"* (Isaiah 43:25). *"Thou hast cast all my sins behind thy back"* (Isaiah 38:17). Through the blood, all past sins were blotted out. But although the *fruit* went, the *root* of sin remains. When God saved us, He did not take away our old Adamic, sinning nature, but made us the recipients of a new nature. This accounts for the conflict within: *"When I would do good, evil is present with me"* (Romans 7:21). Had we been left with only one nature, the newness of life, then we would have been perfectly holy, with no evil bias within for Satan to appeal to. But the old man remains, and because the new man is diametrically opposed to his habits and ways, there is continued conflict as to which man is to rule. But victory is assured over the root of sin, which was not eradicated in our acceptance of Christ as Savior. By His death, He saved us from the fruit of the root; now by His life, He is able to save us from any sproutings of the root. *"Sin shall not have dominion over you"* (Romans 6:14).

> *For if, when we were enemies, we were reconciled to God by the*
> *death of his Son, much more, being reconciled, we shall be saved by*
> *his life.*   (Romans 5:10)

What, exactly, did Paul mean by *"his life"*? Not Christ's earthly life. There is no salvation through trying to emulate the spotless life He lived among men. No, by *"his life,"* Paul means not the Christ after the flesh but the Christ who is alive forevermore. And we are saved from sin's attractions, allurements, and affections by His risen, glorified throne-life. Because Christ lives, He enables us to live victoriously. He has no place in His program for sinning saints, seeing as He has illimitable power to lead us to follow Him in the train of His triumph.

Having been cleansed from the guilt of the past by His efficacious blood, are we being daily delivered from yielding to sin through the power of the Savior, who ever lives to make intercession for us?

> Be of sin the double cure,
> Save me from its guilt and power.[34]

Can we say that the moment-by-moment salvation from sin's enticements is ours because we obey Him who *"liveth, and was dead"* (Revelation 1:18)? Or, though we are saved, are we yet miserably defeated, limping along with only one half of the gospel? God has made infinite provision for our *present* as well as our *past*—for our sanctification as well as our salvation. Life from a condition of spiritual death is ours; but are we experiencing the life more abundant?

> Love's resistless current sweeping
> All the regions deep within;
> Thought, and wish, and senses keeping
> Now, and every instant, clean:
> Full salvation! Full salvation!
> From the guilt and power of sin.[35]

---

34. Augustus Toplady, "Rock of Ages," 1775.
35. Frank Bottome, "Full Salvation! Full Salvation!"

I HAVE YET TO BE SAVED

We sometimes sing, "More and more, always more to follow,"[36] and this is true in respect to the salvation provided for us by God through the death, resurrection, and reappearing of His Son who was born a Savior. While it is not within the scope of this meditation, it can be observed in passing that Paul makes it clear that all of Israel will yet be saved. (See Romans 11:11, 26; 9:26.) The passage, however, relevant to the future of those who have been saved, and are being saved, is the one Paul has in the portion dealing with Christian life and service. Exhorting the saints to arouse themselves from their spiritual lethargy, seeing that *the night is far spent,* [and] *the day is at hand*" (Romans 13:12), the apostle announces, "*For now is our salvation nearer than when we believed*" (Romans 13:11). Well, now, what brand of salvation is this? Were we not saved when we first believed? Yes. Are we not kept daily saved, and we keep on believing? Yes. Then what feature of salvation has Paul in mind when he tells us that it is "*nearer than when we believed*"? As the context reveals, it is associated with the return of the Savior to gather His saved ones home.

At the time we first believed, we received salvation from the penalty of sin. As we keep on believing, we experience salvation from the power of sin, but we must also have salvation from the entire presence of sin. We need to be wholly delivered from a sinning nature within us, and from a sinning world around us. We have a redeemed life, but it is in an old body—a prisoner of hope awaiting a redeemed body. This is what Paul calls "*the redemption of our body*" (Romans 8:23), which will be ours when Jesus returns and transforms the body of our humiliation into a glorious body like unto His own. (See Philippians 3:20–21.). Then we will be saved and will sin no more, being forever saved from a sinning world. (See 2 Corinthians 1:10.)

This blessed, final installment of a heaven-provided salvation is certainly nearer than when we first made the acquaintance of Christ as Savior. We live in momentous days, heavy with prophetic significance, and on every hand there are evidences that the coming of the

---

36. Philip P. Bliss, "Have You on the Lord Believed?" 1873.

Lord draws near. *"When these things begin to come to pass...know ye that the kingdom of God is nigh at hand"* (Luke 21:28, 31). Sooner than we expect, He who promised to return for His saved ones may appear. Are we ready to meet Him and receive from Him the completion of our wonderful salvation?

Separated unto Jesus,
Loosed from all the world beside;
Blinded by the advent glory,
Hour by hour would I abide.

So from glory unto glory,
Gladdened by the advent ray;
All the path is growing brighter,
Shining unto perfect day.[37]

---

37. Emily May Grimes Crawford, "In the Advent Light, O Savior."

THEME 5

GALATIANS:
THE WONDROUS CROSS

In many respects, the epistle to the Galatians, sometimes called "the Magna Carta of Liberty," is one of the greatest writings to come from the gifted pen of the apostle Paul. There are several facets to this brilliant diamond of truth. Approaching the letter to the Galatians, we can study the contrast between law and grace, and note Paul's strong emphasis concerning deliverance from legalism. Or we could confine ourselves to the doctrine of the Holy Spirit as unfolded in the epistle, for Paul's classification of this soul-satisfying theme in this letter is unique. Then we might come to Galatians thinking only of arrested spiritual progress and develop a message on the cause and cure of "backsliding," for far too many Christians begin in the Spirit and end in the flesh.

What impresses our minds, however, as we study Galatians, is the fact that it stands out in all the writings of Paul as a cross-exalting epistle. There is no other New Testament book that deals with the cross of Christ in so many ways as this one, which left such an impact upon Martin Luther. If we were to give the epistle a caption, we would write over it, "The Crucified and His Cross." It is essentially "the Epistle of Calvary," relating the cross to life and experience in unmistakable terms.

Take your New Testament, note these allusions to the cross in every chapter of Galatians, and see if Paul is not worthy of being known as the apostle of Calvary. Had he been familiar with the hymnology of our time, his favorite spiritual song might well have been:

> In the cross of Christ I glory,
> Towering o'er the wrecks of time;
> All the light of sacred story
> Gathers round its head sublime.[38]

AN OVERVIEW OF THE BOOK OF GALATIANS

Paul's purpose in writing this matchless letter was to combat the mutilated gospel and the compromising ministry that the Galatian church had countenanced. In forceful and clear terms, the apostle declares that a full understanding of the redemptive work of Christ is the only safeguard against license and legalism of any kind. The following is an overview of what he addresses.

Chapter 1: The Cross and Deliverance from an Evil World

Who gave himself for our sins, that he might deliver us from this present evil world.   (Galatians 1:4)

Christ, by His death and resurrection, not only saves us from eternal judgment, but also from surrounding wickedness here and now.

Chapter 2: The Cross and Co-Crucifixion

I am crucified with Christ: nevertheless I live; yet not I, but Christ liveth in me.   (Galatians 2:20)

The mystic touch of identification with Christ in His death, burial, and resurrection is sadly neglected by churchgoing people today.

---

38. John Bowring, "In the Cross of Christ I Glory," 1825.

Chapter 3: The Cross and Redemption from the Curse

Christ hath redeemed us from the curse of the law, being made a curse for us. (Galatians 3:13)

The One who was always obedient to God, who had never violated His law, was the One who was willing to bear our curse, enduring our penalty.

Chapter 4: The Cross and Adoption into Sonship

To redeem them that were under the law, that we might receive the adoption of sons. (Galatians 4:5)

The Son Himself was willing to die so that we might be called the sons of God. All who are born anew by the Spirit of adoption are sons, and if sons, then heirs of God. (See Galatians 4:6–7.)

Chapter 5: The Cross and Its Continued Offense

Then is the offence of the cross ceased. (Galatians 5:11)

"*Offense*" here actually means "scandal." What, then, is the scandal of the cross? Cicero wrote, "The cross, it is so shameful it never ought to be mentioned in polite society." It was, of course, a most scandalous thing to die as a felon on a wooden gibbet. What do we know about sharing the shame of the cross?

Chapter 6: The Cross and Its Persecution

Lest they should suffer persecution for the cross of Christ. (Galatians 6:12)

If we seek to make a fair show in the flesh, we will miss much of the hostility the preaching of the cross produces. If we live the cross, we will quickly know what it is to have fellowship with His sufferings. Also in chapter 6, Paul discusses the cross and its glory. "*But God forbid that I should glory, save in the cross of our Lord Jesus Christ*" (Galatians 6:14).

Paul had no other boast. Writing to the Corinthians, he said that he determined to know nothing among men save Christ and Him crucified. (See Paul's letter to the Galatians, as well as all his other letters, reveals how he lived at the heart of Calvary.

Some of the old writers were accustomed to speaking of Calvary as "the divine academy of life." No matter how highly educated we may be, our education is not complete unless we have graduated from such an academy. Paul tarried in such a school of spiritual learning while in the desert, and, in his teaching on the cross, he shares with us the treasures of this divine tuition.

It must not be forgotten that all Paul knew about the meaning and message of Calvary was received directly from the Crucified One Himself. Going back to the autobiographical sketch in Galatians 1, Paul, in his emphatic statement as to the authority of the gospel of redeeming love and power, says: "[It] *is not after man. For I neither received it of man, neither was I taught it, but by the* **revelation of Jesus Christ**" (Galatians 1:11–12).

The One who died on the tree knew, as no other, the full import of such a death, and in turn, He gave Paul a distinct revelation of the true significance of "the old rugged cross."

LESSONS OF THE CROSS

What, then, were some of the lessons the apostle learned about the cross from the slain Lamb Himself, leading him to glory in it?

A Law That Had Been Satisfied

This was the initial lesson he had to master in the divine academy, and how overwhelmed Paul must have been as the sinless Substitute for sinners instructed him in the substitutionary aspect of the cross. His mind was not prepared (neither is ours) for the further truth of the cross until this initial aspect is fully comprehended. In the Person of Christ, sin was judged, condemned, and expiated. Thus, without apology, the apostle declares that "*by the works of the law shall no flesh be justified*" (Galatians 2:16). Not only did Paul preach *"that Christ died for our sins"* (1 Corinthians 15:3), but he made it personal: *"The Son of God, who loved **me**, and gave himself for **me"*** (Galatians 2:20).

Combating the legalism that he encountered in Galatia, Paul thunders out a blood-bought emancipation of liberty from the law's curse and condemnation. All who disobey God's ancient law are under a curse. *"Cursed is every one that continueth not in all things which are written in the book of the law to do them"* (Galatians 3:10). In His death, Christ endured this curse. Now by faith, we can know what it is to sing, "Free from the law, O happy condition."[39] Because of this curse, the sinner was under condemnation: *"The soul that sinneth, it shall die"* (Ezekiel 18:4, 20). The Lord Jesus, however, took our death and made it His own. *"That he by the grace of God should taste death for every man"* (Hebrews 2:9). Having no sin of His own, He was yet made sin—*not* a sinner—for us. (See 2 Corinthians 5:21.)

A Love That Had Been Manifested

While the apostle came to learn that the heart of the cross was the very heart of God, he still knew that the aspect of divine love exhibited at Calvary was that of Christ's love: *"The Son of God, who loved me"* (Galatians 2:20). And it was because of this sacrificial love of the Savior that Paul counted himself honored to be known as His love slave.

A Liberty That Had Been Secured

Passages like Galatians 1:4; 4:9; and 5:1 confirm that the cross represents the blood-bought emancipation made available to us. Calvary disposes of all legality. Sin may pursue us right up to the cross, demanding the wages of death, but at Calvary, the claim is disallowed. Justice pursued us up to the cross, demanding vindication; and it received it in Jesus' cry, *"It is finished"* (John 19:30). Liberty from sin and self is the coronation stone of the cross. Paul could join in John's Calvary doxology: *"Unto him that loveth us, and **loosed** us from our sins by his blood"* (Revelation 1:5 ASV; see also 1 John 1:7).

---

39. Philip P. Bliss, "Free from the Law," 1873.

A Life That Must Be Lived

Many who believe in a crucified Christ are not willing to live a crucified life; yet the two are nailed together. In Galatians 6:14, Paul summarizes for us all that he learned about the cross. He reduces his teaching to three crosses:

+ Christ on a cross: *"God forbid that I should glory, save in the cross of our Lord Jesus Christ"* (verse 14).

+ The world on a cross: *"By whom the world is crucified unto me"* (verse 14).

+ The believer on a cross: *"And I unto the world"* (verse 14).

The cross, then, is the divine laboratory where the flesh is cauterized and put to death. (See Galatians 2:20; 5:24.) The burning caustic of the cross must be applied to the world and the flesh as they arise to laud it over us. The cross is the boundary line or terminus between believers and the world. All legal, carnal elements in the world lost their hold on Paul. Is this experientially true of us? Are we content to let the world go by? Is the shame, scandal, and persecution of the cross our glory? No saint can reach for the old life without crossing Christ's grave, for we died in Him. That blessed cross of His, then, is not only the center of the universe, of Scripture, and of history—it must be at the very center of every part of our lives. The cross must be known not only as a doctrine but as a dynamic, bringing every phase of life into conformity with His death.

THEME 6

EPHESIANS: THE UNFOLDING OF GOD

Readers of Paul's prison letter to the Ephesian church can profit from various outlines of the epistle given by different expositors. One of the most serviceable is that which is founded upon the word *heavenly*. (See Ephesians 1:3.) So we have—

+ The heavenly calling of the church (See Ephesians 1–3.)
+ The heavenly conduct of the church (See Ephesians 4–6:9.)
+ The heavenly conflict of the church (See Ephesians 6:10–24.)

The exposition of Ephesians given by Ruth Paxon deals with the "Wealth, Walk, and Warfare of the Christian." My own handling of Paul's letter, however, may appear to be somewhat unusual. Much reading of it led me to classify the majority of the words forming the epistle under the letters of the alphabet. For instance, under the letter *A, apostle* is used three times, *according*, seven times, and so on. By this method, the truths Paul set out to emphasize were alphabetically arranged with the number of their appearances, and consequently there evolved several cameos made up of the exact phrases found in this "epistle of the heavenlies." Shall we let these priceless phrases speak for themselves?

THE WILL OF GOD (SEE EPHESIANS 1:1.)

The divine will was the basis of Paul's call to the ministry, and it was the cause and consequence, ground and background, of all revelation and manifestation the apostle experienced. The *origin* of the call was the will of God; the *organ* was the apostle himself; and the *object* was the edification and enlightenment of the saints and the faithful in Christ Jesus.

Work out the following cameo of *the will of God*—

1. Called by His will (See Ephesians 1:1.)

2. Good pleasure of His will (See Ephesians 1:5.)

3. Mystery of His will (See Ephesians 1:9.)

4. Counsel of His will (See Ephesians 1:11.)

5. Understanding of His will (See Ephesians 5:17.)

6. Accomplishment of His will (See Ephesians 6:6–7.)

THE GIFT OF GOD (SEE EPHESIANS 2:8.)

What a bountiful giver God is! All His gifts are without repentance. In a parenthetic outburst, Paul instructed the Ephesians to know that grace, first and last, was the sole source of their salvation, of which theirs was a present realization. But what was the exact gift Paul had in mind? Was it salvation or faith? Are not both implied—the gift of salvation and the gift of faith to accept salvation? Saving faith is not natural faith but a bestowed gift, enabling the sinner to accept Christ as a personal Savior.

THE HOUSEHOLD OF GOD
(SEE EPHESIANS 2:19–20.)

No other Pauline epistle unfolds the spiritual position of the true church as does Ephesians, and this feature makes it of great doctrinal value. Here, the church is viewed as—

1. The body (See Ephesians 1:22–23.)

2. The household of God (See Ephesians 2:19–20.)

3. The habitation of God (See Ephesians 2:22.)

4. The temple (See Ephesians 2:21–22.)

5. The center of divine wisdom and glory (See Ephesians 3:20–21.)

6. The bride (See Ephesians 5:25, 32.)

As the figure of *"the household"* (Ephesians 2:19) is domestic in nature, that of the church as a "habitation" is spiritual. Under the old dispensation, God localized His presence in the tabernacle and in the temple (see John 4:20–21), and the Jew had to journey there in order to worship Him. Then, God had a tabernacle for His people; now, under grace, His people are His tabernacle, or dwelling place. The church is "the mysterious cabinet of the Trinity." The term *dwell* means "to abidingly make one's abode." (See John 14:20.) What an overpowering thought it is that every believer is "a temple, hallowed by the indwelling Lord." (See Ephesians 2:21.) What a deterrent against any form of sin the recognition of this fact is!

THE GRACE OF GOD
(SEE EPHESIANS 3:2, 7.)

Grace is the first and the last message of this epistle of grace. (See Ephesians 1:2; 6:24.) Paul deemed it an honor to act as a dispensing steward of the undeserved mercy of God. The dual thought dealt with in the passages before us is that grace is a gift, and that it is given to the least. The word *dispensation* means "age or period," and since the coming of the Spirit of grace at Pentecost, we have had the age of grace. Paul was ever jubilant as he expounded God's elective grace in its richness and sufficiency. (See 1 Corinthians 9:17.)

THE WISDOM OF GOD
(SEE EPHESIANS 3:10.)

Because divine wisdom is *"manifold"* (verse 10), it is not confined to one particular sphere but covers all realms. This "much-varied, many-sided, many-colored" wisdom has been entrusted to the church to display before heaven and earth. The wondrous hues of this divine attribute were all personified in Christ, whom God made unto us wisdom. (See 1 Corinthians 1:30.) If we would possess the wisdom—*"pure, then peaceable, gentle, and easy to be entreated"* (James 3:17)—all we have to do is to appropriate it by faith. (See James 1:5.)

THE FULLNESS OF GOD (SEE EPHESIANS 2:19.)

We are *"fill **unto** all the fulness of God"* (Ephesians 3:19 ASV); we are not filled *with* this fullness but *"unto"* it. The grand goal is to be filled according to capacity even as God is full. (See Colossians 2: 9.) In the epistle, Paul presents a triad of fullnesses: *"The fulness of God"* (Ephesians 3:19); *"the fulness of Christ"* (Ephesians 4:13); *"filled with the Spirit"* (Ephesians 5:18). Although we have such wealth at our disposal, we live like spiritual paupers. An ocean of abundance is ours, yet we content ourselves with a mere trickle of the divine resources at our disposal. May grace and willingness be ours to possess our possessions!

THE SON OF GOD (SEE EPHESIANS 4:13.)

This phrase not only declares the deity of Christ, but it likewise emphasizes the divine Fatherhood. Christ is the only Son the world has ever known who did not have a human father. He came as the only begotten Son of God (see Psalm 2:7), and God sent His only Son to earth as a missionary. The glory of the gospel is that the Son of God became the Son of Man, so that He might make the sons of men, the sons of God. (See John 1:12; Ephesians 4:4–7.)

THE LIFE OF GOD (SEE EPHESIANS 4:18.)

This unique phrase staggers the mind. Our Lord described the kind of life God imparts. As He is *"the eternal God"* (Deuteronomy 33:17), He imparts *"life eternal"* (John 17:3). Salvation is the life of God within the soul, and all who are destitute of this kind of life are spiritually dead. (See 1 Timothy 5:6.)

THE SPIRIT OF GOD
(SEE EPHESIANS 4:30.)

Not only is the Holy Spirit from God, but He *is* God! (See Acts 5:3–4.) The Spirit, like the Savior, came from God, and since His advent, He has been in the world as the administrator of the affairs of the church—the Lord's body. The third person of the Trinity shares the holiness of the first person. Over one hundred times, He is referred to as the Holy Spirit. Why? Because He is intrinsically holy, came from a holy God, represents the holy Son, and seeks to transform those He indwells into the holiness of God.

THE FOLLOWERS OF GOD
(SEE EPHESIANS 5:1.)

This arresting phrase literally means "imitators of God." We are to imitate or copy God, especially in His essential attributes of love and forgiveness. It is from the original form of the word *follower—mimeomai—* that we have *mimeograph,* or "a copy." We are to be imitators, not of those who follow God, but of God Himself. This is not mere imitation, trying to live and act in a Godlike way, but involves surrender to God, so that He might live out His life *in* and *through* our lives.

THE KINGDOM OF GOD
(SEE EPHESIANS 5:5.)

Dual dominion is herewith stated, for what is God's is Christ's, who thought it not robbery to be counted equal with God. (See John 5:18; Philippians 2:6.) Paul speaks of the present spiritual kingdom into which we have been translated and in which the sovereignty of God and of Christ must be recognized. (See Colossians 1:14.)

THE WRATH OF GOD
(SEE EPHESIANS 5:6.)

Arthur May's translation of this passage speaks of this wrath as "ever descending upon the sons of disobedience," who are *"children of wrath"* (Ephesians 2:2–3; see also Romans 2:5). Divine wrath is not inconsistent with divine love. God is holy and righteous, and as a perfect and moral Governor and Lawgiver, He demands obedience and punishes those who transgress His commands. Divine wrath is never unjust. God cannot be guilty of spite. Divine anger is ever subordinate to divine mercy. (See Psalm 30:5; 103:8; 145:8.)

THE FEAR OF GOD (SEE EPHESIANS 5:21.)

Some of the best manuscripts read, *"The fear of Christ,"* such as the *New American Standard Bible.* Either phrase is true, for the Father and He are one. This "fear" is not the kind experienced under the rule of a tyrant. God is not a cruel, merciless dictator. The kind of fear we are to exhibit is that of reverential trust, obedience, and worship— a holy fear that hallows every aspect of life. Fear the Lord, you His saints!

THE ARMOR OF GOD (SEE EPHESIANS 6:11, 13.)

The Pauline Epistles are rich in their use of military metaphors. Close and long contact with Roman guards provided the apostle with effective illustrations of Christian conflict. The complete armor of a Roman soldier included shield, sword, lance, helmet, greaves, and breastplate. Paul does not mention a "spear," but he adds girdle and shoes, which, although not reckoned as a part of armor, were necessary for the soldier. What a magnificent and elaborate description Paul gives us of the full panoply of God! Because of the craftiness, shrewdness, and careful planning of the devil, as well as his methodical devices of error, we must have divine protection. And all that is necessary has been provided. But it must be *"put on"* (Ephesians 6:11) or appropriated by faith. (See 2 Timothy 4:7.) It will be noted that no armor is provided for the *back,* for we are meant to face the foe, not to retreat from him. The knees also are unprotected, seeing as the armor for them is constant, believing prayer—the mightiest weapon of all against every satanic assault. As good soldiers of Jesus Christ, we can be more than conquerors only when fully armed.

THE WORD OF GOD
(SEE EPHESIANS 6:17.)

This offensive weapon of the Christian is absolutely of God and is one that Jesus used most effectively against Satan in the wilderness. (See Matthew 4:1–11.) The infallible Word is the Spirit's two-edged sword. (See Hebrews 4:12.) This same phrase, *"The word of God,"* is used of Christ as He came revealing God to man and reconciling man to God. (See, for example, Luke 3:2.) Thus, the written Word, also known as the living Word, is a mighty weapon to put to flight the powers of evil. Sin and error and heresy cannot exist where Christ and the Scriptures are fully obeyed. (See 2 Timothy 3:16.)

While the designation *God* is used over thirty times in Ephesians, that of *Father* is employed some eight times, and both terms imply that He is the source or spring of any and all blessing. *"All my springs are in thee"* (Psalm 87:7). Each of the references to divine Fatherhood carries its own significance.

GOD OUR FATHER (SEE EPHESIANS 1:2.)

As a Father, He is perfect and, therefore, not subject to the frailties of human fatherhood. As our *Father*, He understands all our needs because we are His children, and as our *God*, He can meet those needs.

THE FATHER OF OUR LORD JESUS CHRIST (SEE EPHESIANS 1:3; 3:14.)

How near and dear the relationship was between Father and Son! As He died, Jesus surrendered His spirit to His Father. As a Son, He never failed to obey His Father's will.

THE FATHER OF GLORY
(SEE EPHESIANS 1:17.)

God is always characterized by glory. (See also Acts 7:2.) This Pauline expression can imply the Father's manifested presence. (See Psalm 108:5.) He is not only essentially glorious in Himself but the source of all true glory.

THE FATHER OF ALL
(SEE EPHESIANS 4:6.)

There is a good deal of unbiblical talk about the fatherhood of God these days. God is certainly the Father of all men in respect to creation, just as He is spoken of as the Father of the rain. (See Matthew 5:45.) But He is not the Father in heaven that our Lord spoke about *unless* we have sonship based upon redemption. God is the heavenly Father only of those who have received the Spirit of adoption. (See Romans 8:15.) Access to the Father is only through the mediation of His Son. (See John 14:6; Ephesians 4:5–7.)

THANKS TO THE FATHER
(SEE EPHESIANS 5:20.)

If an earthly father is grieved over the ingratitude of his children, how do we think our heavenly Father feels when so many of His children forget to praise Him at all times for His unfailing goodness?

PEACE AND LOVE FROM THE FATHER
(SEE EPHESIANS 6:23.)

Blessings from God come to us with the love of His fatherly heart. There are no prayers in Paul's epistles surpassing the two in Ephesians in depth and intensity, in spiritual breadth and elevation. (See Ephesians 1:15–23; 3:14–19.)

THEME 7

EPHESIANS: THE UNFOLDING OF CHRIST

Ephesians is a Christ-magnifying as well as a God-glorifying epistle. Over sixty times, Paul mentioned Christ in the six chapters that form this letter. Then, of the divine pronouns used for God, "His" is most prominent. Everything is His, and the Holy Spirit delights in taking all that is His and making it ours. The striking phrase common to the epistle is *"in Christ,"* suggesting its central theme, namely, that all things are summed up in Christ. He is the element of the believer's life, the One in whom he lives, moves, and has his being. (See Acts 17:28.) A Christian is one who is in Christ and indwelt by Him. Here, again, let us collate the exact phrases and note their implications.

THE APOSTLE OF CHRIST (SEE EPHESIANS 1:1.)

Paul's apostleship was not of man. (See Galatians 1:1.) All the apostles were disciples of Christ, but not all disciples were apostles. An apostle was a disciple who was called and named thus, one who had seen and heard Christ and had witnessed His resurrection. (See Matthew 10:2; Acts 1:21–22.) Paul both saw and heard the risen Christ on that Damascus road. (See Acts 9:4–5; 1 Corinthians 15:8.)

THE FATHER OF CHRIST
(SEE EPHESIANS 1:3, 17.)

"The Father glory clad" was the only Father Jesus had. Although He came as the Son of Man, He was not a son of a man. When He was but twelve years of age, He spoke of God as His Father. (See Luke 2:49.) What love, adoration, obedience, and submission are wrapped up in the tender phrase He often used: *"My Father"*! (See, for example, Luke 22:29; John 6:32.)

THE BLOOD OF CHRIST
(SEE EPHESIANS 1:7; 2:13.)

The Bible is a crimson book, and Paul's Epistles drip with the ruby blood of the Redeemer. The modern, cultured mind may reject all reference to blood-shedding and blood-washing as being repugnant, but the fact remains that *"without shedding of blood is no remission* [of sins]" (Hebrews 9:22; see also 10:18). Because *"the life of the flesh is in the blood"* (Leviticus 17:11), when Christ shed His blood, He gave His life on our behalf. (See Matthew 26:28.) The efficacy of His death abides. (See 1 John 1:7.)

THE PRISONER OF CHRIST
(SEE EPHESIANS 3:1; 4:1.)

As an ambassador in bonds, Paul looked upon himself not as Nero's prisoner but as the Lord's. The apostle had committed no crime meriting punishment. He was in prison for preaching to the Gentiles. As Paul recognized that the will of the Lord controlled all events in his life, and he knew that it was His permissive will that he should suffer captivity. His bonds made for the furtherance of the gospel, and they were used as the ground for an appeal to a closer walk with God in the lives of those to whom he wrote.

THE MYSTERY OF CHRIST
(SEE EPHESIANS 1:9; 3:3–4, 9; 6:19.)

By the use of this term *"mystery,"* Paul implies not something mysterious or difficult to understand, but rather a matter previously hidden but now brought to light, a secret revealed. What exactly was the mystery of Christ? In this narrative, Paul is dealing with the composition of the church, and he reveals that it was the redemptive purpose of Christ to fashion both Jews and Gentiles into one body. It was no mystery or secret in Old Testament days that God would save Jews and likewise save Gentiles. The mystery hidden from the ages was that both Jews and Gentiles would be woven into the mystic fabric, as the church of the living God. This was the mystery revealed to Paul by the Head of the church Himself. (See Galatians 1:12.)

THE RICHES OF CHRIST
(SEE EPHESIANS 1:7, 18; 2:4, 7; 3:8, 16.)

The expressive word Paul uses to describe heavenly riches in Ephesians 3:8 is *"unsearchable,"* meaning "untraceable." We cannot trace its source completely. We do not fully know *"whence it cometh, and whither it goeth"* (John 3:8; see also Job 5:9). Grace is like an inexhaustible mine whose treasures can never be completely explored. What wealth is ours! Riches of glory! Richness of mercy! Riches of grace! The question is, Are we appropriating all we have in and through Christ? For *"all that* [we] *have is* [His]" (Luke 15:31). Let us live on our bountiful inheritance.

THE LOVE OF CHRIST (SEE EPHESIANS 3:18–19.)

The reader will find it profitable to link together all the love passages in Ephesians. (See Ephesians 1:4, 15; 2:4; 3:17; 4:2, 16; 5:2, 25; 5:28, 33; 6:23–24.) Among the paradoxes of our faith is the ability to know the unknowable and to see the invisible. (See Hebrews 11:27.) How comforting are the four dimensions or the rectangular measure of Christ's love! Its proportions are foursquare, like the heavenly Jerusalem John wrote about. (See Revelation 21:16.) This eternal, sacrificial, and immeasurable love of Christ can only be measured by the *"golden reed"* (Revelation 21:15) of man's emptiness and weakness, gilded with His glory. There is the *breadth* of love, and its manifoldness of provision, which is worldwide, including lost souls wherever they may be found. There is the *length* of love, extending to all ages, from eternity to eternity, and enduring as long as God Himself. There is the *depth* of love, which cannot be fathomed, and which is deeper than all human need. It is so profound that no creature is able to fully understand it. (See Romans 11:33.) There is the *height* of love, which is beyond the reach of any foe to deprive us of it. Height can also suggest the exalted position of those whose lives have been claimed by such an embracing love.

> It passeth knowledge, that dear love of Thine,
> My Savior, Jesus; yet this soul of mine
> Would of Thy love in all its breadth and length,
> Its height and depths, its everlasting strength,
> Know more and more.[40]

THE GIFT OF CHRIST (SEE EPHESIANS 4:7.)

Among Paul's favorite words, *gift* holds a prominent place, especially in this epistle, in which he used it fourteen times. In the narrative at this point, the apostle is expounding the manifold gifts the ascended Lord bestowed upon His church. A diversity of graces and offices are given to the members of His body according to each person's measure of faith. (See Romans 12:3.) *"Unto every one of us is given grace according to the measure of the gift of Christ"* (Ephesians 4:7); in other words, there is no born-again believer who lacks a regeneration-imparted gift to be used in the Lord's service. The tragedy of the church is nonuse of unrecognized gifts. There is no Christian without a gift. Have you discovered yours? And are you using it to the utmost limit?

THE BODY OF CHRIST (SEE EPHESIANS 4:12.)

The three figures Paul uses of the church are *"the bride"*—expressing love, union, and intimacy; *"the body"*—indicating the ideas of life and interdependence; and *"the building"*—speaking of unity, cohesion, and utility. *"The body"* was Paul's favorite term for believers. (See Ephesians 1:23; 2:16; 3:6; 4:4, 12, 16; 5:25, 30.) Christ, as the Head of the body, is well able to control all its affairs and direct its actions. (See Ephesians 1:22; 5:25.) A human body is not only a living organism but an organization of many

40. Mary Shekleton, "It Passeth Knowledge," 1863.

members and functions. It is so with the body that is His church. The apostle makes it clear that the church is a holy temple—not a corrupt one like the temple of the goddess Diana (see Ephesians 2:21), and she is a glorious habitation, existing for the glory of her Head, who loves her as a bride (see Ephesians 5:25, 29).

A profitable division of Ephesians is—

1. The church before the Lord (See Ephesians 1–3.)
2. The church before the world (See Ephesians 4–6:9.)
3. The church before Satan (See Ephesians 6:10–18.)

It must be made clear that a person may be a member of a church as an organized assembly of professed religious people and yet not be a member of the church that is His body. The only membership the apostle stresses is membership in the body. Thus, the question of paramount importance is, Are we in Christ, as well as in a visible house of worship as members?

THE FULLNESS OF CHRIST
(SEE EPHESIANS 1:10, 23; 3:19; 4:13; 5:18.)

Our blessed Lord was, and still is, *"the fulness of the Godhead bodily"* (Colossians 2:9). Arthur Way translates the phrase *"The stature of the fulness of Christ"* (Ephesians 4:13) as "The standards of Messiah's own perfection." The word Paul used for *"fulness"* is *pleroma*, expressing the fullness of the divine nature. (See Colossians 1:19.) "He fills all" (see Ephesians 1:23) implies "He filleth for himself." As the Creator, Preserver, and Governor of the world, He fills the *entire* universe with *all* things. He is our fullness, and we are to be His fullness. (See Colossians 2:10; Ephesians 5:18.) Is ours the fullness of the blessing of His gospel? (See Romans 15:29.)

THE KINGDOM OF CHRIST
(SEE EPHESIANS 5:5.)

Another translation of this verse puts it, "The kingdom of Christ who is God." As Emmanuel, He is "God with us." The context here contains a solemn warning against indulgence in the sins of idolaters. Works of darkness are incompatible with membership in the kingdom of heaven. The unworthy Christian has indeed an inheritance in the Lord's present spiritual kingdom and in His coming visible kingdom to his own awful responsibility. But if his life is not in harmony with the principles of the kingdom, then in a spiritual sense, he is one who *"hath not, from him shall be taken away even that* [which] *he hath"* (Matthew 13:12).

THE NAME OF CHRIST (SEE EPHESIANS 5:20.)

There is more in Paul's admonition than the mere recital of a name. The word *"name"* in this verse represents manifested character, the integrity of the one bearing the name. It represents what the person actually is, not only a label by which he is known. When our thanksgiving is offered in the name of Christ, we are really asking God to hear us on the basis of all Christ is in Himself; and on the merits of His accomplishments, God hears and answers prayer. As Rev. Alfred Barry suggests, use of the name suggests identification "in perfect unity with Him—that we have adoption to sonship which is the ground of such thanksgiving. So also in the same unity...we have the ground of perfect confidence in prayer"[41]

Is ours the spirit of habitual thanksgiving? Do we give thanks for *all* things, even the most unpleasant and unwelcome things of life? If we cannot give thanks *for* all things, we can certainly be thankful *in* all things. We may not be able to read the meaning of many of our tears, but we can bless God, even as we weep, because we trust that He knows what is best for His children. "Ill that He blesses is our good."[42] If there is nothing within the heart to disturb our fellowship with the Lord, then no matter what circumstances may prevail, we can live on Thanksgiving Street.

THE SERVANTS OF CHRIST
(SEE EPHESIANS 6:6.)

The words Paul uses for servants are *bondsmen* or *slaves*. In Ephesians 6:5–9, his example of the relationship between slaves and their masters

41. Charles John Ellicott, ed., *A New Testament Commentary for English Readers by Various Writers*, vol. 3 (London: Cassell & Company, 1884), 51.
42. Frederick W. Faber, "I Worship Thee, Most Gracious God," 1849.

portrays one of the hardest forms of subjection; still, it is used under the same idea that both are "in Christ." "The slave is the servant of Christ in obeying his master, the master is a fellow-servant with his slave in the same Divine Lord."[43] To quote Rev. Alfred Barry again—

> To be a slave, looking on his master's authority as mere power imposed by the cruel laws of man, this "eyeservice" is found to be an all but irresistible temptation. It is only when he looks on himself as "the slave of Christ"—who Himself "took on Him the form of a slave" (Phil. ii. 7) in order to work out the will of God in a sinful world, and to redeem all men from bondage— that he can possibly serve from the heart.[44]

Paul always practiced what he preached. When he wrote this epistle, he himself was a bondsman, or slave, but grace was given him to glory in his bonds. What the world counted as ignominy, he counted as the highest honor, and he was thus more proud of his shackles than a king of his diadem. A slave in Christ was actually the Lord's freeman, and he entered "a service which is perfect freedom." (See 1 Corinthians 7:22.)

> He is the freeman whom the truth makes free,
> And all are slaves beside.[45]

We have thus seen how full Ephesians is of Christ's worth and work. How Paul loved to magnify the Lord he so faithfully served! May our lives and lips ever extol the same glorious Lord!

What do we know about spiritual slavery? Do we look upon ourselves as slaves of Jesus Christ? Who and what is a slave? Over one hundred years ago, they practiced slavery in America. Who was a slave then? A slave was a person who had no right to anything he possessed. His body was at the disposal of his master; if he had any talents, they also were at the disposal of his master; if he had offspring, they also were looked upon as the possession of his master. A slave had no right to anything he possessed.

---

43. *A New Testament Commentary for English Readers by Various Writers*, vol. 3, 55.
44. Ibid.
45. William Cowper, *The Task*, "Winter Morning Walk" (1785), lines 732–733.

Paul says that we are slaves of Christ. (See Ephesians 6:6.) Are we? When people are urged to be fully yielded to the Lord, they sometimes protest, "Well, I can do as I like with my time; it is no business of yours what I do with my leisure and money." But we cannot do as we like with all we represent if we are His slaves. Our talents are not our own; they are the Lord's. When people are asked to give their money, they reply, "That is no business of yours. I can give as I like with what is my own." But they cannot if they are the Lord's. As slaves, we have no right to anything we possess. All we are and have has been redeemed by the blood of Christ; we are not our own. Calvary has the prior claim on our lives. Nothing we have is ours; all is based on trust. This was the truth George Matheson had in mind when he wrote,

> Make me a captive, Lord,
> And then I shall be free;
> Force me to render up my sword,
> And I shall conqueror be.[46]

---

46. George Matheson, "Make Me a Captive, Lord."

THEME 8

EPHESIANS: THE UNFOLDING OF THE SPIRIT

One of the most profitable methods of studying a book or chapter of the Bible is to gather all that is recorded on a particular theme. The marvel of the Word is that more than one glorious topic or doctrine can be found in almost every book. Take, for example, the epistle of Paul to the Ephesians. A. T. Pierson fittingly called it "the Alps of the New Testament," for here we scale heights and span breadths unknown. Talk about variety of truth! Ephesians has it. Some of these days, I would like to write a commentary on this matchless epistle. What heart-inspiring hours one will have expounding the cameos of God, Christ, grace, the divine will, saints, and sinners found in Ephesians! Why, there is no end to the ways we can approach this epistle. Here, however, we must content ourselves with but one aspect of truth in Ephesians, namely, cameos of the Spirit. Where can we find another book as God-glorifying, Christ-exalting, and Spirit-magnifying as the epistle to the Ephesians? Altogether, it presents some thirteen references to the Spirit.

THE BLESSINGS OF THE SPIRIT (SEE EPHESIANS 1:3.)

The phrase *"blessed us with all spiritual blessings"* (verse 3) can also be translated "the benediction of all blessings of His Spirit."[47] The verse

---

47. Arthur Way translation.

as a whole offers a proof of the three Persons forming the Godhead. A close study of Ephesians 1:1–14 reveals many blessings of the Spirit. Mark these in your Bible:

1. An unbroken relationship (See verse 4.)

2. An unquestioned acceptance (See verse 6.)

3. A redemption none can rob us of (See verse 7.)

4. A union never to be dissolved (See verse 10.)

5. An unfading inheritance (See verse 11.)

6. A seal, never to be disowned (See verse 13.)

Blessings innumerable are ours in and through the Spirit. Let us not, however, be taken up with the blessings to the exclusion of the Blesser Himself. A subtle scheme of Satan is to have us occupied with a gift rather than with the Giver.

> Once it was the blessing,
> *Now* it is the Lord.[48]

THE SEALING OF THE SPIRIT (SEE EPHESIANS 1:13; 4:30.)

Paul's two references to this aspect of the Spirit's ministry are worthy of prayerful meditation. The Spirit is the seal, and the sealer is God. Therefore, because the believer is divinely sealed, no person or thing can break the seal. Among other things, a seal indicates ownership, and once we are sealed with the Spirit, we become the Lord's forever. The sealing is eternal. (See Ephesians 4:30.)

It is also important to realize that the saving and the sealing synchronize. The moment a believing sinner receives Christ as Savior, the Holy Spirit enters as the evidence of a finished transaction. Being sealed with the Spirit is not some post-regenerative experience, as the wording of the King James Version would imply: *"After that ye believed, ye were sealed"* (Ephesians 1:13). The American Standard Edition of the Revised Version says, *"Having also believed, ye were sealed with the Holy Spirit of promise"* (verse 3 ASV).

---

48. A. B. Simpson, "Once It Was the Blessing."

Attention must also be given to the title Paul uses in this verse of the Spirit: "*The Holy Spirit of promise*" (verse 3 asv). Why is He named thus? Well, He came as the promise of the Father and as the promise of the Son. He also inspired holy men of old to write all the promises the Scriptures present, and He alone can enable us to understand and appropriate the precious promises of the Word.

THE EARNEST OF THE SPIRIT (SEE EPHESIANS 1:14; 2 CORINTHIANS 1:22; 5:5.)

The Holy Spirit is our foretaste of heaven, the advance portion of a glorious inheritance. The Scotch have a very expressive term for "earnest." It is the word *arle*. A farmer buys a field from a neighbor. Once the transaction is completed, the buyer scoops up a handful of the earth and puts it in a bag. This is the *arle*, the earnest, or pledge, that he bought the entire field and can possess it when he desires. In like manner, the Spirit is our *arle*, the earnest or pledge of all that we will inherit.

I have a heritage of joy
That yet I must not see,
But the hand that bled to make it mine
Is keeping it for me.[49]

THE ILLUMINATION OF THE SPIRIT (SEE EPHESIANS 1:17.)

When Paul mentioned the Ephesian believers in his prayers, he interceded for them, that they might know what it was to experience the ministry of the Spirit as "*the spirit of wisdom and revelation in the knowledge of* [Christ]" (verse 17). As there is not one useless word in the Bible, there must be a distinction between "*wisdom*" and "*revelation.*" The terms indicate that God's Spirit operates in a twofold way. As the Spirit of wisdom, He works in and upon the mind. Comprehension of a divine revelation is impossible apart from Him through a Spirit-possessed and enlightened mental faculty. Christ opened the *understanding* of His disciples (see Luke 24:45) as He also opened unto them

---

49. Anna L. Waring, "My Heart Is Resting, O My God," 1854.

the *Scriptures* (see Luke 24:32). The opening of the one is necessary to accomplish the other. As the Spirit of revelation, He opens the truth of God; as the Spirit of wisdom, He opens our minds, or understanding, to receive the revelation. And all His ministry in this twofold way is to bring us a deeper knowledge of Christ. (See John 16:14.)

ACCESS BY THE SPIRIT (SEE EPHESIANS 2:18.)

The immediate context at this point is the introduction of both Jew and Gentile, who together form the mystic fabric that we know as the church of God, into His presence. The Spirit, who is responsible for the formation of the church, introduces her to the Father. In this age of grace, we approach God through the agency of the Spirit. We worship Christ by the Spirit. God can only be worshiped in the Spirit.

THE BUILDING OF THE SPIRIT · (SEE EPHESIANS 2:22.)

What a master builder the Spirit is, and how effectively Paul assisted Him! But what is the sacred task of the Spirit? Is it not the completion of the church, the Lord's body? Christ is the chief cornerstone of this invisible structure, and in Him we are fitly framed together: *"In whom ye also are builded together for a habitation of God in the Spirit"* (Ephesians 2:22 ASV).

Is the Spirit near the end of His sacred task? Possibly the scarcity of results in gospel work is an evidence that He is. Once a builder is almost at the end of building a brick church, he does not require as many bricks for the tower as he did for the walls. The question of paramount importance is, Have you been built into the temple of God? It is sadly possible to be in the church organization and not be a part of the organism, the true and invisible church.

THE INSPIRATION OF THE SPIRIT (SEE EPHESIANS 3:5.)

The mystery of Christ, or the mysteries hidden from the ages, is the composition of the church. It was no mystery to Old Testament readers that Jews would be saved, or even that some Gentiles would be saved.

What was hidden from them was the truth that saved Jews and saved Gentiles would form one mystical body, the church. (See Ephesians 3:6.) Paul was the one privileged to reveal such a mystery: *"By revelation was made known unto me the mystery"* (Ephesians 3:3 ASV). And this sublime revelation was given to the apostle by the Spirit.

All truth is revelation. Phases of truth can only be discerned by the Spirit. (See 1 Corinthians 2:13–15.) He was the one who inspired the truth. (See 2 Timothy 3:16.) Peter also affirms that the Holy Spirit is the source of revelation. (See 1 Peter 1:11; 2 Peter 1:21.)

THE POWER OF THE SPIRIT (SEE EPHESIANS 3:16.)

In one of his superb prayers, Paul prayed that the saints might be strengthened with power through Christ's Spirit in the inner man. Arthur Way translates it, "Strong will power infused by His Spirit into your innermost nature." (See Ephesians 3:16.) How different such power is to the energy of the flesh! A good deal that passes for spiritual power today is merely fleshly energy.

Let us be careful never to separate the power from the Person of the Spirit. Power is not *something* but *Someone*. Often, misguided saints plead for "power" as if it's an intangible force that God can be persuaded to pour out upon them. Our Lord said, *"Ye shall receive power, after that the Holy Ghost is come upon you"* (Acts 1:8). The Spirit *is* the power.

What is power? It is the manifestation of the presence and purpose of the Spirit. May ours be the experience of Micah, who was full of power by the Spirit. (See Micah 3:8.)

THE UNITY OF THE SPIRIT (SEE EPHESIANS 4:3–4.)

The Spirit, as the One, is the only person who can make possible "one body." In verses 4–6 of this chapter, Paul enumerates seven ways by which the Spirit unifies believers. It is also our responsibility to "maintain the unity of which the Spirit is the author." Paul urges us to endeavor to keep the unity. (See Ephesians 4:3.) Alas, we are miserably failing in such a commendable endeavor! What divisions, estrangements, bitter feuds, and separations characterize the church today! "We are not divided, all one body we"[50] is one of the lies that we sing on Sundays. While we have little sympathy with much of the union of denominations, we *must* strive for a spirit of unity among believers.

THE GRIEF OF THE SPIRIT
(SEE EPHESIANS 4:30.)

This great passage teaches us many things about the Spirit. First of all, it offers a proof of His personality. Grief is possible only by a person. We know, then, that He is not a mere influence or emanation from God, for an influence cannot be grieved. Grief is an element of the heart. Where there is no love, there can be no grief. Because the Spirit, then, can be pained, we know that He is the Spirit of love. In verses 31–32, Paul sets forth those things pleasing or painful to the tender Spirit.

Then the apostle speaks of the Spirit as holy. Over one hundred times in the Bible is He thus defined. Why is He called holy? Because of His inherent holiness—He comes from a holy God, represents the holy Son, inspired the Holy Scriptures, and transforms us into the holiness of God.

> Every thought of holiness
> [Is] His alone.[51]

All believers are sealed with the Holy Spirit of God unto the day of redemption, which is the day when our bodies will be redeemed. The Spirit is our "perpetual Comforter and our eternal Inhabitant," as Augustine described Him.

THE FRUIT OF THE SPIRIT
(SEE EPHESIANS 5:9.)

The American Standard Edition of the Revised Version renders this verse, "*The fruit of the light is in all goodness and righteousness and*

---

50. Sabine Baring-Gould, "Onward, Christian Soldiers," 1865.
51. Harriet Auber, "Our Blest Redeemer, ere He Breathed," 1829.

truth" (Ephesians 5:9 asv). There is no contradiction, however, between "Spirit" and *"light."* Christ came as *"the light of the world"* (John 9:5). The Holy Spirit is referred to as *"the Spirit of Christ"* (1 Peter 1:11). Thus, by deduction, He is the Spirit of light. Sowing the light, we reap a golden harvest—*within* us there is goodness; without, righteousness and truth.

- *The fruit of the light is in all goodness.* It is grace embodied. All that is alien to the Holy Spirit is burned out of the soul.

- *The fruit of the light is in all righteousness.* Here we have the sanctification of the conscience, which makes possible unswerving loyalty to God's holy and perfect law. We scorn to stoop to anything crooked or doubtful.

- *The fruit of the light is in all truth.* Truth is not only in our speech but in our thoughts. Ours is no make-believe faith. We are delivered from sham service and sham orthodoxy.

Living in blissful harmony with the will of the Spirit, we are enabled to walk day by day with the unseen Savior, who is the Light of light.

THE FULLNESS OF THE SPIRIT
(SEE EPHESIANS 5:18.)

The observant reader will have noticed a threefold fullness in Ephesians: *"The fulness of God"* (Ephesians 3:19); *"the fulness of Christ"* (Ephesians 4:13); and here, the fullness of the Spirit: *"Be filled with the Spirit"* (Ephesians 5:18). As the continuous, present tense is used, the apostle implies that the Spirit-filled life should be the unvarying, perpetual experience of the believer. There is only one baptism with (not *of*) the Spirit, but there are many in-fillings. The following verses in the chapter set forth, in no unmistakable terms, the evidences of the Spirit-filled life. Paul's contrast *"Be not drunk with wine"* (Ephesians 5:18) is expressive. One can have too much of the cursed liquor, which runs like water in America—but a believer can never have too much of the Spirit, or rather, the Spirit cannot have too much of us. Would that we could be as God-intoxicated as those of whom it was said, *"These men are full of new wine"* (Acts 2:13).

THE SWORD OF THE SPIRIT
(SEE EPHESIANS 6:17.)

How true it is, as Paul reminds us, that the weapons of our warfare are not carnal but mighty through God to the pulling down of strongholds! (See 2 Corinthians 10:4.) The Word of God is our mightiest weapon in such a spiritual conflict, seeing that it is *"the sword of the Spirit"* (Ephesians 6:17). We can say of it what David said of Goliath's sword, with which he consummated his decisive victory over the giant and the Philistine host: *"There is none like that; give it me"* (1 Samuel 21:9). The infallible Word of God is the two-edged sword, which is well able to conquer its foes, slay error, and destroy sin.

THE INTERCESSION OF THE SPIRIT
(SEE EPHESIANS 6:18.)

It is in the goodness of God that we have two divine intercessors— one within (see Romans 8:26–27) and the other above (see Hebrews 7:25). In verses 10–20, Paul describes the armor of the believer. The covering for the knees is *"praying always with all prayer and supplication in the Spirit"* (Ephesians 6:18). If it be true that an army moves on its stomach, it is likewise true that the church lives, or should live, on her knees. An old saint of God spoke of our knees as "heaven's knocker." In the military setup of the Salvation Army, they have what is known as a "knee drill."

There is, of course, a vast difference between saying prayers and praying. Jude speaks about praying in the Spirit, which coincides with Paul's teaching about the Spirit being the inspirer of true, effectual intercession. (See Jude 1:20; Ephesians 6:18.) We do not know how to pray as we ought, but the Spirit makes intercession for the saints according to the will of God. (See Romans 8:26.) He alone can create the prayers that we should offer to God.

> Pray, always pray; the Holy Spirit pleads
> Within thee all thy daily, hourly needs.[52]

---

52. "Master, the Tempest Is Raging."

THEME 9

EPHESIANS: THE UNFOLDING OF GRACE

Paul is prominent among the apostles as the apostle of grace. In his epistles, the term *grace* appears twice as often as in all the rest of the New Testament. Some twenty-two times he speaks of "the grace of God" and "His grace"; fifteen times he speaks of "the grace of Christ" or "the grace of the Lord Jesus Christ"; and once he mentions *"the grace of our God and the Lord Jesus Christ"* (2 Thessalonians 1:12).

As the chief of sinners, the apostle gloried in divine grace. (See 1 Corinthians 15:9; 1 Timothy 1:13–15). How he reveled in such an evangelical truth, and commended the same grace to a world of sinful men! (See Acts 20:24). The epistle we are considering is full of grace. Because the word is used thirteen times in Ephesians, the letter is known as the gospel of the grace of God.

THE NATURE OF GRACE (SEE EPHESIANS 1:2; 6:24; GALATIANS 1:11–12.)

To Paul, God's grace included the sum of all blessings that come from God through Christ. What is *grace?* It is free favor, the sovereign, undeserved, unmerited mercy of God. It is a fearless, comprehensive word that reveals the heart of God and the gospel.

Grace is a direct opposite to sin, works, the law, and all human merit. It is God's way of meeting and conquering man's sin. (See Romans 5:20; 6:1, 15.) Grace and works can never be mixed. Salvation is all of grace, and, once saved, we work for the Savior. Grace deals with all men upon one common ground, that of being sinners. *"All have sinned"* (Romans 3:23). Grace levels their moral condition and reaches only those who feel their need of it. (See Luke 5:31–32.) "Grace is the unmerited favor of God bestowed upon those who justly merited the judgment of God."

Grace does not imply God's passing by sin, but supposes sin to be so horribly vile in God's sight that He cannot tolerate it. If man was able, by his own deeds, to patch up his ways so as to be acceptable to God, then there would be no need of grace. Grace, however, reveals the utterly ruined and hopeless state of the sinner, and also God's graciousness in dealing with sin and the sinner. Thus Paul is jubilant as he expounds the richness and suffering of God's grace. (See Ephesians 1:3–14.) How forcibly he reminded the Ephesians that grace, first and last, was the cause of their salvation. Paul also put his character at the back of his assertion that his gospel of grace was received directly from the Lord Himself. (See Galatians 1:11–12.)

THE SOURCE OF GRACE (SEE EPHESIANS 1:2.)

Grace is God's pitying, forgiving disposition toward men as weak and wretched, guilty and lost. God provided grace, and Christ personified it. (See John 1:14–17.) He came as the expression and vehicle of the grace of God, and He completely identified with God in unmerited, unrestrained love toward sinners. Although sin was inconceivably repulsive to God's holiness, yet the soul was inconceivably precious to Him, leading Him to provide a way of reconciliation for every sinner.

This first chapter is notable for its "doubles":

1.   A double blessing—grace and peace

2.   A double source of blessing—God and Christ

3.   A double designation of recipients—the saints and the faithful

4. A double authority—the apostle and the will of God

The association of grace with peace is interesting to note. Peace is united with grace, like a mother and daughter or twin sisters. These two virtues are the source of all blessings from God, which are revealed and operative in Christ. Grace is the foundation of peace. Grace is the source, and peace is the consummation. There can be no peace without grace, revealing as it does the divine character.

Used as an acronym, the word *grace* can be profitably developed in this fashion:

God is its author (See Titus 2:11.)

Righteousness is its basis (See Romans 6:13.)

Atonement is its channel (See Romans 3:24.)

Christ is its glorious sum (See 2 Corinthians 8:9.)

Eternity is its duration (See Ephesians 2:7–9.)

Some writers have seen in the two expressions "grace" and "peace" the two divisions of Ephesians. Dean Alford says that this epistle is made up of "God's grace toward us and our faith towards Him." Grace from God—peace for us. Campbell Morgan expressed it well when he wrote, "Grace is the river flowing from the heart of God. Peace is the resulting consciousness of the filling of the heart of the trusting soul. The river and the peace alike come from the Lord Jesus Christ."

THE GLORY OF GRACE (SEE EPHESIANS 1:6.)

Paul's love for superlatives is clearly evident in this letter to the church at Ephesus. *Grace* is a tremendous word in itself. Wherein consists the glory of such grace? The acknowledgement of all God's creatures of the gloriousness of God's grace is the emphasis of the exhortation before us. God's essential glory is best manifested in His grace. His almighty power is declared chiefly in the revelation of mercy and pity. (See Exodus 33:18–19; 34:5–7.) "God considers His glory best realized in the spectacle of souls redeemed and regenerated by His grace, and to decree that it should be thus realized for our sakes."

Glory is an attribute of grace, and grace grandly displays itself in glory. No wonder Paul uses extravagant language as he meditates upon the plenitude and splendor of redemption. Glowingly, he extols the transcendent riches of divine grace. Here is the ultimate aim of foreordination. Praise is called forth from the saints as grace displays itself in glory. Grace is not only a favor or gift, but the revelation of the divine character. Grace designates the active principle in God of man's salvation through the Lord Jesus Christ. Thus God is praised for what He *is* as well as for what He *does*. Glory, another ruling word in Ephesians, is linked with "riches" and "fullness." Language seems to fail the apostle as he describes the matchless grace of God.

When God glorifies His grace, He glorifies His whole character; and the glory of grace is that human merit does not help it and demerit does not hinder it. The brilliance of this grace is also seen in its unlimited nature and perfection. Grace has no limits, no bounds. Neither our joy nor our peace depends upon what we are to God, but on what He is to us, and this is grace. How deep in debt we are to God's unfathomable grace!

THE RICHES OF GRACE (SEE EPHESIANS 1:7.)

"Riches of grace and riches of glory are material enough for the sermons of a Methuselah." "Riches" is another thoroughly descriptive Pauline term. (See, for example, Ephesians 2:7; Romans 2:4; Colossians 1:27; 2:2; Philippians 4:19.) Ephesians is saturated with the undeserved bounty of redemption, the surpassing riches of His grace. Man is saved not according to his merits but according to the riches of such grace.

"The idea of richness in grace, glory, mercy, is especially frequent in this Epistle."[53] "In relation to praise," says Rev. Alfred Barry, "stress is laid on the gloriousness of God's grace, so here, in relation to enjoyment of it, on its overflowing richness."[54] (See Ephesians 2:7; 3:8, 13; Romans 3:24; 9:23.) We are saved not according to the narrowness of our own hearts (see Colossians 1:11) but according to His might and the wealth of His grace. God does not promise something He is unable to perform.

---

53. *A New Testament Commentary for English Readers by Various Writers*, vol. 3, 25.
54. Ibid., 17.

He is sure of His own resources before bequeathing His wealth to His own. He never runs short when it comes to the deliverance of the soul from sin. He is abundantly able to save. H. A. Ironside used this simple illustration of "according to":

> It does not say "out of" His riches, but "according to" His riches. Here is a millionaire to whom you go on behalf of some worthy cause. He listens to you and says, "Well, I think that I will do a little for you," and he takes out his pocket-book and selects a ten-dollar bill. Perhaps you had hoped to receive a thousand from him. He has given you "out of" his riches, but not "according to" his riches. If he gave you a book of signed blank checks all numbered, and said, "Take this, fill in what you need," that would be "according to" his riches.[55]

The pity is that with so much guaranteed wealth at our disposal, we yet live as spiritual beggars. God's grace abounds, overflows, and has no fixed limit. In His bank, there is more than enough for all the destitute of earth.

THE SALVATION OF GRACE (SEE EPHESIANS 2:5.)

It is all because of grace that we were saved and kept in a state of salvation. The two phrases "justification by faith" and "salvation by grace" are popularly identified and substantially identical in meaning. Perhaps the more advanced stage of the process of redemption in Christ is associated with salvation—past, present, and future—which is all of grace. Justification is the release of a prisoner on his pronounced pardon; salvation, a continuing state of liberty.

The triumph of grace is seen in the fact that man's sin and hatred of God are overcome by His triumphant love and mercy, which the cross reveals. The believing sinner is saved by grace alone. This is all his plea. The great mountain peak of Ephesians, then, is that grace is the cause, the spring of salvation. Sin can drag a man down to the lowest depths; grace can raise him to the highest heights.

---

55. Henry Allan Ironside, *In the Heavenlies*.

Because in our natural state we were dead in sin, our salvation, or a spiritual resurrection, is all because of grace, which is God's free gift. Human worth and works are unavailing to save, and the unifying of law with grace is "another gospel." (See Galatians 1:9.)

Until our last breath, there will be need of grace, and, bless God, there will always be grace for every need. The bestowal of grace never impoverishes God.

Examining the true nature of grace, two basic thoughts emerge, which require constant emphasis. First, behind the conception and initiative of grace is the undeserved mercy or generosity of God. What the sinner could never possibly merit or deserve has been generously and freely provided by God. Grace is everywhere spoken of as something man can never acquire but only appropriate. (See Ephesians 3:7; 1 Corinthians 1:4; 2 Corinthians 6:1; 8:1, 9.)

Paul contrasts grace and debt (see Romans 4:4), the latter representing payment, a contract that men are obligated to meet; the former, something unearned and undeserved. The apostle also contrasts grace and works. If works could save, then there would be no need of grace. (See Romans 11:6.) But because grace is all-sufficient, works are rejected. (See Ephesians 2:5–9.)

This brings us to our second basic idea: Grace needs no supplement. Nothing else is necessary for man's salvation. To add anything destroys the purpose of the cross. Paul learned the great secret that the grace of God requires no human additions to be effective for salvation, and in all his letters, he is enthralled and dominated with the conviction that the sinner can neither earn nor achieve favor with God. He can be saved only by grace.

THE PURPOSE OF GRACE (SEE EPHESIANS 2:7.)

The saints of God are to be His display cabinet. The end of grace is not only our salvation, future certainty, and eternal happiness, but also the display of God's glory. (See Ephesians 3:10–21.) Both here and hereafter, we are to show forth the surpassing riches of His grace. "*The ages to come*" (Ephesians 2:7) can be translated, "the ages which are coming on."

Time and eternity are looked upon in one great continuity, and the saints are conspicuous as monuments of God's exceeding grace. *Exceeding* means "overshooting the mark." Grace gives us more than we deserve.

The manifestation of the riches of God's grace is looked upon as His special delight, His chosen way of manifesting His own self to His creatures. Grace springs from His love and is displayed in all His benefits.

THE CHANNEL OF GRACE
(SEE EPHESIANS 2:8.)

The peerless grace of God avails nothing for the sinner unless all that such grace has provided is appropriated by faith. Grace made salvation possible, but it is only faith that can make this salvation the actual experience of the sinner. We are saved *by grace* (God's part) *through faith* in Christ (our part).

Are grace and faith both gifts of God? The answer is yes! As Rev. Alfred Barry puts it, "This attribution of all to the gift of God seems to cover the whole idea—both the gift of salvation and the gift of faith to accept it."[56] Salvation is all of grace. God does not save on a fifty-fifty basis, partly grace, partly good works. Salvation is all of grace, lest any man should boast. It is only by the faith the Spirit inspires and imparts that such salvation can be realized. Man is so helpless that of himself he has not even the faith necessary for his salvation.

THE STEWARDSHIP OF GRACE
(SEE EPHESIANS 3:1–14.)

Having dealt with God's elective grace in the previous chapter, Paul reminds the Ephesians that he was in prison because he proclaimed such a message. The origin of his captivity is traced back to the jealousy of Jewish leaders over the free admission of Gentiles into the church of Jesus Christ. So the apostle declares that his bonds were profitable on behalf of the Gentiles. (See Ephesians 3:13; 2 Timothy 3:10.)

By using the phrase *"I, Paul"* (Ephesians 3:1), he identifies himself as the agent employed by the Spirit to enlighten the Gentiles, after

56. *A New Testament Commentary for English Readers by Various Writers*, vol. 3, 26.

having been first enlightened by the same Spirit. (See Ephesians 3:3, 5, 9.) Having experienced the boundless grace of God, he communicates the good news to others (see Ephesians 1:9), and thus he becomes a dispenser, or a *"steward"* (see 1 Peter 4:10). The word *dispensation* means "the office of dispensing." The admission of Gentiles into the church was a Spirit-given revelation, and one that Paul had to share. (See Ephesians 1:9–10; Galatians 1:12). All who are saved by grace should function as dispensers of another's property, meaning, of course, that efforts must be made to bring others to share in the grace of God. "The revelation of salvation to the Gentiles was 'the dispensation,' that is…, the peculiar office in the ministration of the grace of God to the world, assigned to St. Paul by His wisdom."[57] (See Ephesians 1:10; 1 Corinthians 1:17–24.)

THE PREACHER OF GRACE
(SEE EPHESIANS 3:7–8.)

Paul deemed it a high privilege to be called to preach the gospel of redeeming grace. How wonderfully he was enabled by the Spirit to extol God's grace! A deep sense of unworthiness overcame Paul as he thought of God's special grace and favor to him. How unworthy a vessel he was to hold such a treasure. (See 1 Corinthians 15:9–10; 2 Corinthians 4:7; 11:30; 12:9–11; 1 Timothy 1:12–16.) Three times over, Paul blesses God for the honor of preaching among the Gentiles the inexhaustible wealth of grace. (See Ephesians 3:2, 7–8.)

It is said that D. L. Moody, the renowned American evangelist, once studied the word *grace*. Moved by the subject, he ran into the street and, with characteristic impetuosity, seized the arm of the first passerby and said,

"Do you know about grace?"

"Grace who?" asked the amazed man.

Then Moody poured out his soul on the subject of God's love.

Such an approach to people would possibly not be appreciated today, but the same sort of bubbling-over enthusiasm would be really effective.

---

57. Ibid., 32.

THE RECIPIENTS OF GRACE
(SEE EPHESIANS 4:7.)

Grace is not for a select few, but for all men. If you take away the *g* from *grace*, you are left with *race*, and grace is for the race. In the narrative, however, Paul associates grace with gifts. *"Unto every one of us is given grace* [the one "grace of the Lord Jesus Christ"]*"* (Ephesians 4:7). Grace was "given in the Divine purpose in the regeneration of the whole body, although it has to be received and made our own, separately in each soul, and gradually in the course of life."

Grace manifests itself in different gifts, and the diversity of gifts functions in the one body. (See 1 Corinthians 12:4; Romans 12:4–8.) The gift and gifts of grace are all alike connected with Christ's ascension, and these gifts to men must be exercised under the Spirit's direction. In his expression of the universal sweep and power of God in men's lives, Paul urges the recipients of grace to employ their heaven-inspired gifts to the full, so that other lives can be enriched.

THE LIFE OF GRACE (SEE EPHESIANS 4:29.)

It is the solemn obligation of all who are saved by grace to have a life fragrant with such grace. While grace is certainly an act of God, it must become a state in which we live, move, and have our being. As used in this passage, *grace* has the meaning of "goodness" or "graciousness." If people's lips are clean, then they can supply what is necessary in the hearer's spiritual condition. When we are right with the Lord, then we can note by the quick insight of love what each man's need is and, hastening to speak accordingly, "give grace" or blessing to meet that peculiar need. (See 2 Corinthians 1:15; 1 Thessalonians 3:10.)

Grace is received not only from God, but it should be shown by us to others. When God's grace has been poured into our lives and lips, then there will be the manifestation of pleasantness, charm, and winsomeness of bearing and speech. The phrase *"a gracious woman retaineth honour"* (Proverbs 11:16) implies a woman of grace, that is, one of attractive appearance and manner. Alas, too many are saved by grace and have gifts of grace but are far from gracious in

their actions. The sins of egotism, pride, self-honor, self-aggrandize-
ment, criticism, and belittlement of others rob so many of the children of grace of graciousness. (See Luke 4:22.) Are we good to those
who do not deserve kindness? Do we give graciously and freely? Are
we forgiving and tenderhearted, emulating thereby the God of all
grace—and graciousness? It is of little use preaching grace if we do
not practice it.

THE BENEDICTION OF GRACE
(SEE EPHESIANS 6:24.)

Paul's peculiar and favorite signature in his letters was the salutation *"Grace be with you"* (Colossians 4:18; 2 Timothy 4:22), and its various forms. (See 2 Thessalonians 3:17.) This characteristic "token" closes
all of his epistles. Many biblical scholars attribute the book of Hebrews
to Paul because this signature appears at the end. Here in Ephesians
6:24, the benediction is at once general and conditional: "[To] *all them
that love our Lord Jesus Christ in sincerity."*

In one Bible, the word *sincerity* in this verse is given as "incorrupt-
ibility" in the margin, a word applied to the immortality of heaven (see
Romans 2:7; 1 Corinthians 15:42; 15:50, 53–54; 2 Timothy 1:10), and
also to human character on earth (see Titus 2:7; Ephesians 6:24). As
used by Paul, the term means "'with a love immortal and imperishable,'
incapable either of corruption or of decay, a foretaste of the eternal communion in heaven."[58]

God's undiminishing grace embraces the saints of every age, and
will endure throughout the eternal ages. Such grace—so rich and full
and free—not only saves us from sin but sustains us in the dark and
difficult hours of life. No matter what crises may arise, His grace is ever
sufficient. Oceans of grace surround us; let us, therefore, plunge deep
into such a bountiful provision.

> And a new song is in my mouth
> To long-loved music set;

---

58. *A New Testament Commentary for English Readers by Various Writers*, vol. 3, 60.

Glory to Thee for all the grace
I have not tasted yet.[59]

All the figures of speech Paul uses of believers convey the truth so prominent in the epistle—namely, our unity in Christ.

---

59. "My Heart Is Resting, O My God."

THEME 10

PHILIPPIANS: THE PORTRAIT OF CHRIST

Paul's priceless epistle to the Philippians was probably written during the period of his two-year imprisonment in Rome around 61–63 AD. (See Acts 28:30.) This is why there are allusions in this epistle to the apostle's strict imprisonment and to the uncertainty of any release. Bishop Handley Moule says,

> Occasioned on the one hand by present circumstances, and on the other guided by the secret working of the Holy Spirit to form a sure oracle of God for the Church for ever, the Letter was dictated, and the greetings of the Writer's visitors were added, and the manuscript was given over to Epaphroditus, to be conveyed across Italy, the Adriatic, and Macedonia, to the plain and hill of Philippi.

Philippi was near the head of the archipelago; now the city is a scene of ruins. Bishop Lightfoot wrote:

> The city has long been a wilderness....Of the church, which stood foremost among all the apostolic communities in faith and love, it may literally be said that not one stone stands upon another. Its whole career is a signal monument of the inscrutable

counsels of God. Born into the world with the brightest promise, the Church of Philippi has lived without a history and perished without a memorial.

Yet the spiritual influences of that church will never pass. The letter
Paul wrote in his Roman dungeon has been a cheerful guide to saints of
every age and nation along the most rugged paths in life.

Philippi took its name from Philip of Macedon, 359–336 BC, who
made it a town of importance and military strength. He also worked
most vigorously the silver mines in the district. Thus it became *"the chief
city of that part of Macedonia"* (Acts 16:12). Conspicuous in this city of
prestige was Lydia, *"a seller of purple"* (Acts 16:14). A vivid account of
Paul's work in Philippi is recorded in Acts 16. He maintained communication with his Philippian converts. Messages were frequent between
them (see Philippians 4:16), and they reveal an affectionate and untroubled intimacy.

There are various ways by which we can approach this remarkable
epistle, which assumes soundness of doctrine and stresses Christian
experience. There was little in the Philippian church to set right. The
believers there formed a normal New Testament assembly.

The epistle indicates the position and influence of women in the
Christian life of the church. In Acts 16:14–19, Luke mentions two
females who were brought to Christ by Paul. Then in Philippians 4:2,
two more, who evidently held important influence in the church, are
named. Freely Paul speaks of his debt to spiritually minded women.
Women were held in reverent regard by Macedonian men.

Another striking feature of the Philippian epistle is the pecuniary
liberality of the Philippians themselves. Paul, always a grateful man,
deeply appreciated the material provisions with which his converts supplied him. The majority of those making up the gift were poor, for "the
poor help the poor." The giving of the comparatively poor to missionary
causes is vastly greater than that of the rich. If the wealthy gave in the
same degree as the poor working people do, there would be no scarcity
of money for the Lord's work.

Many expositors draw attention to the emphasis on *joy* in the book of Philippians. And it is, indeed the epistle of rejoicing. There are five references to *joy*, and twelve references to *rejoicing*. Paul did not fail to serve the Lord with joyfulness and gladness of heart. C. I. Scofield groups the teachings in Philippians around the subject of joyous triumphs over trials:

1. Christ, the believer's life, rejoicing in suffering (See Philippians 1.)

2. Christ, the believer's pattern, rejoicing in lowly service (See Philippians 2.)

3. Christ, the believer's object, rejoicing despite imperfections (See Philippians 3.)

4. Christ, the believer's strength, rejoicing over anxiety (See Philippians 4.)

Our own personal study of the epistle, however, convinces us of the fact that Paul's object in writing it was to exalt Christ, whom he specifically mentions forty-seven times in the book. Around the apostle were those Judaizers who held "lowered and distorted views" of the person of our blessed Lord. These views later developed into Ebionite Christology, which Irenaeus identified as a heresy during the second century. There were two phases of Ebionism.

The Pharisaic Ebionites held the belief that Jesus was born in the ordinary course of nature, but that, at His baptism, He was "anointed by election and became Christ," receiving power to fulfill His mission as Messiah, but still remaining man. They believed He had neither pre-existence nor deity. What we now know as "Modernism" is the present form of this Ebionism.

Then there were the Essene Ebionites, who were, in fact, Gnostics, and who held the view that Christ was a superangelic, created Spirit, incarnate at many successive periods in various men; for instance, in Adam, and finally, in Jesus. At what point this Spirit entered Jesus in His existence on earth was never clarified by the know-it-alls.

In this Christ-exalting epistle, Paul presents the Lord in His preexistence, voluntary humiliation, vicarious death, and victorious triumph over all foes. The aspects of Christ and our relationship to Him are emphasized by Paul in this letter, and sparkle like the facets of a diamond. Let us try to summarize the apostle's Christology.

ENCIRCLED BY CHRIST

Seven times Paul uses the pregnant phrases "in Christ Jesus" and "in the Lord," in this epistle. An old scholar has reminded us that "every Christian is a Christ-enclosed man," and no New Testament writer understood this truth as much as Paul did. A. T. Pierson informs us that the three short words "in Christ Jesus" are the key not only to Paul's epistles but to the whole New Testament. As "a very small key may open a very complex lock and a very large door, and that door may itself lead into a vast building with priceless stores of wealth and beauty," so this brief phrase expresses the mutual relation of the believer to Christ.

Paul uses the phrase and its equivalents, *"in Christ," "in Christ Jesus," "in Him,"* and *"in whom,"* almost 150 times in his writings. Such phrases indicate our new life in Christ, declared by Himself in the memorable words, *"Abide in me, and I in you"* (John 15:4). Christ is the sphere of our being. It is in Him that we live, move, and have our being. Pierson draws a distinction between a *sphere* and a *circle*. A circle surrounds us, but only on one plane. A sphere encompasses, envelopes, and encircles us in every direction and on every plane.

> If you draw a circle on the floor, and step within its circumference, you are within it only on the level of the floor. But, if that circle could become a sphere, and you be within it, it would on every side surround you—above and below, before and behind, on the right hand and on the left.

The sphere surrounding us separates us from whatever is outside of it. It also protects whatever is within it from all that is without. Furthermore, it supplies what is necessary to those within. How real these facts are when applied to Christ, who is the sphere of our whole lives and beings! In Him, we are surrounded by Him. In Him, we are separated from all external foes, secure in any peril that may arise, and supplied with all that we need.

Paul found himself in two spheres. As he wrote, he was in *"bonds"* (Philippians 1:13), and yet he was *"in Christ"* (verse 13). Had he not been in Christ, His adversity would have been unbearable. John was *"in the isle that is called Patmos"* (Revelation 1:9), but he was likewise *"in the Spirit"* (verse 10), and the latter encirclement made his prison a palace.

Paul starts his letter by affirming that *all* of the saints, not *some* of them, are *"in Christ Jesus"* (Philippians 1:1). His benediction ends with a salute to *"every saint in Christ Jesus"* (Philippians 4:21). The saints, or devotees of God, are kept saintly by Christ who encircles them. He is between them and sin. Surrounded by the Holy One, all in Him are holy ones.

The characteristic Pauline signature appears again in a most unusual fashion. True, Paul was in bonds, but he thought of himself not as a prisoner of Nero but a prisoner of Christ: *"My bonds in Christ"* (Philippians 1:13). What was manifest about Paul's captivity was that it was *"in Christ"*; it was due to no political or social crime, but to his union with his Lord. Christ, Paul knew, was between him and his foes. Thus, his fetters made only for the furtherance of the gospel. Chained as he was to soldiers of the Praetorian Guard, he witnessed to all who were thus close to him and spread the gospel through the whole Praetorian. His indifference to adversity inspired the saints to take on more courageous endeavors. Paul's brethren in the Lord waxed confident by his bonds. (See Philippians 1:14.) They leaned on a leadership that proved strong by self-sacrifice. Out they went to be more lavish in their efforts and ventures. The fearless apostle could preach Christ in spite of his bonds, so why should they not venture all for Him, as well?

As Paul was confident that Christ was His security, he assured his friends that, in spite of his imprisonment, he could abide and continue in his witness and ultimately return to them, which should cause them to abundantly rejoice *"in Jesus Christ"* (Philippians 1:26). It is blessed to know that Christ is between us and all that would hinder our supreme joy! He knows how to overrule the forced separations of life. As we await reunion, consolation is ours *"in Christ"* (Philippians 2:1).

All who are in Christ must manifest His disposition. He died to self-interest. His meat was to do the will of the Father. He emptied Himself and *"became obedient unto death"* (Philippians 2:8). This mind *"in Christ Jesus"* (Philippians 2:5) must also be our mind. Humility, patience, and sacrifice must characterize us. Grace must be ours to "lay in dust life's glory dead"[60]

Several times over, Paul reminds us that Christ is the sphere of our perfect joy and satisfaction. He says, *"Rejoice in the Lord"* (Philippians 3:1; 4:4). Paul had nothing to rejoice over in his prison cell, but he was happy in the consciousness that the Master, for whom he had counted loss as gain, was near at hand. Pierson says of this epistle,

> [It is] like one long *song in the night*, a kind of prolonged echo of that midnight prayer and praise which marked Paul's first experience in the city of Philippi....The man who sang and prayed in his inner jail is the man who in this epistle, a prisoner at Rome, sings, "Rejoice in the Lord, alway! and again I say, Rejoice!" (chapter 4:4). If this epistle has any special keynote which is the controlling thought, in all these melodies of a holy heart, it is this: *in Christ Jesus satisfied*.

Bishop Moule says, "Self has yielded the inner throne to Christ, and the result is a Divine harmony between circumstances and the man, as both are seen equally subject to, and usable by, Him."

What perfect encirclement is ours! With Christ within us, around us, above us, and beneath us, how safe we are! He is between us and all hostile influences; between us and all anxieties and cares; between us and all unholy forces; between us and all discontent; between us and all self-advantage; between us and all possible need.

> Not a single shaft can hit
> Till the God of love sees fit.[61]

---

60. George Matheson, "O Love That Wilt Not Let Me Go," 1882.
61. John Ryland.

ENRICHED THROUGH CHRIST

In Philippians, simple prepositions like *by, through,* and *of* speak to us of the spiritual wealth that awaits our appropriation. And the repetition and variety of these words must have some intense meaning. Christ is not only our sphere of being but our source of every blessing. Let us examine the links in this chain of truth.

First of all, Christ is the procuring cause of the fruits of our new life. The fruits of righteousness are ours by Jesus Christ, and these fruits must be borne unto the glory and praise of God. (See Philippians 1:11.) The righteousness that Paul mentions is the rightness of the regenerate will, regarded as in accord with divine law. Christ, who personified this law, is the true basis of righteousness in our lives.

It is also "by" or "through" Christ that we enter into possession of all we need here, with the riches of glory as our vast reservoir of supply: *"My God shall supply all your need according to his riches in glory by Christ Jesus"* (Philippians 4:19). The glory of both grace and providence is lodged *in* Him for His people. *By* Him, all spiritual and material needs can be fully met.

Relief from all unbelieving anxiety can be ours only *"through Christ Jesus"* (Philippians 4:7). What a curious threefold cord the narrative presents: anxiety for nothing, thanksgiving for anything, and prayerfulness in everything! Our only channel of relief from carping care is Christ. He alone can communicate the peace of God to anxious hearts, since He is the representative of the God of peace. (See Philippians 4:9.) What a blessed life this is! Hearts and minds are garrisoned by Christ Jesus. Bishop Moule says, "Even the details of our mental action, as we plan, reason, judge, and the like, shall be shielded from evil by the peace of God....The Lord is the Place of peace."

Further, "through Christ," we find strength for all things. He is between us and all weakness: *"I can do all things through Christ which strengtheneth me"* (Philippians 4:13). We receive ability to do all things through Him who is all-powerful. It is only as we are in vital union with the Head that, as members, we are able to do or to bear His will. Paul's strength was not only made manifest in his weakness but was also made perfect. Paul provided the weakness; Christ perfected His strength. A. T. Pierson said, "Omnipotence needs impotence for its sphere of working." Man's extremity is God's opportunity. Paul's ability to do all things was not acquired by frequent exercise; it was a disposition that he had by grace. It was all *"through Christ."*

While meditating upon Paul's priceless letter to the liberal-hearted Philippians, one is impressed with the various cameos of Christ that are displayed by the apostle. Each of these beautiful cameos is worthy of comment, but they will simply be set forth for the reader to study. All together, they demonstrate how Christ is the cause, the channel, and the consummation of all things:

1. The servants (slaves) of Christ (See Philippians 1:1.)
2. The day of Christ (See Philippians 1:6, 10; 2:16.)
3. The bowels (heart) of Christ (See Philippians 1:8.)
4. The Spirit of Christ (See Philippians 1:19.)
5. The gospel of Christ (See Philippians 1:27.)
6. The belief of Christ (See Philippians 1:29.)
7. The name of Christ (See Philippians 2:10.)
8. The things of Christ (See Philippians 2:21.)
9. The work of Christ (See Philippians 2:30.)
10. The knowledge of Christ (See Philippians 3:8.)
11. The faith of Christ (See Philippians 3:9.)
12. The apprehension of Christ (See Philippians 3:12.)
13. The cross of Christ (See Philippians 3:18.)
14. The grace of Christ (See Philippians 4:23.)

THE RESPONSIBILITIES OF ALL BELIEVERS

Going over the four chapters of the epistle again, we cannot fail to observe how Paul emphasizes the believer's obligation toward Christ. All He is to the believer is fully stated. But all Christ is to His own, and has for His own, is balanced by what they must do for Him. Our responsibility is of a ninefold nature.

1. Preach Christ (See Philippians 1:15–16, 18.)

Paul mentions two kinds of preachers: those who are prompted by good will and love, and those who are guilty of envy, strife, and contention. Judaistic teachers preached a mixture of law and grace, yet Paul rejoiced because they did convey to pagan hearers the primary fact of salvation— Jesus Christ. The apostle, however, never ceased to warn believers that the teaching of the Judaizers was pregnant with spiritual disaster. Commenting on these verses, Bishop Moule remarks, "It is a sorrowful paradox, but abundantly illustrated, that the true CHRIST could be emphatically and in a sense earnestly proclaimed with a wrong motive." May grace be ours to preach Christ by lip and life, in a way pleasing to Him, and fruitful in results! Let everyone take to heart these lines of Grace Noll Crowell:

> Preach Christ, O men—His blood, His saving power!
> Never the need was greater in an hour
> Than in this hour! Cry out His blessed name.
> O preachers, teachers, set the world aflame
> For Christ, that those who walk earth's darkened roads
> May feel His hand beneath their heavy loads;
> May come to know Him as their Saviour, Friend,
> Who will walk with them until the journey's end.
>
> Preach Christ, O men! Their hunger is so great!
> The days are swift—there is no time to wait.
> You hold the bread of life within your hands,
> And the living water for their thirst. The lands
> Of earth cry out for what you have to give:
> The living Christ—preach Him, that they may live.

2. Magnify Christ (See Philippians 1:20.)

Like Count Zinzendorf, Paul's one passion was Christ. He was a Christ-consumed being. Thus, life and death to him were a dilemma of blessings "in Christ." Here he desired to manifest Christ so as to have Him praised. Paul wanted to make his Lord bright and beautiful to eyes that otherwise saw nothing desirous or attractive about Him.

Physically scarred and imprisoned, Paul longed to have Christ glorified both in and through it his body. He knew that his body was "the soul's necessary vehicle for all action on others. Through the body alone could others 'see' how the man had peace and power in his Master, living or dying; through the words of his lips, the looks of his face, the action or patience of his limbs." We cannot but think of John and Betty Stam, and of the influence Paul's courage had on them as they faced brutal martyrdom in China.

3. Live Christ (See Philippians 1:21.)

The alternative of life or death is still in the mind of Paul, and his words take on a new luster when we remember that he wrote them at a time of suspense regarding the issue of his trial. Whether it would be life or death he did not know, and apparently he did not care. His was a "holy equanimity."

To Paul, Christ was life: "*I am...the life*" (John 14:6). He was completely full of Christ, wholly occupied with and for Him! How a person completes the phrase "For me to live is..." shapes his character and determines his destiny. Evidently, the apostle had a preference for death. He knew it would be better for him to depart and to live with Christ, but it was more needful for the Philippians and others whom he had won for Christ to live and encourage them by his life and labors. He knew that he would have more time for fruitful toil for the Christ he dearly loved if he continued to live his earthly life.

4. With Christ (See Philippians 1:23.)

A born-again believer is one who is *in* Christ, *like* Christ, *for* Christ, and *with* Christ. Once union with Christ is brought about, companionship with Him never ceases. The redeemed are *with* Christ, here and hereafter. Paul endured as seeing Him who is invisible. To fold up his earthly tent, however, and to find himself in the actual presence of Christ would be "*far better.*"

5. Confess Christ (See Philippians 2:10.)

The apostle's declaration regarding adoration ascending from creation in its totality must be examined in the light of its context. (See Philippians 2:5–11.) Although equal with God, Christ made Himself of no reputation, humbled Himself, and died as a felon on a cross. His humiliation, however, is to be rewarded with exaltation. Animate and inanimate, personal and unconscious, creation is said to worship the exalted Christ. Heaven and hell, demons and angels, saved and lost, all alike will recognize the lordship of Jesus.

Paul makes it clear that the Father is to be the ultimate object of adoration. The Christ of God, as the Nicene Creed reminds us, is at once divinely adorable in Himself and the true medium for our adoration of the Father.

The question of present concern is, Are we confessing Christ as we should as we linger amid the shadows? Too many who name His peerless name are guilty of hiding their light under a bushel.

6. Trust Christ (See Philippians 2:19, 24.)

A peculiar affection existed between Paul and Timothy. It was young Timothy who sought to keep Paul well informed as to the welfare of the churches the apostle had founded. There was no other like him in natural fitness for such a task. As for both his and Timothy's visit to Philippi, Paul trusted the Lord to guide and direct their steps. Paul would do nothing on his own initiative. He trusted the Lord to make the way clear and to provide all that was necessary for the journey.

7. Win Christ (See Philippians 3:8.)

In order to understand what Paul means about "winning Christ," we must follow his train of thought as he wrote verses 4–9. Much credit and respect had been his because of his Jewish stock, his zealous attachment to the law, and to the traditions of the elders; but all prestige and power were counted as loss for Christ. Paul came to understand that Christ crucified could alone profit him. Privileges, Jewish or otherwise, yes, all that the apostle had counted valuable or gainful, upon which he had depended for favor with God, he now counted as loss for Christ. After enumerating past advantages, he set everything on the scale, which Christ outweighed. All prospects of personal, national, and ecclesiastical distinctions were freely and fully sacrificed for Christ's sake. Paul suffered the loss of all, so that Christ might become his gain.

Paul's contempt for past gains is expressed in the phrase, *"I count all things but loss...do count them but dung"* (Philippians 3:8). The word he uses for *"dung"* means the vilest dross or refuse of anything, the worst kind of excrement. It also implies "the leavings of a feast." Bishop Lightfoot says,

> The Judaizers spoke of themselves as banqueters seated at the Father's table, of Gentile Christians as dogs greedily snatching up the refuse meat which fell therefrom. St Paul has reversed the image.

The language used shows how utterly insignificant and unavailing the apostle esteemed everything alongside the gain of Christ. Would that we could share Paul's contempt for all self-honor, self-glory, self-advantage, and advancement, and seek Christ *only*!

8. Know Christ (See Philippians 3:10.)

There are two precious phrases that we can join as we meditate on verses 9–10: *"found in him"* (verse 9) and *"know him"* (verse 10). In order to know Christ, we must be found in Him. Position comes first; then privilege becomes ours. Intimacy and fellowship form fruit from the root. Forsaking his own righteousness, Paul accepted the righteousness that had its origin in God, and then he passed on to assimilation "in Christ." He went on from the crisis of knowledge to the process of growing knowledge, and he became lost in Him whose love passes knowledge. Spiritual harmony with the sufferings, death, and resurrection of Christ became Paul's passion.

9. Expect Christ (See Philippians 3:20.)

Paul, knowing that the seat of his citizenship was in heaven, eagerly anticipated the coming of Christ, so that he could have a redeemed, glorified body to appreciate all the glories of heaven. Time and life were fast sinking away into the shades of death for the apostle, but he was upheld by the "blessed hope." He looked for the Lord, who had been the center and circumference of all things in his life, to come from heaven. Amid his extreme sufferings, he triumphantly witnessed for Christ, knowing that the effulgence of the dawning glory of the eternal world would soon be his.

Enough has been written to show what a Christ-exalting epistle Paul sent to the Philippians. It reveals his determination to know nothing among them except Christ and Him crucified. Paul loved and lived Christ. His work and writings were saturated with his passion to glorify his Lord. Paul, like Hudson Taylor, believed that if Christ "is not Lord *of* all, He is not Lord *at* all."

THEME 11

THESSALONIANS:
THE SECOND ADVENT

Thessalonica, a city of Macedonia now known as Salonica, was previously called Thermae, so named because of its famous hot springs. On account of its marine and geographical position on the Thermae Gulf, it not only commanded a share of the commerce of western Asia and southern Europe but was also a logical starting place for the gospel to reach Europe.

The church in Thessalonica was founded by Paul during his second missionary tour and was the second church established by him. (See Acts 16–17; 27:2; Philippians 4:16; 2 Timothy 4:10; 1 Thessalonians 1:1; 2 Thessalonians 1:1.) During one of the apostle's evangelistic tours, a revival broke out. The spiritual upheaval was so great that the world seemed to be "turned upside down."

The two epistles Paul sent to the Thessalonian church mark the beginning of his writing ministry. Many scholars affirm that 1 Thessalonians was the first New Testament book to be written and is, therefore, the earliest piece of Christian writing. Certainly it was the first of Paul's letters. It was penned around 54 AD, some twenty-one years after Calvary, and sixteen years after Paul's miraculous conversion.

Some have wondered why, if 1 Thessalonians was among the first New Testament books to be written, it was not placed earlier in the

New Testament. The Holy Spirit, who superintended the arrangement of Scripture, did not follow any chronological order but rather gave a progressive revelation.

The epistle to the Romans was written some six years after 1 Thessalonians; yet it comes first in the order of Paul's epistles simply because Romans commences with the foundational truths of the faith. The superstructure of Christian living and experience follows and reaches a climax in 1 Thessalonians, which contains the clearest presentation of Christ's return in the New Testament.

It is interesting to trace the occasion of the Thessalonian letters. Paul's dynamic presentation of Jesus as Christ resulted in his arraignment on a charge of treason against Caesar. (See Acts 17:3–8.) Driven from the city, which grew to greatness under Rome, Paul left Silas behind to carry on. Later on, he sent Timothy to Thessalonica to bring him word as to the condition of the church. Timothy returned to Paul at Corinth and reported on their loyalty under grave persecution. The church became renowned for its doctrinal purity and spiritual power. Timothy also reported concerning the death of some of the faithful believers at Thessalonica, and Paul responded by writing a letter commending the church for its loyalty to the Word and consoling those who mourned. Vividly he depicted the second advent of Christ, assuring the bereaved members that their dead would not be overlooked at His return. The second epistle was written a few months later, after Paul's banishment from Thessalonica by unbelieving Jews.

A reading of both epistles reveals that there are no Old Testament quotations or allusions, seeing that the bulk of the converts were Greeks who had left paganism for Judaism. There were, of course, some Jews among the members of the church in that city. (See 1 Thessalonians 1:9; 2:14.) Being addressed to young believers, the epistles contain no elaborate arguments. Prominence is given to practical exhortations and admonitions about common duties. Both letters are personal in tone, proving the close bond between Paul and his spiritual children. He commended them as examples of the highest evidence of Christianity.

The two letters must be studied together, seeing that both of them are taken up with the second advent, which is distinctly mentioned twenty times. Thessalonica was noted for its materialism; inscribed upon the tombs of numerous citizens were the words "Death Is an Eternal Sleep." But Paul reassured the saved but sorrowing saints of a glorious resurrection. The style of the letters is the same, and one letter is bound to the other. (See 1 Thessalonians 3:12; 2 Thessalonians 1:3.) The first three chapters of 1 Thessalonians are personal and historical; the last two, didactic and hortatory. The second epistle gives consolation under persecution (see 2 Thessalonians 1); consummation of evil (see 2 Thessalonians 2:1–12); and a closing exhortation (see 2 Thessalonians 2:13–3).

Looking at the epistles separately, we find Paul developing in the first one various doctrines in connection with the second advent. Doctrines such as election (see 1 Thessalonians 1:4), the Holy Spirit (see 1 Thessalonians 1:5–6; 4:8; 5:19), assurance (see 1 Thessalonians 1:5), the Trinity (see 1 Thessalonians 1:1; 5:6; 5:23), conversion (see 1 Thessalonians 1:9), the Christian walk (see 1 Thessalonians 2:12; 4:1), sanctification (see 1 Thessalonians 4:3; 5:23), man's threefold being (see 1 Thessalonians 5:23), and resurrection (see 1 Thessalonians 4:16) are discussed in the light of Christ's return. The word *parousia*, or personal presence, is used some twenty-four times, as a comfort in death, a motive to patience, a help to purity, the ground of rejoicing, and a separating and sanctifying power. All problems are to be solved in the light of such expectancy. The saints must abstain from sin and practice holiness, seeing that the Lord Jesus is coming again. The bereaved can bury their dead with joy and hope because of the rapture awaiting them. Christ is coming for His own, which constitutes the first stage of His second advent.

The second epistle followed as the result of the first. Some of the members were swept away by fanaticism, believing that Paul had informed them that Christ was coming instantly. Work was abandoned. Many became idlers and visionary. In their unconverted state, these deluded souls had been accustomed to myths and delusions, and they became an easy prey to their own imaginings. So Paul wrote 2 Thessalonians to correct the fanatical views erroneously deducted from his first epistle. He rebuked the idle Thessalonians, exhorting them to continue in the constancy and faithfulness that they had previously manifested. Paul gives a clear view of the man of sin and of events associated with the second stage of Christ's second advent. In 1 Thessalonians, Christ is seen coming for His church; in 2 Thessalonians, He is seen coming with His mighty angels and His own to take vengeance upon His foes. The keyword in both epistles is *"waiting"* (2 Thessalonians 3:5; see also 1 Thessalonians 1:10.)

Let us give ourselves to a fuller consideration of the first epistle, written as it was with the tenderness of a nursing mother, the authority of a father, the devotion of a friend, and the courage of an apostle. (See 1 Thessalonians 1:2; 5.) Conduct, we are told, is always affected by conception. If, therefore, we scorn the great truth of the rapture, as set forth in this first epistle, what else can we have but soiled garments and unlit lamps? If it is true that "the power of any life is in its expectancy," then those expecting Christ to return should live the most powerful and fruitful lives. It is with these considerations in mind that we now turn to the practical outworking of the second coming of Christ, as given in 1 Thessalonians.

In this first epistle, Christ's return is mentioned at the close of each chapter, and these different instances suggest a fivefold relationship:

+ In 1 Thessalonians 1:9–10, the blessed hope is connected with our salvation, and the message of patience is prominent.

+ In 1 Thessalonians 2:19–20, the return of Christ is associated with joy and service, and the rewards of it are here unfolded.

+ In 1 Thessalonians 3:12–13, Christ's appearing is connected with love, and our conduct godward and manward is in view.

+ In 1 Thessalonians 4:13–18, His coming is declared to be the spring of comfort. Here suffering and sorrow resulting from death are uppermost.

+ In 1 Thessalonians 5:23, the descent of Christ is joined to holiness, for Paul outlines the true character of a saint to guide and inspire the Thessalonians.

Now let us examine these five chapters with their fivefold advent relationship more closely.

AS A BELIEVER

In 1 Thessalonians 1:9–10, the believer is a "turning" one, and patience is the virtue emphasized. The threefold view of the believer's life involves *turning, serving,* and *waiting,* and he has a full-orbed experience if he is characterized by all three. Some turn but do not serve. Others turn and serve but do not wait, for they either neglect or reject the extremely practical truth of the second coming.

It is interesting to observe how this threefold phase of the believer's life dominates this first chapter of the book. In verse 3, there is the *"work of faith"* (1 Thessalonians 1:3), which is seen in their turning to God from idols; then there is the *"labour of love"* (verse 3), as seen in their serving of the living and true God; and finally there is the *"patience of hope"* (verse 3) as expressed in their waiting for God's Son from heaven.

The past is characterized by salvation; the present, by occupation; and the future, by expectation. Faith rests on the past; love works in the present; and hope endures as seeing the future. And the fact that we serve as we wait goes to prove that the truth of the coming of Christ does not cut the nerve of effort but only serves to strengthen our hands for all legitimate labor.

The order of these old-fashioned conversions is significant; the Thessalonians *"turned to God from idols"* (1 Thessalonians 1:9), not "from their idols to God." The motive in their salvation was not repulsion, occasioned by the grossness of idols, but the attraction of the character of God as presented by Paul. Our great task is not to tamper with idols belonging to unconverted people, but to point the people to God.

Moreover, the preaching of this threefold message would make for the same result today. One reason why the church is flirting with the world is because she has put out of her mind the expectation of God's Son returning from heaven. Activity she has in plenty, but this third attitude is missing.

Michelangelo, because of his prolonged and unremitting toil upon frescoed domes, acquired such a habitual upturn of countenance that, as he walked the streets, strangers, observing his bearing, set him down as a visionary and eccentric. If we profess to be Christians, with our citizenship in heaven, let our faces be set thitherward. Instead of looking at the earth, as the man with the muckrake did, let us walk the dusty lanes of life with that upward look, keeping ourselves unspotted from the world.[62]

AS A WORKER

In 1 Thessalonians 2:19–20, the believer is a *serving one*, and the joy that results from service is in view. Thessalonian converts were to be Paul's *"crown of rejoicing"* (1 Thessalonians 2:19) at Christ's return.

Someone has translated verse 19 as, "It is the thought of presenting you to Him that thrills us with hope, joy, and pride—the thought of wearing such a decoration before Him." Paul was to be prouder of these newborn souls than a king of his crown or a champion of his laurels. There are other crowns to earn, but this one is the great incentive to service—that souls will be in glory because of our influence and testimony. Would it not make for a mighty revival if every believer truly lived and labored in the light of this promised reward? Mother, what about your daughters? Father, what about your boys? Sunday school teacher, what about your scholars? Will they be with Christ because of your witness? Possibly you have all your heart may wish for here: a comfortable home in which you are unafraid of poverty or loneliness; children rising up in love and loyalty. But what of the future? Will you experience the joy and thrill of the apostle? Will there be any stars in your crown? Is yours to be a joyless meeting with the Savior, with no rewards from His gracious hand? Or are you among the number who hasten the coming by "gathering in the lost ones for whom our Lord has died"?

---

62. This refers to a character obsessed with worldly profit in John Bunyan's *Pilgrim's Progress*. "There stood also one over his head with a celestial crown in his hand, and proffered to give him that crown for his muck-rake; but the man did neither look up nor regard, but raked to himself the straws, the small sticks, and dust of the floor."

AS A BROTHER

In 1 Thessalonians 3:12–13, the believer is a *loving one*, and love in its godward and manward objects is outlined. "Multiply you in love until you have enough and to spare of it."[63] One is afraid that there is not much love to spare among Christians. "So that you may not only love one another abundantly, but all mankind."[64] In the narrative, Paul illustrates his deep love for the Thessalonians. *"Night and day"* (1 Thessalonians 3:10) they were upon his heart, and *"as a nurse"* (1 Thessalonians 2:7) he sought to cherish them. And brotherly love, he urges, leads to a life of holiness (see 1 Thessalonians 4:9); for a loveless heart can never succeed in the quest after holiness. True love sanctifies the one who loves.

Paul urges these Thessalonian saints to increase and abound in love, or, as Weymouth expresses it, "Grow and glow in love." (See 1 Thessalonians 3:11 WEY.) And surely we can never have too much of this fruit of the Spirit! The tragedy is that much sweet fruit is frosted.

Paul prays that his converts might be loving in a superlative degree—overflowing with love. And such a message is needed in these days of spiritual coldness. As we get nearer to the moment of our Lord's return, it would seem that the devil is active, drying up the spring of love, for never was such a loveless feeling prevalent among professing Christians as is apparent today.

We heartily sing, "We shall know each other better when the mists have rolled away."[65] But why wait until the future for a better understanding of each other? If we are to live together up yonder, let there be more unity here. Let us get put right with each other, and then keep right with each other until the Lord Jesus comes. *"Be at peace among yourselves"* (1 Thessalonians 5:13). The old-time way of expressing love was by a kiss—to greet one another with a holy kiss. (See 1 Thessalonians 5:26.) Kicking rather than kissing is our attitude. A revival of love among God's people, in view of Christ's coming, would make for a great ingathering of the lost!

---

63. *A New Testament Commentary for English Readers by Various Writers*, vol. 3, 136.
64. Ibid.
65. Annie H. Barker, "When the Mists Have Rolled Away," 1883.

AS A SUFFERER

In 1 Thessalonians 4:13–18, the believer is a "weeping" one, and comfort in view of death is in mind. Many of these Thessalonians were troubled about their dead. The prevalent, pagan idea is expressed in a heathen inscription discovered at Thessalonica:

> After death, no reviving;
> After the grave, no meeting again.

Ignorance may cause unnecessary sorrow and despair. A mother, not having learned that her little one who had fallen asleep is safe in the arms of Jesus, will be tormented by unnecessary and unreasonable pain. It was so with the sorrowing believers in Thessalonica who were ignorant concerning the Lord's return and the condition of their blessed dead. So Paul sends this letter to comfort the sorrowing in the assembly, stating that both the dead and the living will participate in Christ's coming. He alleviates their sorrow, suffering, and separations by showing that they are not worthy to be compared with the glory of Christ's return.

The secular life of today is without much hope, as was the pagan life of old. Attention is fixed upon the present world, and all discussion as to the future is avoided. People are content to have a good time and risk what is to come. The saints of God, however, can comfort one another with these words written in this chapter, although it may sound strange to the ears of the world when God's servants say that they "*love his appearing*" (2 Timothy 4:8).

AS A SAINT

In 1 Thessalonians 5:23, the believer is described as one who is holy, and the sanctifying influences of the blessed hope are brought before us. What a fitting climax this is!

James Moffatt translates the verse, "*May the God of peace consecrate you through and through! Spirit, soul, and body, may you be kept without break or blame till the arrival of our Lord Jesus Christ!*" (1 Thessalonians 5:23 MOFFATT).

The phrase *"without break"* tells us that this is godward relationship; communion, holiness, and prayer being kept intact *"through and through."* The phrase *"without…blame"* tells us this is our manward relationship; fellowship, conduct, and testimony all operating until He comes. Paul urges us to have all parts of our complex being ready for Christ's return.

1. *Our Bodies.* These, as temples of the Holy Ghost, are to be delivered from all pampering, excess, and neglect, and are to be used only for His service and glory. We are to have holy hands, continually doing good; holy feet, running incessantly upon His errands; and holy lips, pleading His cause afar.

2. *Our Souls.* All the powers of thought and imagination are to be consecrated to Him. All unholy, wrong thoughts are to be banished. Our consciences and self-life must be disciplined by His Word and Spirit, until they obey His dictates without murmur.

3. *Our Spirits.* We are to have pure worship and devotion that is worthy of God, and we are to have worthy reverence and trust. Thus our complex nature, outward, inward, and upward, must be sanctified in view of our Lord's return.

> With such a blessed hope in view
> We would more holy be.[66]

And what He commands, He supplies. He calls us to holiness and supplies it. *"Faithful is he that calleth you, who also will do it"* (1 Thessalonians 5:24). Augustine expressed it well when he said, "Give what Thou commandeth, then command what Thou wilt."

---

66. Robert Boswell, "Behold, What Love!"

THEME 12

SECOND TIMOTHY: THE CHRISTIAN WORKER

Special significance is attached to this second epistle to Timothy, seeing it was the last letter written by Paul. It is for this reason that it has been called "the Swan Song of Paul." Shortly after writing it, the apostle faced martyrdom for Christ's sake, and thus the epistle bears the stain of the writer's blood. A good deal of sentiment is attached to the last letter from a friend before his home-call, and Paul's last message was to his much-loved son in the faith, his companion, Timothy the evangelist. How this young man must have treasured it!

It was written from a cold, damp, dark Roman dungeon about 67 AD, toward the end of Nero's reign. Paul was scheduled to appear before the emperor, and his immediate motive in writing to Timothy was his intense desire to see him once again before death parted them. This urgent wish is expressed several times in the epistle. (See 2 Timothy 1:4; 4:9, 11, 21.) Paul was alone—friendless among foes. Demas, a one-time close follower, had forsaken him, and Alexander the coppersmith had been evilly disposed toward him, all of which induced Paul to send this request for his son in the faith to hurry to him, to be with him in his last hours. How true and tender was the affection that bound these two valiant hearts together! With no Christian friend near to console him except, probably, Luke, it was to Timothy that Paul turned for sympathy and aid. But whether Timothy reached Rome in time to comfort his devoted friend and spiritual father before his bitter end is not revealed.

One of the objects of this last will and testament was to inform Timothy of the dangers that threatened the writer, and to fortify his courage. He bade Timothy hasten to his aged friend and to bring with him Mark from the east. Evidently, Paul had previously appeared before Nero, but his case had been adjourned. (See 2 Timothy 4:16–17.) He expected to appear again in the winter and wrote Timothy, whose liberty from prison made it possible for him to come at once (see Hebrews 13:23) to bring with him the necessary articles Paul had left elsewhere (see 2 Timothy 4:9, 11, 13, 21). Expecting a speedy martyrdom (see 2 Timothy 1:8, 16; 4:6), and uncertain whether Timothy would arrive in time, the apostle sends him a farewell warning as to heresies he must combat, and also a parting message encouraging him to zeal, courage, and patience. Not knowing whether he would be spared to give last instructions with his own lips, Paul fills his last letter with fatherly exhortations applicable to Timothy in his continuing witness for the Master.

With a calm resignation, Paul said that he was *"ready to be offered"* (2 Timothy 4:6). Written under the shadow of death, this epistle is full of light and shade, shadow and hope. Expressing his affectionate regard for Timothy, and his ardent desire to see him, Paul counsels his beloved son in Christ not to shrink but to share his spiritual father's shame and suffering for Christ and His truth. By the grace and power of God, Timothy must endeavor to fill the gap and to function as a faithful minister of the Word of God, an opposer of false teachers, a prophet in perilous times, a sufferer in Christ's cause, and a saint eagerly anticipating Christ's return.

Among the matchless epistles of Paul, there are three that are grouped together and known as the Pastoral Epistles, namely 1 and 2 Timothy, and Titus. All three belong to his old age, and bear his mature thought. They also carry an imperative stamp, being made up of ministerial imperatives, such as, *"Guard the truth"* (2 Timothy 1:14 RSV),

"Hold fast the form of sound words" (2 Timothy 1:13), *"Preach the word"* (2 Timothy 4:2), and so forth. Sound doctrine and practical piety are the prominent interests in these epistles. Paul's creative days are over; his battles are fought; his course is run. Completing touches remain to be added and a final seal remains to be set to the work and teaching of his long and honored life. These three letters emphasize that purpose.

Taking 1 and 2 Timothy together, we observe how one epistle complements the other. In the first epistle, Paul draws us a picture of the ideal church every pastor should have. In the second epistle, we see the ideal pastor every ideal church should have. In the first epistle, Timothy is urged to preach a straight gospel and to guard the doctrine, which was his message from God. This is the silver trumpet. In the second epistle, Timothy is exhorted to live a straight life and to guard his testimony, which was his life from God. Here is the player behind the silver trumpet. The first epistle reveals the internal condition of the church at Ephesus, over which Timothy was pastor. The second epistle depicts what kind of pastor Timothy was to be. Paul, in no uncertain terms, describes what pastor and church must be like, both then and now. Pure churches—pure pastors! May they be ours in increasing numbers!

Written especially for young Timothy, the personal element in the second epistle is strongly marked. *"Timothy, my dearly beloved son"* (2 Timothy 1:2). This is why there is a moving, paternal touch about this farewell letter. Here we have the veteran worker's final advice to a younger fellow laborer. In no other epistle does the true, loving, undaunted, and trustful heart of the great apostle speak in more consolatory yet touching accents as in this most human document. Because it is made up of four chapters, we have the suggestion of a fourfold gaze in 2 Timothy:

+ In chapter 1, the apostle looks back over the past. There is the remembrance of Timothy's affectionate grief at parting, his faith, his family associations, and his spiritual gift received at ordination.

+ In chapter 2, Paul looks at the present and gives directions to Timothy on how to conduct himself amid the manifold difficulties of his position.

✦ In chapter 3, Paul looks forward to the future and forewarns and forearms his friend against the dangers and troubles he foresees in the history of the church.

✦ In chapter 4, the gaze is lifted from earth to heaven, for though the apostle is a chained, persecuted, deserted, and suffering warrior, he awaits martyrdom; his sky is bright with the dawn of a coming, glorious day.

As 2 Timothy is one of the three Pastoral Epistles, we prefer to see in Paul's "Swan Song" the fourfold obligation of the Christian pastor, teacher, or worker.

THE MINISTER AND HIS MISSION
(SEE 2 TIMOTHY 1.)

Among the descriptions given of those who labor in the gospel, none is as expressive as that which Paul uses of Timothy: *"Minister of God"* (1 Thessalonians 3:2). Such a title is not to be limited to one who has had a college education, who holds a certain ecclesiastical position, such as "Reverend," and who is distinguished by a certain dress. This appellation applies to all who are saved by grace, who are called and equipped by the Holy Spirit to serve God in some divinely appointed sphere, and who by His power make full proof of this ministry. Further, this is a calling, not a profession: *"Who hath saved us, and called us with an holy calling"* (2 Timothy 1:9).

Paul is careful to put conversion before calling, salvation before service. God calls none to serve Him who have not been saved according to His purpose. The sons of Eli served Him but did not know Him, so their professional service was not divinely accepted. We must be born anew by the Spirit as a prerequisite to a divine call to serve God. Saved, we must serve, for we were saved to serve.

Because of the sacredness of their task, all who minister unto the Lord must guard themselves against the threefold danger of slackness, stagnation, and the fear of man. These marked features are associated with making our calling and election sure—

1. The presence and power of the Holy Spirit (See 2 Timothy 1:7.)

2. The partaking of afflictions (See 2 Timothy 1:8; 3:12; 4:5.)

3. The promise of eternal security; double committal (See 2 Timothy 1:9, 12, 14.)

4. The possession of fundamental truths (See 2 Timothy 1:13; 2:2.)

THE MINISTER AND HIS MASTER
(SEE 2 TIMOTHY 2.)

If the motto of the previous chapter is "Be brave," the suitable motto of this second chapter is "Be thorough." As this chapter is prominent in the way it outlines the Christian worker's relationship to his Lord, its opening words constitute the key verse, *"Be strong in the grace that is in Christ Jesus"* (2 Timothy 2:1). He who calls us equips us to serve Him aright. *"Faithful is he that calleth you, who also will do it"* (1 Thessalonians 5:24). He is the source of strength for service. He never sends us forth to warfare on our own charger. The phrase "in Christ Jesus" was one of Paul's favorites; he used it some 160 times in his epistles. Whether "in Christ," "in Christ Jesus," "in the Lord," "in whom," or "in Him," such expressions convey the truth that Christ Jesus is the fountainhead of all the power and patience we need to witness for Him in an apostate age. It will be found that the second chapter contains a series of metaphors illustrating our relationship to Him who called us to follow and labor.

1. He is the commander; we are the soldiers (See 2 Timothy 2:3–4.)

2. He is the umpire; we are the athletes (See 2 Timothy 2:5; see also 1 Corinthians 9:24.)

3. He is the husbandman; we are the laborers (See 2 Timothy 2:6.)

4. He is the employer; we are the workmen (See 2 Timothy 2:15.)

5.   He is the owner; we are the vessels (See 2 Timothy 2:20–21.)

6.   He is the master; we are the slaves (See 2 Timothy 2:22–25.)

We are to flee the negative and follow the positive. As those, then, called to serve the One who saved us, we have—

+ Strength for the fight (See 2 Timothy 2:1.)

+ Wisdom for the work (See 2 Timothy 2:7.)

+ Prospect of a glorious reward (See 2 Timothy 2:11–12.)

THE MINISTER AND HIS MESSAGE (SEE 2 TIMOTHY 3.)

Over this chapter we can write, "Be watchful," for the minister of God, having looked to his charge, then to his Lord, must now think of his relationship to the Scriptures. Perilous times and false voices make it imperative for him to abide in, and to constantly study, God's Word. Thus, the key verse of the chapter reads, "*All* [holy] *scripture is given by inspiration of God*" (2 Timothy 3:16). In this wonderful portion, Paul declares unequivocally his faith in the Scriptures as being divinely inspired. All (or every) Scripture affirms that the Bible not only contains the Word of God but is His infallible Word from beginning to end. "*Holy men of God spake as they were moved* [borne along] *by the Holy Ghost*" (2 Peter 1:21). Any worker will be perplexed and badly equipped if he fails to—

+ Admit the Scriptures to be inspired by God

+ Submit to the Scriptures in order to be sanctified

+ Commit the Scriptures to memory to draw upon in need

+ Transmit the Scriptures to others for their salvation

A perusal of 2 Timothy 3 reveals these features of Scripture—

A Source of Comfort and Guidance in Perilous Times (See 2 Timothy 3:1–13.)

In these remarkable verses, we have an ancient mirror of modern events, a description of the last days preceding the coming of the Lord.

What a somber outline the passage is of the deplorable character of man, which is outstandingly common today. Never in the course of history has life become so evil. Paul was among those who William Cowper wrote of in *The Task*:

> Thy prophets speak of such; and, noting down
> The features of the last degenerate times,
> Exhibit every lineament of these.

The word Paul gives us for *"perilous"* (2 Timothy 3:1) is equivalent to the phrase Jesus used of the conduct of the two demon-possessed men: *"exceeding fierce"* (Matthew 8:28). Thus, we can freely paraphrase the apostle's opening verse of the chapter before us, "Demonized times shall come." And there is no other way to describe the terrible crimes, the bloody revolutionary elements, and the abounding iniquity of our times, reflecting as they do the catalog of infamy and vices Paul gives us. Knowing his time is short, Satan is manifesting great wrath.

Believers, discerning the times, are not perplexed—although they are saddened—by the prevailing features of these last days. They are not sidetracked by false voices, for, living near the *"more sure word of prophecy"* (2 Peter 1:19), they discern how the condition and character of human society is heavy with prophetic significance. God's inerrant, infallible Word is a light unto their paths, enabling them to watch and pray amid the gathering clouds. They study the Word and thereby show themselves approved unto God.

A Source of Salvation of the Lost (See 2 Timothy 3:15.)

The only hope the slaves of sin and apostates have of emancipation from their fetters is through the Savior the Scriptures present. Holy Scripture alone can make them wise unto salvation through faith in Christ Jesus. The gospel of His redeeming grace and power is the sole medium of deliverance from the guilt and thralldom of sin. And, in these iniquitous days, we have need to get back to the preaching of ruin by the fall, repentance for sin, redemption by the blood, and regeneration by the Holy Spirit.

At the turn of this century, General William Booth, founder of the Salvation Army, stated, "The chief dangers in the twentieth century will be religion without the Holy Spirit, Christianity without Christ, politics without God, heaven without hell." What a true prophet the old general turned out to be! All the more reason for us to preach his gospel of blood and fire, and to fling the message into the face of a godless world: *"Ye must be born again"* (John 3:7)!

A Source of Spiritual Knowledge (See 2 Timothy 3:16.)

One evidence of Scripture as the divinely inspired Word of God is its profitability in the understanding of doctrine, reproof, correction, and instruction in righteousness. That a person may have a mental knowledge of Scripture without a deep spiritual experience is seen in the case of Nicodemus, of whom Jesus asked, *"Art thou a master of Israel* [a man who was familiar with Old Testament Scripture], *and knowest not these things?"* (John 3:10). It is sadly possible for one to know the Book of God, yet not know the God of the Book. Because the truth of Holy Writ is spiritually discerned, the Spirit, who inspired holy men to write Scripture, must be within us as the source of our sanctification and illumination: *"That which I see not teach thou me: If I have done iniquity, I will do no more"* (Job 34:32).

A Source of Spiritual Equipment (See 2 Timothy 3:17.)

The minister of God is likewise a man of God or a man who is God-possessed and God-controlled; and the more such a man lives in the Scripture given by inspiration of God, the more complete and thoroughly furnished unto all good works he becomes. No man in the ministry who neglects personal Bible meditation and study is fully furnished for the task he assumes, namely, a minister of the word. If he preaches essays on various secular themes instead of proclaiming the blood-red evangel, he will never make full proof of his ministry. His supreme mission in the world is to rescue the perishing by telling them of Jesus, who is mighty to save. God never fails to manifest His power through such preaching. (See Titus 1:3.) Therefore, the unceasing, solemn obligation of the man of God is to preach the Word!

THE MINISTER AND HIS MOTIVE
(SEE 2 TIMOTHY 4.)

What a mighty spiritual upheaval the church and the nation would experience if only all ministers lived by this chapter in which Paul portrays the features of a preacher after God's own heart! It is a chapter every preacher should daily read in the solitude of his own study if he would be delivered from mere lip-preaching. Paul preached in the light of eternity, hence the quality and results of his utterances. He never preached to please, but always for the prize—the *"crown of righteousness"* (2 Timothy 4:8). Confidently and unashamedly, Paul confesses that the constraining motive or incentive in all untiring loyal service for the Master was the prospect of seeing Him and receiving from Him the commendation *"Well done, good and faithful servant"* (Matthew 25:23). The apostle found stimulus in the blessed hope: *"This one thing I do...I press toward the mark for the prize of the high calling of God in Christ Jesus"* (Philippians 3:13–14). The key phrase of 2 Timothy 4 is "Be strenuous."

To live and labor in the light of the judgment seat of Christ, with its rewards for dedication and devotion to His cause, enables one to serve Him to the limit. Paul loved the thought of his Lord's appearing, and thus his last epistle is dominated by such a glorious prospect.

+ He believed that Christ had brought not only life but also immortality to light through His gospel. (See 2 Timothy 1:10.)

+ He ever kept before him the day of the Lord's return for His own. (See 2 Timothy 1:12, 18; 4:8.)

+ He anticipated the privilege through grace of sharing the throne of his reigning Lord. (See 2 Timothy 2:13; 4:1.)

+ He had an insight into the portents of his Master's second coming advent signs. (See 2 Timothy 3:1–9.)

Paul loved the very mention of Christ's appearing. Not only had his mind grasped all the facets of such a truth, but his heart, likewise, was held captive by the hope of seeing Him he dearly loved and sacrificially served. (See 2 Timothy 4:8.) This is the key verse of this chapter. Untold numbers of preachers have found that there is nothing as revolutionary in their ministry as to live and labor in the light of the judgment seat, before which all saints are to appear. (See 2 Timothy 4:18.)

The few autobiographical touches Paul gives us as he closes his farewell letter reveal him to be the happy warrior he was. Without doubt, he stands out as the magnificent hero of the faith and as the apostle extraordinary.

+ He was the *lamb* ready to be offered. (See 2 Timothy 4:6.) His martyrdom was near, but he had no fear. His frail bark was about to be loosed from its moorings.

+ He was the soldier who had fought *"the good fight"* (2 Timothy 4:7 RSV). He had lived out his exhortation to young Timothy: *"Fight the good fight of faith"* (1 Timothy 6:12).

+ He was the athlete who had finished the race with great honors. What a remarkable course he had run! (See 2 Timothy 2:5; 4:7.)

+ He was the trustee who had preserved the sacred deposit of the whole body of revealed truth. *"I have kept the faith"* (2 Timothy 4:7; see also Jude 1:3).

Truly these assertions describe a noble end to a most noble life! Sealing his remarkable testimony with his blood, Paul entered the presence of his Master to receive the laurel that was safely "laid up" for him from the scarred hands of his living Lord—

> We live in deeds, not fears; in thoughts, not breaths;
> In feelings, not in figures on a dial.
> We should count time by heart-throbs. He most lives
> Who thinks most, feels the noblest, acts the best.[67]

This is how Paul, the greatest Christian in church history, lived. May grace be ours to follow in his train!

---

67. Philip James Bailey, *Festus.*

THEME 13

PHILEMON: CHRISTIAN COURTESY

Lord Byron, in *Don Juan*, has the expressive lines—

> Though modest, on his unembarrassed brow,
> Nature had written "gentleman."

How true a sentiment of the apostle Paul is Byron's couplet! His modesty is seen in his self-depreciation, calling himself *"less than the least"* (Ephesians 3:8) and "the chief of sinners" (see 1 Timothy 1:15). Paul's epistle to Philemon reveals his gentlemanliness. Without doubt, he belonged to heaven's spiritual knighthood. He was one of God's gentlemen. Grace made him gracious in his dealings with others. He never forgot his obligation to adorn the gospel. Tennyson's words fit Paul's manners—"O selfless man and stainless gentleman."[68]

Too many preachers, conservative in their theology, are most ungracious in their behavior. They lack gratitude, unselfishness, kindness, and those finer traits and attractive courtesies commendable in every person, especially in a Christian. It was not so with Paul. Whether he dealt with master or slave, rich or poor, Christian or heathen, his approach was kind and thoughtful, considerate and courteous. "He bore without abuse the grand old name of gentleman."[69]

68. Alfred Lord Tennyson, *Idylls of the King*, "Vivien."
69. Alfred Lord Tennyson, *In Memoriam*.

We might well ask what a gentleman is. Charles Dickens put this conception of a gentleman on the lips of Oliver Twist: "I shall be a gentleman myself one of these days, perhaps with a pipe in my mouth, and a summerhouse in the back garden." But possessions do not make a gentleman. As the old proverb says, "It is not the coat that makes the gentleman." Edmund Burke claimed, "A king can make a nobleman, but he cannot make a gentleman."

One who is not well-born and lacks a good education and social position can yet be a gentleman after the Bible order. He can have that refinement of manners, attractive behavior, finesse, and courtesy born of the Spirit. He can be like the Master of whom old Thomas Dekker wrote in 1604—

The best of men
That e'er wore earth about him was a sufferer;
A soft, meek, patient, humble, tranquil spirit,
The first true gentleman that ever breathed.[70]

Christ was the "finished Gentleman from tip to toe," whom Lord Byron speaks of in *Don Juan*. And Christlikeness and gentlemanliness are akin. Courtesy is a trait of a Christ-possessed Christian. The dictionary describes a gentleman as "one who belongs to a stock." The "gens-men" in Roman law were only those who had a family name, were born of free parents, had no slave in the ancestral line, and had never been degraded to a lower rank. Paul had such a pedigree, but it was grace that made him a nobler gentleman.

Shakespeare, in *Winter's Tale*, has the line, "We must be gentle, now we are gentlemen." Paul, however, could change the thought and say, "We must be refined, now we are regenerated." His epistle to Philemon is a beautiful cameo of knightliness. One of its peculiar features is its aesthetic character. It is a model of delicacy and skill in the effort to reconcile parties at variance. It reveals the triumph of love. "It is a precious relic of a great character." Philemon is unique as a perfect masterpiece of pure politeness. The courtly manners of Paul and the benevolence and

---

70. Thomas Dekker, *The Honest Whore* (1604), Part 1, Act 1, Scene 12.

hospitality of Philemon himself illustrate that distinctive character of the early disciples that compelled the heathen around to exclaim, "See how these Christians love one another!" (See John 13:35.)

Bishop Handley Moule, comparing this epistle with the much-admired letter of Pliny to his friend Sabinianus to ask pardon for a young freedman, who had offended Sabinianus, says,

> It is a graceful, kindly letter, written by a man whose character is the ideal of his age and class; the cultured and thoughtful Roman gentleman of the mildest period of the Empire....His heart has not the depth of Paul's, nor are his motives those of the Gospel, which taught Paul to clasp Onesimus in his arms, and to commend him to Philemon's, as a friend in God for immortality.

Because of its infinite charm, and the fact that it is simple and inartificial in style, the epistle to Philemon has been called "a little idyll of the progress of Christianity." Other writers, because of its graceful and delicate courtesy, have spoken of it as the "Polite Epistle." Within it there is no insincere compliment. In a manly, straightforward, yet captivatingly persuasive way, Paul presents his case to Philemon. The apostle gives us a specimen of the highest wisdom as to the manner in which Christians ought to manage social affairs.

Alexander Maclaren says,

> The incomparable delicacy of this letter of Paul's has often been the theme of eulogium. I do not know that anywhere else in literature one can find such a gem, so admirably adapted for the purpose on hand. But beyond the wonderful tenderness and ingenuity born of right feeling and inbred courtesy which mark the letter, there is another point of view from which I have been in the habit of looking at it, as if it were a kind of parable of the way in which the Master pleads with us to do the things that He desires. The motive and principles of practical Christianity are all reducible to one—imitation of Jesus Christ. And therefore it

is not fanciful if here we see, shining through the demeanor and conduct of the Apostle, some hint of the manner of the Master.

It is the consensus of opinion that Paul wrote Philemon during his first Roman imprisonment, around 62 AD, at the same time he wrote Colossians; both epistles were delivered by Onesimus. This may account for some of "the undesigned coincidences" between Philemon and Colossians. In both, Paul and Timothy head the epistle, Archippus is addressed, and Paul appears as a prisoner. In none of his epistles, however, does Paul reveal his great heart and care for every member of the church as he does in Philemon, which is a personal letter fragrant with a sense of honor and politeness. In many ways, this epistle proves that "gentleman is written legibly on Paul's brow." Let us summarize it in this sevenfold fashion:

1. HIS FRAGRANT REMEMBRANCE OF OTHERS

If "memory is a paradise from which we cannot be driven,"[71] then Paul was sublimely happy, for he was rich in his friendships and in his remembrance of them. In *Seven Lamps of Architecture*, John Ruskin calls gentlemanliness another name for intense humanity. Well, Paul shared this quality in an unusual degree. He was keenly alive to the value of Christian friendship, and as a prisoner, he depended on others for personal needs. Onesimus supplied both wants and won the apostle's heart, so that he became much attached to the onetime slave. When, reluctantly, he sent Onesimus back to Philemon, Paul, because of his natural craving for human sympathy, found the parting painful.

It may be worthwhile to form a closer acquaintance with Paul's friends named in this short epistle, many of whom were, to adapt John Dryden's phrase, "God Almighty's gentlemen." First on the list is—

Philemon (See Philemon 1:1.)

The recipient of the letter bearing his name is tenderly referred to as *"our dearly beloved,"* or "beloved friend," and *" fellowlabourer."* Many Bible

---

71. John Lancaster Spalding.

names are full of significance. The name *Philemon* means "friendly," and this trait is, as we see, one that Paul commends. Philemon's prayers, love, generosity, and hospitality were always in Paul's mind. (See Philemon 1:5, 7, 21–22.) As a "*fellowlabourer*," Philemon had assisted in the cause of Christ in many ways.

All we know of Philemon is in this letter Paul sent him. Evidently he lived in Colosse, was a believer, possessed considerable wealth (see verse 22), and was held in high esteem by Paul. Philemon's house was the rendezvous of believers. "The church" met in his home, and as the head of the Christian congregation in Colosse, Philemon's influence must have been considerable. It has been suggested that Philemon was led to Christ by Paul during the apostle's ministry in Ephesus. Philemon might have visited Paul, seeing the apostle had not visited Colosse up to this time.

Apphia (See Philemon 1:2.)

Because of her association with Philemon, it is felt by many scholars that Apphia was the wife of Philemon. Otherwise, she would not have been mentioned on such a domestic matter. As a "beloved sister," Apphia is identified as a sincere believer, since the name means "faithful."

Archippus (See Philemon 1:2.)

While his name signifies "leader of horses," and may be indicative of his employment or pleasure, yet it was in a spiritual warfare that he was a sharer of similar dangers and hardships. (See 2 Timothy 2:3.) Living amid military sights and sounds in Rome, it was only natural for Paul to employ such terms. There is no biblical support of the view that Archippus may have been the son of Philemon, even though he may have lived in his home and was an active worker in the church at Colosse; hence Paul's exhortation to Archippus: "*Take heed to the ministry which thou hast received in the Lord, that thou fulfil it*" (Colossians 4:17).

A further word is necessary regarding "the church in the house," in which Archippus was an active part. Originally, believers met in large houses of wealthy Christians. Some would provide plenty of room for the gathering of saints. Not until long after the apostolic age were separate buildings for worship erected. These early assemblies were characterized by unity (see Psalm 133) and consisted of—

1. Messages from the apostles announced or read (See Colossians 4:16.)

2. Prayers offered for the apostles and all men (See 1 Timothy 2:1.)

3. Singing of psalms and spiritual hymns (See Colossians 3:16.)

4. Scriptures read and explained (See 1 Timothy 4:13.)

5. Commemoration of the Lord's Supper (See Acts 20:11.)

6. Collections taken for pressing needs (See 1 Corinthians 16:2.)

Onesimus, in his unconverted state, must have often witnessed these gatherings in Philemon's home, and wondered what they were all about. This we know: the runaway slave's heart was not touched nor won for Christ until he heard the gospel from the lips of the prisoner Paul in Rome.

Epaphras (See Philemon 1:23.)

Although *Epaphras* is the same name as *Epaphroditus*, this was not the same person who brought the contribution from Philippi to Rome about this time. (See Philippians 2:25.) Epaphras lived in Colosse. (See Colossians 4:12.) Epaphroditus lived in Philippi and held office in the church there. Paul speaks of him as a "fellow servant." (See Colossians 1:7.) This does not mean that he had been cast into prison on Roman authority, but that he became a voluntary companion-captive in exile. To remember the brethren in bonds was accounted the same thing as being bound with them." (See Hebrews 13:3.) Willingly, he took up residence with Paul in the lodging where he was guarded by the soldier who kept him.

Mark (See Philemon 1:24.)

This is the same Mark whose surname was John, the man Paul had disagreed with Barnabas about. (See Acts 15:37–39; 1 Peter 5:13.)

Whatever it was in Mark that made Paul disapprove of him joining the missionary crusade, he eventually made good and became a valuable helper to Paul in the closing days of his life (see Colossians 4:10; 2 Timothy 4:11), as well as the writer of the gospel bearing his name.

Aristarchus (See Philemon 1:24.)

From the various references to Aristarchus ("excellent chief"), we gather something of his work and worth. He was a fellow laborer (see Acts 20:4), a fellow prisoner (see Colossians 4:10), and a fellow traveler of Paul (see Acts 19:29; 27:2). Tradition has it that he became the bishop of Apamaca.

Demas (See Philemon 1:24.)

Although Demas is mentioned as Paul's fellow laborer (see verse 24), along with Mark and Luke, and a companion during the apostle's first Roman imprisonment (see Colossians 4:14), Demas was one friend who gave Paul a good deal of heartache at the end of his life. The most poignant words Paul ever penned were, *"Demas hath forsaken me, having loved this present world"* (2 Timothy 4:10). Love of worldly ease and home comforts became his snare—a sad contrast to Paul's lot and to *"all them also that love* [Christ's] *appearing"* (2 Timothy 4:8). The one love blasts the other.

Luke (See Philemon 1:24.)

The beloved physician was doubtless a great help to Paul in his later years. As a loyal companion and fellow laborer, his medical attention must have been deeply appreciated. Luke was the writer of the third gospel and of the book of Acts. (See Luke 1:1–4; Acts 1:1; Colossians 4:14; 2 Timothy 4:11.) In Paul's last imprisonment, when others forsook him, Luke remained loyal to the end. *"Only Luke is with me"* (2 Timothy 4:11). Evidently of Gentile parentage, Luke was the only Gentile among the writers of the Bible. Tradition tells us he suffered death by martyrdom between 75 and 100 AD. As we look back over these and other friends of Paul, the words of Pollock, the poet, come to mind—

Some I remember, and will ne'er forget;
My early friends, friends of my evil day;
Friends in my mirth, friends in my misery too;
Friends given by God in mercy and in love;
My counsellors, my comforters, and guides;
My joy in grief, my second bliss in joy.

2. HIS SINCERE APPRAISAL OF CHARACTER

With all the grace of a spiritual knight, Paul knew how to give honor where honor was due. He deeply appreciated kindnesses bestowed upon him, and he was quick to commend those who did so. Yet, lovingly but with justice, he condemned those whose defection from truth and holiness were apparent. The epistle to Philemon is a striking example of Paul's insight into character, and of his ability rightly to evaluate the true worth of those who surrounded him.

Take, for example, Paul's approach to Philemon in verses 4–7. With instinctive kindliness and conscious diplomacy, he praises Philemon for his Christian life and labors. From the lips of Onesimus he had heard so often of Philemon's love, faith, and liberality. The tired hearts of the poor or otherwise distressed and harassed saints had found in Philemon a haven of rest, and Paul, without flattering, extols the one whose life was the fruit of a loving heart.

We can readily see how Paul's recommendation of Philemon prepared his mind for the apostle's request on behalf of Onesimus. Paul purposely puts Philemon's love first, seeing it was an act of love he planned to ask him to demonstrate. "Love and faith" are not the right theological order. Faith has the precedence, then love—the fruit of faith. When Paul asked for the communication of faith (see Philemon 1:6), he requested liberality from faith—the sharing of what he had (see Hebrews 13:16).

The same assessment of human worth is seen in Paul's estimation of Onesimus. (See Philemon 1:10–17.) No matter what the runaway slave had been, grace had transformed his life, and Paul extols the virtues supplanting the past vices of Onesimus. Paul was not blind to the fact that Onesimus belied the name he bore. *Onesimus* means "profitable"; but he had been not only unprofitable, but positively injurious—he had wronged his master, possibly by stealing from him. But now Onesimus was highly profitable in spiritual as well as practical things. Skillfully, Paul covers a once-hated name with two protective designations, "my son" and "begotten in bonds." The onetime slave was now a son and a partner. No longer must Onesimus be dealt with as a chattel but as a Christian. Paul plays on the name of Onesimus and says, in effect, "He did not show himself truly as Onesimus; but he is changed now, and become worthy, yea, twice worthy…of that expressive name."

3. HIS TENDER APPEAL FOR FORGIVENESS

The kingly heart of Paul begs forgiveness for Onesimus. How could Philemon spurn such a gracious overture? Paul strengthened his plea in several forceful ways. (See Philemon 1:9.) First of all, it was Paul who was presenting the plea—Paul, the well-known apostle, whose praise was in all the churches and who was held in high esteem everywhere. Second, he pleads his age. Nearing seventy, with his weakness of age being aggravated by his suffering in prison, he must therefore be listened to with respect. In the plea of his age there may be a suggestion that Philemon was a good deal younger than Paul. Third, the apostle speaks of his bonds. And we can imagine how Paul's hardship would appeal to Philemon's heart. Further, Paul did not have much longer to live. The shadow of martyrdom was over his path. Perhaps the strongest plea for Philemon's forgiveness of Onesimus was the fact that Philemon owed his own salvation to Paul's faithful witness. (See Philemon 1:19.) In urging Philemon to take back Onesimus as if he were Paul, the apostle presents the case as if he himself had been guilty of the wrong done to Philemon. Such an appeal was backed up by the reminder that he was Philemon's father in Christ. He was under obligation to comply with Paul's request, seeing he owed all he had in grace to him. Martin Luther's commented on this plea: "[Paul] strips himself of his right, and thereby compels Philemon to betake himself to his right."

Paul also wanted Philemon to know that there must be nothing done halfhearted. His forgiveness of his former slave had to be warm, full, and free. *"Receive him, that is, mine own bowels"* (Philemon 1:12). Paul counted Onesimus as dear as his own heart. Such language implies the intense affection of a parent for a child. It is more than certain that Paul's fervent plea did not fall upon deaf ears. Paul's recommendation for clemency met with a favorable reception. (See Colossians 4:9.) It is said that Philemon liberated Onesimus and became the bishop of Berea, ultimately at Rome.

4. HIS LOFTY ESTIMATION OF SUFFERING

Paul, more than any other man, knew how to glory in his tribulations. He never groaned under his burdens. His shackles could not bind his spirit. True, he was a prisoner—but a prisoner in Jesus Christ. (See Philemon 1:1, 9.) Roman fetters bound hands and ankles, but they were the bonds of the gospel. (See verse 13.) It was Christ's cause, and no infringement of Roman laws, that had put him in chains. Paul traced everything to the Master he dearly loved and sacrificially served. Samuel Rutherford used to date his letters from his Scottish prison—Christ's Palace, Aberdeen. Outwardly, Paul was Nero's prisoner. Inwardly, he was Christ's. Some of the Moravian missionaries sold themselves into slavery that they might preach Christ to the slaves. Paul treated his bondage as a God-given opportunity for the furtherance of the interests of the gospel. (See Philippians 1:12–13.) "Stone walls do not a prison make."[72] (See Acts 28:20.)

Can we say that although prison walls, tangible or intangible, shut us in, we yet have a heart enfranchised? If in a sick chamber, or in some restricted sphere, there are letters we can write and a sweet resignation we can maintain—the influence of which can reach far and live long. Bound in some way or another, we can yet be God's freeman.

> Make me a captive, Lord,
> And then I shall be free;
> Force me to render up my sword,
> And I shall conqueror be.[73]

---

72. Richard Lovelace, "To Althea, from Prison," 1642.
73. George Matheson, "Make Me a Captive, Lord."

5. HIS NOBLE CONSIDERATION FOR PROPRIETY

There was never anything rude or crude about Paul's dealings with those around him. He was never off guard. Everything about his speech and action was proper. True, in a moment of passion, he insulted the high priest by calling him a *"whited wall"* (Acts 23:3). Learning, however, that it was the high priest he had addressed, he humbly apologized with all graciousness.

Of Paul's approach to Philemon, Bishop Ellicott remarks,

The exquisite tact with which [Onesimus'] fraudulent conduct towards Philemon is alluded to (ver. 18),—the absence of everything tending to excuse or palliate the misdeed, yet the use of every expression and sentiment calculated to win the fullest measures of Philemon's forgiveness,—has never failed to call forth the reverential admiration of every expositor of this Epistle from the earliest times down to our own day.[74]

Martin Luther also wrote of Paul's manners with characteristic human tenderness and Christian insight.

Philemon showeth a right noble lovely example of Christian love. Here we see how Paul layeth himself out for poor Onesimus and with all his means he pleadeth his cause with his master and so setteth himself up as if he were Onesimus and had himself done wrong to Philemon.

Would that we could exhibit the same tact, wisdom, and spiritual guile when faced with the problems of others. (See Philemon 1:8, 10, 14, 19.)

C. A. Joyce, the well-known British educationalist and popular broadcaster, has given a fascinating insight into life among prisoners, especially of young offenders in need of corrective training, in his book

---

74. Charles John Ellicott, *A Critical and Grammatical Commentary on St. Paul's Epistles to the Philippians, Colossians, and to Philemon, with a Revised Translation*, vol. 2 (Boston: William H. Halliday and Co., 1868), 215–216.

Thoughts of a Lifetime. Possessed of a firm religious faith and a sincere concern for others, he reveals what a deep understanding of basic human nature he has. Fully convinced that, in setting Christian standards, the first rung of the ladder is courtesy, the author firmly states that all he mentions in his book applies not only to work among young offenders but to society in general. He says,

> There is no home, no office, no works that could fail to be improved by this thing called courtesy, and the essence of the whole thing seems to me to be just this: in private life, in industry nationally or internationally, when we really sort it out, everything depends on personal relationships.

And that—in 1971—is as timely a statement as one could expect to hear!

6. HIS UNCEASING LOVE FOR SOULS

Paul had long practiced the art of watching over the souls of others. His long and loyal witness was an exhibition of his own exhortation to serve the Lord in and out of season. D. L. Moody's determination was, "I must speak to one soul each day about Christ." Paul never waited for opportunities to win souls to come his way—he made them, as Philemon proves. (See Philemon 1:10, 12, 16.)

Without hesitation, Paul speaks of Onesimus as his son whom he had begotten in his bonds. He knew Onesimus had been a slave. His name was that of a common slave. But Paul knew that in the matter of salvation, all men were sinners and had to be treated as such on equal terms. It may be pointed out here that in the latter days of the Roman Empire, slaves of Roman masters were immensely numerous. It was difficult for a Roman to pass muster in society if he had less than ten slaves. None of the apostles sanctioned slavery; neither did they stir up animosity in slaves against their masters. They emphasized the spirit of love toward each other. Thus Alexander MacLaren wrote of Philemon, "By the principles which the Epistle expresses, by the results which it involved, this little letter became the Magna Carta of freedom throughout the world."

Untiring in his labors for the Master, Paul won Onesimus. As Christ on the cross preached to the thief, so the apostle witnessed to the runaway slave, who, after his conversion, proved his worth. Paul would have retained Onesimus, for he had implicit trust in him as a *"brother beloved"* (Philemon 1:16). Faithfully, Onesimus cared for Paul as a son for his father, and such a bond between the two helped to remove any dislike Philemon might have had in the reception of Onesimus. Now he would be "much more unto thee," as Paul put it. Through grace, master and servant had been brought nearer and into a more lasting relationship. God had overruled past evil for the ultimate good of all.

While Onesimus had actually run away from Philemon, Paul uses the softer term of *"departed"* and that *"only for a season"* (Philemon 1:15). The word *"perhaps"* (verse 15) suggests God's overruling providence. God has His own designs—His own secret stairs. An old Scottish saint said, "I thought He would come by the way of the hills, and lo, He came by the way of the valleys." How true it is that there is a divinity shaping our ends, rough hew them though we may! Onesimus absconded of his own accord, yet a higher will was in operation. From the human side, the slave foolishly and fearfully left his master. From the divine side, God was guiding Onesimus to the prison cell to meet one whose love for souls was to change his whole life. Onesimus went back to Philemon, who, agreeing to Paul's request, received his onetime slave as a brother in the Lord. All was forgiven. The two were perfectly reconciled. Nothing could divide them again, for now they were bound together in an undying life. (See Genesis 45:5.) While they lived, Philemon and Onesimus would be partners in spiritual interests, partakers of the same faith.

Paul speaks of Philemon as owing him his own life, which is but another way of saying that Philemon owed his salvation to the apostle. So master and slave alike had been won for Christ. Then, Timothy, Paul's companion (see Philemon 1:1), was also his son in the faith. How very many stars will adorn the apostle's crown! Can we say that we are borne along by the same passion for souls? Irrespective of their position and condition, do we approach men and women as those who are lost in sin, who can be delivered only by the Savior's power?

7. HIS UTTER DISREGARD FOR SELF

Selflessness is a conspicuous trait of true refinement, and such a trait was Paul's to an eminent degree. In *King Lear*, Shakespeare says, "The prince of darkness is a gentleman." While he can transform himself into an angel of light, the satanic prince has no innate gentlemanliness. It is only a false veneer—a make-believe. Paul, however, was never guilty of manufactured courtesy to attract attention to himself. His knightliness sprang from his Christlikeness, and colored all his actions.

As an apostle, Paul could have commanded Philemon to take Onesimus back, but because of the love between them, he besought him: *"For love's sake I rather beseech thee"* (Philemon 1:9). Paul would not impose his apostolic authority. Philemon must willingly concur in Paul's request. (See verse 14.) Delicately, Paul bases his appeal on all that Onesimus had done for him. What Philemon would have done for Paul, in his prison cell, Onesimus had done as a living substitute. Using a softer term for "robbed," Paul said he was willing to make good any wrong Onesimus had been guilty of. He said, *"I will repay it"* (Philemon 1:19). Unselfishly Paul is ready to assume all the indebtedness of Onesimus. There is, of course, a significance beyond this application of Paul's words to Philemon. All of us are deep in debt to Christ. There is a sense in which we owe ourselves to those who won us for Christ. There is a bond of tenderness between the two. But it was Christ who paid our debt. A man raised up from some crippling disease owes his life to the doctor. Christ redeemed us at great cost to Himself, and we owe Him all we are and have.

Paul's unselfishness comes out in many ways in this precious letter of emancipation. For instance, he displayed no sense of superiority. He took no advantage of his apostleship. He looked upon others as equals. So we have the terms "fellow prisoner," "fellow laborer," "fellow soldier," "partner," and "brother." Too many preachers lack this spiritual attractiveness. They are too much taken up with their own prestige, position, and superiority. It is foreign to them to think of others as being better than themselves.

Paul was also humble enough to confess that he depended on the prayers of others. He, himself, had his prayer list of those he constantly remembered (see Philemon 1:4), and in turn, he wanted to be prayed for (see verse 23). He urged Philemon to pray that he might be liberated and then enjoy the loving hospitality of his home. (See verse 22.) We can imagine how the prospect of such a visit to Philemon would secure a kindly reception for Onesimus. Once Paul reached the home, he would see how Onesimus fared after being welcomed back by Philemon. Had he treated him as Paul's other self?

How fitting it is that this epistle, which illustrates such courtly manners, should end with a benediction of grace! Paul tells us that he wrote Philemon with his own hand. (See verse 19.) Bishop Lightfoot reminds us that "a signature to a deed in ancient or mediaeval times would commonly take the form, 'I, so-and-so.'" Paul meant by his epistle, then, coming as it did from his own hand, not only to ease the way for the return of Onesimus to his wronged master, but to show us how to act in all graciousness toward all men. There is a proverb that condemns us if "you have good manners, but never carry them about with you." Paul, however, shows us how to always carry good manners about with us, and to live and act as those belonging to the aristocracy of heaven.

THEME 14

HEBREWS: BETTER THINGS

The epistle to the Hebrews is one of the most important books of the Bible in that it contains the most exalted presentation of Christ to be found anywhere. A prayerful, careful study of the epistle leads to a greater reverence for the Captain of our salvation, who is the chief subject of this New Testament counterpart of Leviticus. Here we see Jesus magnified above all others as one above and apart from all others. The design of the writer was to prove that Jesus of Nazareth, whom Jewish rulers put to death, was none other than their Messiah, the Son of God, superior to everyone who preceded His incarnation. No one can meditate upon this epistle without being deeply impressed with the matchless grandeur and superiority of Him who was the express image of the Father.

It is from Hebrews that we discover how Old Testament shadows find their substance in Christ, and that the gospel is the full and final revelation of God to man. The Law given by Moses is shown to be the divinely appointed preparation for Him to whom all the Old Testament gives witness. Leviticus, with its priesthood and offerings, was God's picture book for His ancient people; and in Hebrews, the pictures are explained for the spiritual benefit of those He redeemed by grace. The sacrifices and services of old were *"figures of the true"* (Hebrews 9:24) or *"a shadow of good things to come"* (Hebrews 10:1).

A striking feature of the epistle before us is the way it opens—abruptly. There is no name, no introduction, no salutation, no thanks, and no prayer, as the other epistles have. It opens as sublimely and majestically as the first book of the Bible—*"In the beginning God"* (Genesis 1:1). Hebrews begins, *"God...in time past"* (Hebrews 1:1). Godet, the renowned French theologian, says,

> This epistle without introduction or subscription is like the great High Priest of whom it treats, who was without beginning of days or end of years, abiding an High Priest continually. It is entirely fitting that this book should remain anonymous.

As to its authorship, Origen said, "God alone knows who wrote it." Volumes have been written in the discussion of who penned it. The title giving it to Paul is not found in the oldest manuscripts. Some have assigned the epistle to Barnabas. Martin Luther favored Apollos as its author. Yet others ascribe it to Luke. G. Campbell Morgan contended that the book has Paul's thinking in Luke's language, which may account for similar terms in Acts and Hebrews. From early church days, its Pauline authority has been accepted. Whoever wrote it, we like him, because he put God *first.* If, as it has been said, we can trace the anonymous to God, whoever the writer was, he was inspired of God, for every sentence bears the authorship of the Holy Spirit.

As the title describes, the epistle was addressed to the Hebrews—Hebrew Christians of some definite community, who were in danger of going back to Judaism. (See Hebrews 10:25; 13:7, 17.) The writer proves in every respect that the Christian faith and the church mark a great advance over the Jewish system and so urges the Hebrew professors of Christianity not to go back but to go on. Hence, the epistle adapts itself especially to those Jewish converts who were exhorted to let go of everything and hold fast the faith. Christian progress is the consistent appeal of the epistle, as demonstrated by the repeated challenge, *"Let us go on"* (Hebrews 6:1). We never remain static in Christian experience; if we are not going forward, then we are going back.

While there are many features of Hebrews we would like to deal with, our present concern is with its key word, *better.* This word occurs thirteen times in the thirteen chapters that form the epistle, and it is used to express the contrast between the old and new dispensations, stressing the superiority of the latter. Here, "the old is *not* better." The key verse of this book gives us an epitome of the whole epistle: *"God having provided some better thing for us, that they without us should not be made perfect* [complete]" (Hebrews 11:40). Let us, then, examine the chain of references where *better* is found.

BETTER THAN ANGELS (SEE HEBREWS 1:4.)

The word *better* means "greater, stronger, more powerful." Jesus became greater than angels after He had made "purification of sins." In His past glory, He was superior to the highest created angelic being. (See Ephesians 1:21; Philippians 2:9.) God had, in ancient times, declared His law through the media of angels (see Hebrews 2:2), but grace and truth came in the person of Jesus. By inheritance, He obtained a more excellent name than the angels. By essential right, He was the Son of God and worthy to receive the worship of angels (see Hebrews 1:6), who are not to be worshiped (see Revelation 22:8–9). No angel ever received the title "Son of God." True, they are spoken of in an inferior sense as *"sons of God"* (see Job 1:6; 38:7), but the word *Son,* as used of Jesus, is unique. Angels were employed to carry out divine purposes, but the Son of God is the one addressed in the phrase *"Thy throne, O God, is for ever and ever"* (Psalm 45:6).

But the adulation "much better than angels" seems to contradict the assertion *"Thou madest him a little lower than the angels"* (Hebrews 2:7; see also Psalm 8:5). The margin of Hebrews 2:7 has it, "A little while inferior to angels." Ellicott, however, affirms that the true rendering of the Hebrew should be restored. Becoming "God manifest in flesh," Jesus, because of the limitations of His human form, appeared to be a little less than God. Jesus, then, is greater than angels in name, in kind, and in degree. He is superior to all His creatures, and angels were a part of His creation. His character and conduct, work and worth, give Him an excellency that transcends and eclipses that of the angels of God who minister to the heirs of salvation.

BETTER THINGS (SEE HEBREWS 6:9.)

This verse is introduced by one of those important, pivotal *buts* of Scripture. The writer had been describing the terrible state of apostates. Then he gives the warning about the peril of those who follow those whose end is "nigh unto a curse." (See Hebrews 6:8.) For those who truly believe, there are better things, things accompanying their salvation, to experience. Among these "better things" are our labor of love, our fruitfulness in service, our kindness to fellow saints, our unceasing and full assurance of hope, and our inheritance of the promises of God. (See Hebrews 6:10–12.)

Surely it is *better* to be an apostle than an apostate, a possessor than a professor, a redeemed believer than a rejecter. If we constantly seek all the blessings arising from our salvation, and that ought to accompany it, there is no fear of us ever putting the glorious Captain of our salvation to an open shame. The first part of this chapter is a solemn warning to those who have never gone the whole way in surrender to the claims of Christ and are in danger of becoming willful rejecters of the Crucified One. If they do reject Him, their end is destruction. The "better thing" God foresaw for His own was their being perfected together in perfect consummation and bliss. (See Hebrews 11:40.)

BETTER HOPE (SEE HEBREWS 7:19.)

Actually, there is no contradiction between the psalmist's declaration "*The law of the* Lord *is perfect*" (Psalm 19:7) and that which is given in the verse "*The law made nothing perfect*" (Hebrews 7:19). The word "*perfect*" carries the idea of completion, and the Law in itself was not complete. Because of things it could not do, it was called "*weak*" (see Romans 8:3) and was characterized by "*weakness and unprofitableness*" (Hebrews 7:18). The Law could proclaim, but it could not provide righteousness. Its function was to point us to Christ, whose righteousness was applied to us. (See Galatians 3:24.)

The better hope, then, is the coming of the Righteous One as "*the end of the law for righteousness to every one that believeth*" (Romans 10:4). The Law is now annulled, and in its place we have a better, or greater, hope. This more powerful hope stands connected with the *"better covenant"* and the *"better promises"* (Hebrews 8:6). It is only through this *"better hope"* (Hebrews 7:19) that we can draw near to God. Under the Law, only anointed priests were allowed to participate in the service of the sanctuary. But now, with a nobler meaning, priesthood belongs to all God's people who are saved by grace. In addition, they have, as the result of this *"better hope,"* the prospect of the *"blessed hope"* (Titus 2:13).

BETTER TESTAMENT (SEE HEBREWS 7:22.)

The terms *testament* and *covenant* are more or less the same; thus, "testament" is given in the margin as an alternative translation for the phrase *"a better covenant"* (Hebrews 8:6). If there is any distinction to be drawn between the two words, a "covenant" is a contract or bond between living persons, while a "testament," or "will," only comes into effect after the death of the testator. For the *"better hope"* (Hebrews 7:19), we now read a "better testament"; the new idea is not different in substance, but it is more definite and clear. The very promise of the "other priest" brought with it a "better hope"; the recollection of the divine oath is fitly succeeded by the mention of a covenant, or testament.

What a compelling phrase this is: *"By so much was Jesus made a surety of a better testament"* (Hebrews 7:22). In English law, a surety is a bondsman, or one bound with and for another who is primarily liable—the *principal,* or the one legally liable for the debt, default, or failure of another. At Calvary, Christ made Himself liable for our debts and defaults and paid them in full. He blotted out the bill of default against us. Elsewhere in the epistle, "surety" is given as *"mediator."* (See Hebrews 8:6; 9:15; 12:24.) "As through the Son of Man the covenant becomes established, so in [Christ, our Great High Priest,] it remains secure; the words addressed by God to Him as Priest and King contain the pledge and [the covenant's] validity and permanence."[75] The Old Testament ends with the word *curse,* but the New with the better word *grace.*

The New Testament is better because it is *absolute,* not *conditional* as was the Old, and it is *internal,* not *external* as it was. The former

---

75. *A New Testament Commentary for English Readers by Various Writers,* vol. 3, 310.

days, then, are not better than those under grace. (See Ecclesiastes 7:10.) Under the better testament, there are no *ifs*, no injunctions we must observe to do. There are only "I wills": *"I will make a new covenant"* (Hebrews 8:8); *"I will put my laws into their mind"* (verse 10); *"I will be to them a God, and they shall be to me a people"* (verse 10); *"I will be merciful to their unrighteousness, and their sins and their iniquities will I remember no more"* (verse 12). The former covenant received its dissolution at the cross. It has vanished away. Under grace, we are free from the law—"O happy condition!"[76]

BETTER PROMISES (SEE HEBREWS 8:6.)

The ministry of Jesus as the Mediator of a better covenant is more excellent than that of the imperfect priests of the Old Covenant. His ministry is above all others because His testament excels their law; it is better because it is established upon better, or greater, promises, which are given by God. Being based upon the better covenant, this then becomes the law of His kingdom and the declaration of His procedure. The man who accepts the promises by entering into the conditions laid down is dealt with according to this law.

Israel was God's earthly people, and thus He promises to them an earthly city and kingdom. The promises of the old Law were of an earthly and temporal nature. But the redeemed who form the church of the living God are a heavenly people, seated with their glorious Head in the heavenlies. Thus, the promises of the New Covenant, sealed with the blood of the Mediator, are heavenly, spiritual, and eternal. What exceedingly great and precious promises belong to those who have been made partakers of the divine nature! (See 2 Peter 1:4.)

BETTER SACRIFICES (SEE HEBREWS 9:23.)

In the previous part of the chapter, the writer contrasts the first covenant and its ministrations of the tabernacle with the greater and more perfect Tabernacle, not made with hands. The High Priest had to enter the most holy place once every year with the blood of sacrifice to atone

---

76. Philip P. Bliss, "Free from the Law," 1871.

for his own sin and the sins of the people. Jesus, the High Priest of good things to come, holy, harmless, and undefiled, shed His own blood to atone for sin and entered into the holy place of heaven, having obtained an eternal redemption for us.

The sacrifices of old were patterns, or parables of *"better sacrifices"* (Hebrews 9:23). The use of the plural here need not confuse us. It arises from the studious generality of the terms of the verse. To "these things," the natural antithesis is *"better sacrifices."* The ministry of Christ, the true High Priest with His presentation of but *one* sacrifice, is clearly emphasized in the context: *"Christ was once offered to bear the sins of many"* (Hebrews 9:28).

> Not all the blood of beasts
> On Jewish altars slain
> Could give the guilty conscience peace
> Or wash away the stain.
>
> But Christ, the heavenly Lamb,
> Takes all our sins away;
> A sacrifice of nobler name,
> And richer blood than they.[77]

BETTER SUBSTANCE (SEE HEBREWS 10:34.)

In the references to afflictions, bonds, and recompense of reward, the Pauline touch is evident. The context covering verses 32–39 is certainly reminiscent of many of the sufferings Paul says he endured for Christ's sake. Phillips' translation of the verse before us is helpful: *"You knew that you had a much more solid and lasting treasure* [in heaven]" (Hebrews 10:34 PHILLIPS). We can take joyfully the spoiling of our earthly possessions when we have the assurance of a better possession beyond—the one that no man can rob us of.

Patient endurance is to be rewarded when we see *"he that shall come will come, and will not tarry"* (Hebrews 10:37), for He will be our eternal treasure. Earthly riches and reputation may appear to be solid and

77. Isaac Watts, "Not All the Blood of Beasts," 1709.

lasting, but no matter what their nature, they are only temporal. All that awaits us in heaven is eternal.

> Heaven and earth may fade and flee,
> Firstborn light in gloom decline;
> But, while God and I shall be,
> I am His, and He is mine.[78]

BETTER COUNTRY (SEE HEBREWS 11:16.)

Their sojourning in the land God brought them into was to the patriarchs of old a constant symbol of their sojourning upon the earth as strangers and pilgrims. But they all died in faith, for they looked for a city without foundation whose builder and architect is God. Are strangers and pilgrims the same? No, a stranger is a man away from home, while a pilgrim is one on his way home. And the saints of old, as well as ourselves, if saved by grace, are both. Here below, in this sinful world, we are strangers away from home, for our citizenship is in heaven; but as pilgrims, we are on the way home to a better country, in which sin, sickness, sorrow, and Satan cannot enter.

The marvel is that before they desired that heavenly country, it had been provided, for "he prepared for them a city." But because of the lofty desire those ancient saints had, or, rather, because of their faith and love toward God in which the desire was founded (and of which the longing for a better or heavenly country was the expression), God was not ashamed to be called their God. (See Genesis 17:7; 26:24; Exodus 3:6.)

> I have a heritage of joy
> That yet I must not see;
> But the hand that bled to make it mine
> Is keeping it for me.[79]

BETTER RESURRECTION (SEE HEBREWS 11:35.)

In this verse, reference is made to *"women [who] received their dead raised to life again"* (Hebrews 11:35). The two women so miraculously

---

78. George Wade Robinson, "Loved with Everlasting Love."
79. "My Heart Is Resting, O My God."

blessed were the widow whose son Elijah was raised from the dead (see 1 Kings 17:22–23) and the Shunammite whose son Elisha was brought back from the dead (see 2 Kings 4:35–37). But these two resurrected boys, along with those whom Christ raised from the dead, did not remain alive forevermore, but died again. Yet all those past heroes of the faith, some of whom died terrible deaths, believed in a better resurrection than those who were raised from the dead. They believed that when raised, at the trumpet sound, they would remain alive forever—that death would no longer have dominion over them.

If we are not among those who are alive when Jesus returns for His own, and we go home to heaven by the way of a grave, then a glorious resurrection will be ours. Then with our risen Lord we will be able to say, "We live, but were dead, and, behold, we are alive for ever more." "When this corruptible shall have put on incorruption, then shall be brought to pass the saying that is written, Death is swallowed up in victory" (1 Corinthians 15:54).

> Hear ye the trump of God resounding,
> Saints, arise! saints, arise!
> Through death's dark vaults its note rebounding,
> Saints, arise! saints, arise![80]

BETTER BLOOD (SEE HEBREWS 12:24.)

Hebrews 12:24 reads, "To Jesus the mediator of the new covenant, and to the blood of sprinkling, that speaketh better things than that of Abel," that is, Abel's blood. The sense here is that the shed or sprinkled blood of Jesus speaks more powerfully than that of the outpoured blood of Abel, which Cain, his brother, was guilty of. Because of the excellent sacrifice Abel offered unto God, although dead, he yet speaks or is spoken of. (See Hebrews 11:4.) But his blood cries out for vengeance, whereas Christ's blood pleads for mercy. Abel was a martyr, and his blood cries out from the ground, and led to his slayer being branded as a murderer. Christ died as a substitute for sinners, and His blood cries out from

---

80. William Hunter, "Soon Shall We See the Glorious Morning," 1867.

heaven for the deliverance from the guilt and penalty of sin in all who repent and believe.

God was the avenger of righteous Abel, but Jesus Christ the righteous is our advocate with the Father, and He is the propitiation for our sins. (See 1 John 2:1–2.) The cultured, unregenerated mind may despise the preaching about the blood of Jesus, but without it, there is no remission of sins.

> Abel's blood for vengeance
> Pleaded to the skies;
> But the blood of Jesus
> For our pardon cries.[81]

---

81. Attributed to Alfonso M. de' Liguori, "Glory Be to Jesus," 1853.

THEME 15

PETER'S EPISTLES: SUFFERING

Every book in the Bible was written for a purpose. The Holy Spirit, controlling the minds and pens of the forty writers of the sacred Word, saw to it that each writer emphasized a particular phase of divine truth. In the realm of ordinary literature, authors do not always disclose their purposes. Some books are written to preserve history, others for edification of another kind, others for scientific reasons, still others merely as entertainment, and so forth.

The penmen of the Bible, particularly those of the New Testament, state the purpose they had in mind as they set out to record divine truth. John Macbeath wrote that they "put on record the words and works of Christ: to persuade to faith in Christ; to give assurance of eternal life; to stimulate hope and glory and love; to correct opinion and belief; to lead to action and obedience."

When we read Peter's epistles, we quickly realize that he wrote in such a way as to warm the hearts of his readers. His first epistle was definitely designed to encourage the saints of God to face a time of suffering and martyrdom with stoutness of heart. And as "one of the martyr fellowship of pain," he was the best man to write such a letter. As this letter was written under the shadow of his own cross, Peter was well qualified to use militant language as he urged the believers of his day to meet the hostility of the Roman Empire without fear or retreat. This letter, which F. B. Meyer called "the child of many tears and much sorrow," was written when persecution was already upon the church. The aim of the apostle, who was feeling the pressure of time, was to fortify the hearts of his readers by sending them a message, not of condolence but of courage. The apostle told them that suffer they would—and must!—for Christ's sake, but he urged them to lift their minds from surrounding trials to the mighty forces of God, which operated on their behalf without lapse of time or power, and to the fact that *"Christ also suffered"* (1 Peter 2:21).

To those who were to suffer "for his sake," the comforting reference to Christ's suffering altered their outlook on their tribulation. Now, to suffer was no longer a penalty, but a priceless privilege. The act of surveying Christ's wondrous cross transformed complaint to courage. This is why Peter's writings are not set in the minor key. Saints, emulating the example of the Master, must always glory in their grief, sing in their suffering, and triumph in their trials!

Time is always on the side of those who suffer for the One to whom one day is as a thousand years and a thousand years as one day. (See 2 Peter 3:8.) The day of reckoning is ahead, when the righteous Judge will deal with those who ill-treat His little flock. Thus, Peter exhorts his readers to keep before them the prospect of the Lord's return and allow the blessed hope to stir them to diligence as they await death. (See 2 Peter 3:14.) This is why, as E. Schuyler English reminds us in his commentary *The Life and Letters of St. Peter,*

> The theme of the epistle is the contrast between present suffering and future glory; and its purpose, to strengthen the brethren who are called upon to bear severe testing as the trial of their faith. It is sometimes called, "The Epistle of the Living Hope."

To their faith, the saints must add virtue (see 2 Peter 1:5), and the word Peter uses for *"virtue"* implies "fearlessness, courage, endurance," or the "Mr. Valiant" whom John Bunyan describes.

Alexander Smellie tells us that there was a moment in the French Revolution when the Republic was ringed round with enemies. The

Prussians were on the Rhine, the Piedmontese in the Alps, the English in the Netherlands; La Vendee had rebelled in the west, and Lyons in the east. But Danton cried, "We need audacity, and again audacity, and always audacity." It was a sanctified audacity that the apostle Peter called for in the holy war in which the saints of his day were engaged. They must be willing to dare anything and everything for Christ's sake, and they must be prepared to die as they dared.

Classifying Peter's teaching on suffering helps us to note its different phases. It is a word he uses somewhat freely, fifteen times, in fact. There are right and wrong kinds of suffering. There are sufferings that are mutual, material, physical, social, personal, beneficial, and vicarious. All of these aspects were dealt with by the apostle in his epistles. Scofield's notes supply us with the following serviceable outline:

Suffering in the first epistle of Peter is set in the light of:

1. Assured salvation (See 1 Peter 1:2–5.)

2. The great glory at Christ's appearing (See 1 Peter 1:7.)

3. Christ's sufferings and coming glories (See 1 Peter 1:11.)

4. The believer's association with Him in both (See 1 Peter 2:20–21; 3:17–18; 4:13–15.)

5. The purifying effect of suffering (See 1 Peter 1:7; 4:1–2; 5:10.)

6. Glorification of Christ in the believer's patient suffering (See 1 Peter 4:15.)

7. Disciplinary aspect of suffering (See 1 Peter 4:17–19; 1 Corinthians 11:31–32; Hebrews 12:5–13.)

Perhaps a running commentary on the suffering of Christ and those whom He redeemed may prove helpful.

THE SUFFERINGS OF CHRIST

Peter repeatedly refers to the vicarious sufferings of Christ. In fact, each chapter of his first epistle carries some allusion to the cross. First of all, he reminds us that our Lord's sufferings were foretold by the Holy

Spirit in Old Testament Scripture, and that angels, with holy curiosity, sought to know more of the mystery of the cross. (See 1 Peter 1:11–12.) Then the apostle makes it clear that Christ suffered for us: *"Who his own self bare our sins in his own body on the tree"* (1 Peter 2:24).

Quintin Hogg, who spent his fortune building the magnificent Polytechnic Institute in London for the spiritual and physical welfare of the young manhood of the city, was once asked what it cost him to erect such a pile of buildings. He replied, "Not much; just the lifeblood of one man." The building of the church—the habitation of God—cost the lifeblood of Him who came as the God-man.

Then, as we will presently see, Peter calls upon the saints to reciprocate the sufferings of Christ: *"Follow his steps"* (1 Peter 2:21). Christ suffered for us in the flesh, and we must arm ourselves with the same mind He had. (See 1 Peter 4:1.) Further, Peter relates the sufferings of Christ to the trials of the saints; then he forewarns his readers of martyrdom and forearms their minds. Our Lord's sufferings were all-sufficient to make atonement. The saints through the ages suffer for His sake, but He *"once suffered for sins"* (1 Peter 3:18); the word *"once"* means "once for all." By His death, Christ procured a perfect salvation for a sinning race. His was a swift, quick death; but for His followers there is a continuous martyrdom: *"I die daily"* (1 Corinthians 15:31). Peter speaks of the long-suffering of God (see 1 Peter 3:20; 2 Peter 3:9), which spells salvation (see 2 Peter 3:15). Discipleship implies the willingness to be *long* in *suffering*. Love to the Lord suffers long. The cross is taken up daily.

The apostle then goes on to tell us that he himself was a witness of Christ's suffering. (See 1 Peter 5:1.) He was present at Calvary when his Lord died. As an apostle, he submits the credential. The Gospels do not record that Peter was at the cross; nevertheless, he was an eyewitness of the crucifixion, and never forgot that a similar fate awaited him. (See 2 Peter 1:13–14.) Isaac Watts has taught us to sing, "When I survey the wondrous cross," but we can do so only by faith. We were not present when our Lord died. Peter's eyes, however, had been fixed upon that cross of shame. The word he uses for *"witness"* (1 Peter 5:1) is from the Greek term *martus*, from which we get *martyr*, and its use was limited in Peter's day to those who suffered a violent death in the cause of truth. The term is employed today in a wider and milder sense, in which some speak of a person as being a martyr to a certain complaint or physical illness.

THE SUFFERINGS OF SAINTS

There are some phases of suffering that we cannot avoid and will never understand here on earth. The dominant theme of the book of Job is the problem of pain and suffering. Not until we reach the land where all tears are wiped away will we be able to penetrate the mystery of so much that our loving God permits. This we do know: A good deal of suffering is our inevitable lot as fallen creatures. The entrance of sin into the world brought with it the multiplication of sorrow. If suffering is not the result of our own sin, then it comes to us as the consequences of another's transgression.

There are times when the saints of God suffer wrongfully. (See 1 Peter 2:19.) Peter's reference is evidently associated with the slavery that was "a universal and unchallenged feature of the social life of the time." Sometimes Christian slaves were harshly treated. So, when Peter urges servants or bond slaves to be obedient to their masters and to endure patiently their unjustified suffering at the hands of men, his exhortation takes on a deep significance. (See 1 Peter 2:18–20.) Their incentive in the patient endurance of forced suffering is the example of Christ. He threatened not. (See 1 Peter 2:23.) He never paid His persecutors back in their own coin. Self-vindication was not His motivation. Enduring the contradiction of sinners against Himself, He left Himself in the hands of God, who *"judgeth righteously"* (1 Peter 2:23). When we are the innocent recipients of any form of suffering, it is comforting to know that vengeance is God's and He will repay.

Not only are we patiently to endure unjust suffering, but Peter goes on to say that, if we suffer for the sake of righteousness, we should sing over our suffering. Cruel forces should never terrorize us, the apostle courageously declares. (See 1 Peter 3:14.) And, further, it is far better to suffer for truth than for evil. (See 1 Peter 3:17.) If, therefore, we are called upon to suffer as Christians, we should not be ashamed of our scars but glorify God in the afflictions. (See 1 Peter 4:14, 16.) This must have been the valiant spirit of John and Betty Stam, martyred missionaries to China, as they faced the terror of their heartless persecutors and executioners many years ago. Here, again, the incentive to a holy defiance amid imposed suffering is the example of our blessed Lord Himself, who suffered in the flesh. Suffering brings us into a unique fellowship. It makes us *"partakers of* [or "partners in"] *Christ's sufferings"* (1 Peter 4:13). It was Paul's ambition to become a fellow of the order of suffering; thus he declared, *"That I may know him...and the fellowship of his sufferings"* (Philippians 3:10). Both Peter and Paul had caught this truth from their Master's own word and life. (See Luke 9:23.) And let it be noted that the taking up of the cross is not the equivalent of enduring "a thorn in the flesh." Christ made clear that a cross consists in the denial of self, in complete obedience to His will.

The truer we are to the Lord, the greater increase of suffering we can expect. If we are not suffering in some way or other for His dear sake, then it is very likely that there is something wrong with our spiritual experience. Yet care must be taken not to court unnecessary suffering, as Peter shows. (See 1 Peter 4:15.) How practical the apostle was! Useless suffering is caused when we thrust our noses into other folks' business. There are too many busybodies in other men's matters these days.

Let us conclude on an inspiring note. If we are partakers of Christ's sufferings now, He will make us *"partaker[s] of the glory that shall be revealed"* (1 Peter 5:1; see also 4:13). Glory followed the sufferings of Christ (see 1 Peter 1:11), and the same glorious future is to be ours (see 1 Peter 1:3–9). The apostle Peter, facing his own cruel death, knew that after his cross, there would be a crown. (See 2 Peter 1:11–14.) The undying wonder of heaven is the nail prints in the hands of the Savior, still visible in His glorified body. And it will be so one day on behalf of the noble band of martyrs and sufferers for Christ's sake—theirs will be a luster, grandeur, and reward far beyond that which any angel can anticipate.

THEME 16

FIRST PETER: THE FEATURES OF JUDGMENT

As the distinctive note of Peter's first epistle is preparation for victory over suffering, it is fitting that its key word is *suffer*, which, with its cognates, occurs eighteen times. Our Lord predicted sorrow and suffering for His own, and when it overtakes them, they are not to be ashamed, but are to glorify God in the fire of persecution. (See 2 Peter 1:11–14.) All through the ages, the church has had to pass through the deep waters of reproach, suffering, and martyrdom. But the rule of providence is that when God brings great evil and sore judgments upon the nations, He begins with it the purging of His own people: *"Lo, I begin to bring evil on the city which is called by my name"* (Jeremiah 25:29); *"Begin at my sanctuary"* (Ezekiel 9:6). And here Peter says, *"Judgment must begin at the house of God"* (1 Peter 4:17). There are at least three features of this particular judgment to discuss.

1. THE SEASON OF JUDGMENT

"The time is come...begin" (1 Peter 4:17). The phrase *"the time is come"* indicates that this particular judgment was about to begin when Peter wrote, and the word *"begin"* shows that in his mind, it would be a long process. The judgment in question was the fierce persecution the

early Christians were to suffer. Under succeeding Roman emperors, countless numbers of saints did perish. Satanic hostility was experienced by Peter's Lord, then by the big fisherman himself, who, like his Lord, was crucified. This torment of the saints will not cease until Satan is cast into the lake of fire. (See Revelation 20:10.)

Judgment has not yet touched sinners. Their pleasure and prosperity seem to be uninterrupted here, but Scripture affirms that unless they repent, they will be suddenly destroyed, and without remedy. God suffers His own to pass through tribulation now. They have their hell now, but heaven hereafter. With the sinner it is the reverse. Judgment for the church, then, represents severe trial and adversity; but the trial of her faith is much more precious than gold that perishes. Suffering for Christ's sake shapes character and proves the reality of our profession.

Stormy days were already overtaking the church when Peter wrote his epistle. Christ had predicted them, and now they were about to break forth in all their terror. But, as F. B. Meyer says in his commentary on 1 Peter,

> Bitter as they were, such times are needed—needed as the north-east wind to break off the dead and useless timber in the spring; needed as the winnower's fan to separate the chaff from the wheat. Without these searching times of judgment, the Church becomes filled with those who make a profession of godliness, but deny its power; whilst without them even the godly and genuine are apt to become too luxurious and self-indulgent, wrapt in slumber, and indifferent to the needs of the world. So from time to time it is needful for God to set Himself to the work of discrimination, of crisis, of judgment.

Has not the time come for the judgment of God upon the life and conduct of the present day church? Is she not in need of a drastic overhaul, a deep searching of heart, and the disciplinary work of the Holy Spirit? We can, of course, speak of the church in general terms, forgetting that it only becomes what its members make of it. Therefore, collectively and individually, the sifting of God is necessary.

2. THE NATURE OF JUDGMENT

It is imperative to distinguish between the many judgments mentioned in Scripture. There are future judgments for nations, saints, sinners, Satan, and apostate angels. There is a present judgment related to the believer. *"When we are judged, we are chastened of the Lord"* (1 Corinthians 11:32). The Spirit is the scrutinizer, examiner, and judge who thoroughly searches the heart; and we need more of His ministry as the Spirit of Judgment, sifting and exposing all that is sinful, carnal, and worldly in our hearts and habits.

A Divine Judgment

Human judgment is not always just or merciful. It is easy to judge one another, and our conclusions are often wrong. But divine judgment is always right and for our present good. Through the Word, read or preached, the Holy Spirit reveals where correction is necessary in character and conduct.

A Minute Judgment

God said that He would search Jerusalem with candles. (See Zephaniah 1:12.) If something small and precious is lost in a corner of the home, then, like the woman in the parable, we take a candle or similar small handy light to search for it. This is the kind of thorough inspection the psalmist had in mind when he prayed, *"Search me, O God"* (Psalm 139:23). Once God takes over the investigation, He leaves no corner unsearched, but goes into every nook of our beings, exposing things large and small. Such an honest search may prove humiliating, but what His light reveals, His blood can cleanse. If deep penitence results from the judicial work of the Spirit, divine mercy operates for our rectification.

A Gracious Judgment

When judgment begins in your life and mine, it is not condemnatory but corrective. Our present judgment is not for destruction but for sanctification; it is not for our condemnation but for consecration.

God never afflicts us willingly, or without cause, but He judges and penetrates our motives, actions, and relationships for our spiritual good. His chastening is always, if not pleasant, profitable.

A Constant Judgment

When it begins with the saint, it never ends during his earthly pilgrimage. At the close of each day, we should check up with God and see where we have come short of His glory. Long accounts are hard to settle. As we walk in the light, it keeps revealing our blemishes, and the blood keeps on cleansing us from them.

3. THE RECIPIENTS OF JUDGMENT

Peter cites the objects of God's judicial work, namely, *"the house of God"* and *"them that obey not the gospel of God"* (1 Peter 4:17). Saints and sinners are both included. The judgment of the church is here and now; the judgment of the lost is at the great white throne—the most awesome of all judgments. Although the disobedient are often found within the church, Peter distinguishes the saved from the lost.

"The house of God" *(See 1 Peter 4:17.)*

The term *"house of God"* (1 Peter 4:17) is equivalent to the church, which Peter describes as a *"spiritual house"* (1 Peter 2:5) and singles out for the commencement of divine judgment: *"Begin at my sanctuary"* (Ezekiel 9:6). Unless the church is living in obedience to the will of God, she cannot influence those outside her borders who do not obey God. As the church, or any local church, is made up of members, we have a personal responsibility to keep right with God. Are we partakers of His holiness? Do we live in accord with His mind and will? Do our afflictions, sorrows, and losses make us less selfish and more fit for His kingdom? God hates sin, and He hates it most in those who are His. He will never rest unless He cleanses them from its defiling touch. Sins of saints are more grievous than sins in those who do not know the gospel, because the sins saints commit are sins against light and knowledge.

Corporately

Taking the church as a whole, or churches in particular, is it not evident that because of their impotence in a world of need, the time of judgment is overdue? Is it not the responsibility of each church to face up to the necessity of regulating its life by New Testament standards? Are practices condoned contrary to the mind of Him who founded the church? In at least three realms, there is need for spiritual readjustment:

1. In the conception of the church's institution and ministry

2. In the methods of support and maintenance

3. In the presentation of modern doctrines

Individually

As any house or church of God is made up of units, it behooves each member to subject himself to heart-searching tests, to go to his knees and discover what hinders the revival the church so sorely needs. Is it not time that the rod of judgment fell upon many hindrances to the manifestation of the mighty power of God? A few of our many hindrances include—

Our spiritual impoverishment. We have profession but no power. We are always confessing our sin but do nothing about its removal. Thus our churches make no difference to the lost world outside.

Our worldly conformity. The miracle of Pentecost was the placing of the church in the world. The masterpiece of Satan has been the placing of the world in the church. Did not Jesus say that His church would be in the world (as a witness) but not of it? Today, however, she is very much of the world. The marks of separation from worldly policies and pursuits are inconspicuous because of their absence.

Our carnal-mindedness. Pride and prejudice, criticisms and divisions mar the atmosphere of love in a church. Instead of fighting together against our common satanic foe, we burn up precious time fighting one another.

Our desecration of God's holy day. What disregard there is for preserving the one day in the week that God claims for Himself! Multitudes of church members feel that if they give God an hour in the morning, that relieves them of their obligation toward Him, and the rest of the day is theirs to do as they like.

We live in an age of increasing worldliness, materialism, and iniquity. Unbelief and agnosticism are rife in theological circles, so that young men enter the ministry doubting their beliefs and believing their doubts. If the church is to be as a signpost pointing the way back to God, there will have to come a thorough searching and cleansing of her courts. Christ established His church in the world to honor Him and to bring lost souls to Him. His declared mission was to seek and to save the lost. Is this not His church's preeminent task as well?

Those Who Do Not Obey the Gospel of God

This aspect of divine judgment is solemn, sure, and certain. If God deals drastically with those who profess to be saved in order to make them channels of blessing, what will the end be of those who willfully reject the gospel? If saints who depart from the revealed will of God suffer, what terrible perdition must befall those who spurn that will altogether? The believer knows that no matter how grievous present judgment may be, that suffering cannot pass the limit of his mortal life. With the unbeliever, however, it is different, because no matter what tempest may break over his head, he knows that it is only the beginning of sorrows for him. For the believer, the best is yet to be. For the unbeliever, the worst is yet to be, seeing that through death he passes into unrelieved misery and outer darkness. For the believer, the sufferings of this present time are nothing in comparison with the seething abyss, or bottomless pit, awaiting the unbeliever.

Peter concludes his paragraph about the righteous and the sinner in judgment with the comforting words about the committal of the soul to God. How safe and strong we are in the hands of such a faithful Creator and Redeemer! None can pluck us out of those mighty and merciful hands of His. "Without anxiety or alarm you may look out from them on the wreck of matter and the crash of worlds. Those hands shall ultimately bear you, as they did your Lord, through all the heavens, and set you down at his own right hand in glory."[82]

---

82. F. B. Meyer.

THEME 17

JOHN'S EPISTLES: THE RAPTURE

At the outset of this summary, it is fitting to ask what we mean when we speak of the rapture of the church. The actual word itself, although constantly used by all lovers and students of prophetic Scriptures, is not found in them. *Rapture* is associated with "rapt," which means the fact or act of being transported from one place to another, which is found four times in the Bible—

1. In the act of the Spirit snatching away Philip (See Acts 8:39.)

2. In the experience of Paul caught up to paradise (See 2 Corinthians 12:2–4.)

3. In the snatching away of the man child (See Revelation 12:5.)

4. In the disappearance of the saints when Christ returns (See 1 Thessalonians 4:17.)

The word *rapture*, which is related to *harpago*, meaning "raptured, or snatched away," is from the Latin *rapio*. A form of *rapio* is *rapus*, which is the root of our English words *rapt* and *rapture*, terms found in English literature. For instance, writing of one who is carried away by violence, Samuel Daniel says, "Now as the Libyan lions outrushing from his fen rapts all away." Then Edmund Spenser, describing waters carried away, sees "the circled waters rapt with whirling spray." Matthew Arnold, in "The Scholar Gypsy," has the lines,

177

> Rapt, twirling in thy hand a wither'd spray,
> And waiting for the spark from heaven to fall.

As the lion outrushing rapts all away, and as the whirling pool rapts with whirling spray, so will the Lion of Judah seize His own from a ruthless world, just as He took Elijah in a whirlwind to the skies. Thus, *rapture* is a proper term to employ when speaking of Christ's return to rapt, or speedily remove, His waiting church to heaven to be with Him forever. (See 1 Thessalonians 4:13–18.)

Another common meaning of the word *rapture* is that of "ecstatic and transporting joy," which, too, will be the experience of the church when rapt aloft to be with Christ. Robert Browning wrote of "the wise thrush," and its "first fine careless rapture."[83] William Wordsworth describes one whose death he had heard of as, "The rapt One, of the godlike forehead."[84] Even Robert Burns used the word in the same sense:

> Ev'n ministers, they ha'e ben kenn'd
> In holy rapture,
> A rousing whid, at times, to vent,
> And nail't wi' Scripture.

But our rapturous joy, when we see Jesus, will far outstrip all forms of ecstatic emotion that men experience here on earth. When transported to the skies, ours will be an ecstasy unknown before.

> What an anthem that will be,
> Ringing out our love to Thee,
> Pouring out our rapture sweet
> At Thine own all glorious feet.[85]

As we have already hinted, it is a most profitable exercise to gather out from any given book of the Bible the various aspects of a selected theme, being careful not to build up a doctrine on it. The Bible is a

---

83. Robert Browning, "Home-Thoughts, from Abroad."
84. William Wordsworth, "Extempore Effusion upon the Death of James Hogg."
85. Frances R. Havergal, "Thou Art Coming, O My Savior," 1873.

progressive revelation, as well as a complete one, and thus attention must be given to what other books record on such a particular theme, and thereby, view it as a whole. We are now to concentrate on what the apostle John has to say about the second advent of our Lord in his epistles. The reader can follow out this plan by studying what he had to say in his gospel and also in his book of the Revelation.

Spoken of as leaning on the bosom of Jesus and as the disciple He loved, John lived near to the heart of his Lord and shared His secrets as, perhaps, no other disciple did. It was he who recorded the memorable promise that Jesus would return to gather His redeemed ones unto Himself. (See John 14:1–3.) Here, then, in his first and second epistles, are the references to the fact and features of the rapture. He makes no mention of Christ's return in the third epistle, an omission shared by Philemon. (These two epistles—3 John and Philemon—are the only two books out of the twenty-nine that form the New Testament which have no direct reference to the promised return of Christ.)

SIGN OF THE RAPTURE

John has much to say about the appearance of the Antichrist and of antichrists as constituting a very definite sign of the second coming of Christ. Listing the verses, we can see at a glance the characteristics of spurious christs:

> Ye have heard that antichrist shall come, even now are there many antichrists; whereby we know that it is the last time.
>
> (1 John 2:18)[86]

> He is antichrist, that denieth the Father and the Son.
>
> (1 John 2:22)

> This is that spirit of antichrist, whereof ye have heard that it should come; and even now already is it in the world.   (1 John 4:3)

---

86. That those described were once in the church is proved by the next verse: "They went out from us, but they were not of us" (1 John 2:19).

*Many deceivers are entered into the world, who confess not that
Jesus Christ is come in the flesh. This is a deceiver and an antichrist.*   (2 John 1:7)

Both the plural and singular are used, for antichrists are the forerun-
ners of the dreaded Antichrist—a term used only by John. Apostates,
like Hymenaeus, Alexander, Philetus, and Diotrephes were caricatures
or counterfeits of Christ. Who or what is an antichrist? The prefix
"anti" means "instead of," or "make-believe, spurious." Paul gives us the
description of the Antichrist he calls the *"man of sin…the son of perdition"* (2 Thessalonians 2:3), who is revealed as being in opposition to or
antagonistic to the claims of Christ. Not only does he manifest hostility toward Him, but he exalts himself as God. Usurping the authority
of Christ, he presents himself in place of Christ, or under the guise of
Christ. Before the coming of the true Christ as the King of Kings, this
false Christ will ape the Christ of God.

As to the manifest features of an antichrist or any anti-Christian
teaching, John says these are the denial of the fatherhood of God and
the eternal sonship of Christ. (See 1 John 2:22–23.) Therefore, being
anti-God or antichrist is a mark of *the* Antichrist, and it would seem
Christ had this in mind when He said that the world would eventually
worship one who would *"come in his own name"* (John 5:43). Our Lord
also prophesied that there would be *"many false prophets"* (Matthew
24:11); and *the* False Prophet is one of the many and becomes head of
them all (see Revelation 13:16; 19:20). As Seiss, the renowned expositor, puts it, "He will be the consummation of all false prophets, as he is
by emphasis *the* false prophet in the same way that the first beast is *the*
Antichrist of the 'many anti-Christs.'" Is it not tragic to reflect that we
have some of these antichrist deceivers in clerical garb today? Openly
they declare that God is dead, and that Christ may have been a son of a
man, but that He was certainly not *the* Son of Man or *the* Son of God.
Too many of our theological colleges are riddled with professors and
tutors who, by their antichristian teaching, are preparing the way for
the manifestation of the predicted Antichrist.

SHAME AT THE RAPTURE

To John, the second coming was not merely a doctrine but a dynamic; it was not only a truth to be accepted by the mind but a hope influencing every phase of life. In fact, he linked exhortations about practical duties to the majority of his references to Christ's return. Here is the aged apostle's appeal: *"And now, little children, abide in him; that, when he shall appear, we may have confidence, and not be ashamed before him at his coming"* (1 John 2:28). J. B. Phillips, in his *New Testament in Modern English*, expresses it this way: *"Little children remember to live continually in him. So that if he were to reveal himself we should have confidence, and not have to shrink away from his presence in shame"* (1 John 2:28 PHILLIPS).

We are not to be afraid at the thought of His coming, and we are not to be ashamed before Him when He appears or when we stand before Him at the judgment seat. John stresses the opposite to fear and shame in his declaration *"Herein is our love made perfect, that we may have boldness in the day of judgment: because as he is, so are we in this world"* (1 John 4:17). If we are living in the light of the rapture, then we will not shrink away with shame because of unconfessed and uncleansed sin; but we will welcome our entrance into the presence of the Redeemer. If we are ashamed of Him now, then we are a shame to Him, and we will be abashed when we ultimately see Him. Such a feeling of disgrace arises from something that has been done contrary to the will and purpose of the Lord. (See 2 Corinthians 10:8; Philippians 1:20.) May we so live as to be ready to meet Him with a joy unspeakable and full of glory! If we allow the "blessed hope" to sanctify us, then no shame will be ours when He comes.

SHARERS OF THE RAPTURE

John uses two precious filial terms to describe those who will participate in the rapture, *"the sons of God"* and *"little children."* How amazed John is that such a privileged relationship is all because of the love of our heavenly Father. (See 1 John 3:1–2.) *"Beloved, now are we the sons of God"* (1 John 3:2). The word *"now"* is not a future anticipation but a present position.

God sent forth his Son...that we might receive the adoption of sons.
And because ye are sons, God hath sent forth the Spirit of his Son
into your hearts, crying, Abba, Father. (Galatians 4:4–6)

We are His sons because we were *"born of him"* (1 John 2:29). Actually, the phrase here means "born *out of* God." We are part of His own being because we were *"born...of the Spirit"* (John 3:5). Through regeneration, we were made partakers of the divine nature. Sons of God, then, is a title that expresses divine life and kinship. Because we are His sons through grace, He will bring us to glory. (See Hebrews 2:10.) No wonder John addressed his readers as *"Beloved"* (1 John 3:2), for this is an amazing truth—because of His love, God calls us His sons!

"Little children" is another designation for those who are the Lord's. The word *"little"* John uses here has no connection with age or size. Six times over in his first epistle, John employs this appellation of tender and caressing love. (See 1 John 2:1, 12, 28; 3:18; 4:4; 5:21.) Possibly it was a reference to John's advanced age—about ninety years old when he wrote the epistle—and, being old, he felt a fatherly care for those who were his spiritual family. The affectionate word for *"children"*—*teknia*—means "born ones," or, as the Scotch would say, *bairns*; the connections of these terms is profitable to observe. C. I. Scofield divides the epistle in this manner:

1. The little children and fellowship (See 1 John 1:1–2:14.)

2. The little children and the secular and religious world (See 1 John 2:15–28.)

3. The little children knowing each other (See 1 John 2:29–3:10.)

4. The little children living together (See 1 John 3:11–24.)

5. The little children and false teachers (See 1 John 4:1–6.)

6. The little children assured and warned (See 1 John 4:7–5:21.)

The thought of shame and misery of sin always melted the loving, holy heart of John, and so he cautioned his spiritual children to *"sin not"* (1 John 2:1). Godet, in his commentary on John, quotes at length the story of Eusebius, one of the early fathers, about the apostle calling a lapsed youth, "My child." This young convert of his turned again to *"the weak and beggarly elements"* (Galatians 4:9) of the world and became a thief. John found his way to the robber's haunt, but the young man, on seeing him, took to flight. John, forgetful of his age, ran after him, crying,

> O my son, why dost thou fly from me thy father? Thou, an armed man—I, an old and defenseless one? Have pity on me! My son, do not fear! There is still hope of life for thee. I wish myself to take the burden of all before Christ. If it is necessary, I will die for thee, as Christ died for me. Stop! Believe! It is Christ who sends me.

How could the backsliding youth resist a passionate appeal like that!

Both terms, *"sons of God"* and *"little children,"* imply a birth relationship. Being the human agent of the regeneration of those he addressed, John speaks of them in language associated with a spiritual family. Only those born anew by the Holy Spirit are the sons, or children, of God. Those out of Christ may be the creatures of God, but they are not His children. Rather, they are children of disobedience. Jesus told those who resisted His authority and claims that they were children of the devil, that he (the devil) was their father, not the heavenly Father. (See John 8:41–44.) How certain we should be that ours is the spiritual relationship qualifying us to participate in the rapture!

SURETY OF THE RAPTURE

Having heard his Lord say, *"I will come again, and receive you unto myself"* (John 14:3), the apostle was fully persuaded that his beloved Master would redeem His promise and appear the second time. John was also present when the heavenly evangelists announced, *"This same Jesus, which is taken up from you into heaven, shall so come in like manner as ye have seen him go into heaven"* (Acts 1:11). There is, therefore, the ring of certainty about the apostle's advent declarations. *"When he shall appear"* (1 John 2:28; 3:2).

"To appear" means "to be evident." "To be manifested" implies something more than appearance. A person may appear under a false guise or without disclosure of his true identity. But when Jesus comes, we are to see Him *as He is.* He will be revealed in His true character. This will be the *parousia,* the Greek word for "personal presence." Jesus said, *"I will come again"* (John 14:3), and John, believing in the personal return of his Lord, could pray, *"Even so, come, Lord Jesus"* (Revelation 22:20). Appearing to His own when He returns, He will not then appear to the world. This final phase of His appearing will take place when He comes back to earth to usher in His millennial reign.

The word *"when"* John used (or *"if,"* as some old texts read: *"If he shall appear"*) does not express any doubt as to the *fact* of Christ's return, but rather uncertainty as to the circumstances. The *fact* is certain, because of all Christ is within Himself as the truth. He was not a man that He should lie. Having said, therefore, that He would come again, He must appear the second time—and He will. But the *time* of His coming is as uncertain as the *fact* is certain, hence the necessity to watch as we wait so we will be ready when He suddenly breaks through the clouds, saying, *"Arise, my love, my fair one, and come away"* (Song of Solomon 2:13).

SIMILARITY AT THE RAPTURE

Without any fear of contradiction, John affirms, *"We know that, when he shall appear, we shall be like him"* (1 John 3:2). Like Him! It is beyond the human mind to fully comprehend all that is implied by this declaration of similarity between Jesus and us. We are to see Him as He is. What will He be like when He comes again? Why, the very same as He was when He ascended on high after His resurrection! The disciples who saw Him disappear were consoled when the two men from heaven told them that *"this same Jesus"* (Acts 1:11) would return in like manner as He vanished. Thus, physically and morally, we are to resemble Him. Is this not the truth Paul taught the Philippians who looked for the Savior from heaven? *"Who shall change our vile body* [or the body of our humiliation], *that it may be fashioned like unto his glorious body"* (Philippians 3:21). Then our likeness to Him will be complete.

The certainty of such a transformation and the unknown glory associated with it is implied in the phrase *"It doth not yet appear what we shall be"* (1 John 3:2). Through matchless love, we are *now* the sons of God, but a still greater divine privilege will be ours when we see the Son of God and are changed into His image. The more we see Him as He is reflected in His Word, the greater is our desire to live like Him now, and the more intense is our longing to awake in His likeness. D. L. Moody was greatly blessed by the ministry of Andrew Bonar at Northfield when he preached with great effect. As he came to leave for his native Scotland, Moody asked Bonar to send a photo of himself, which he did. But on the back of the photograph, Bonar had written, "This is not very good of me, but I expect a better likeness when Jesus comes, for the Bible says, 'I shall be like him.'"

> Upheld by hope—that wondrous hope,
> That I shall see His face.
> And to His likeness be conformed
> When I have run the race.[87]

SANCTIFYING INFLUENCE OF THE RAPTURE

"Hope," it has been said, "is the more of desire." John goes on to say that *"every man that hath this hope in him purifieth himself, even as he is pure"* (1 John 3:3). This is the *"blessed hope"* (Titus 2:13) that Paul wrote about, which enables us to live *"soberly, righteously, and godly, in this present world"* (Titus 2:12). However, the saintliest on earth are not without blame or blemish!

> The highest hopes we cherish here, how fast they tire and faint;
> How many a spot defiles the robe that wraps an earthly saint;
> O for a heart that never sins; O for a soul washed white;
> O for a voice to praise our King, nor weary day or night![88]

Such an aspiration will be fulfilled when we see Jesus, the perfection of purity. It is as *sons* of God that we have this hope, and purity is one of the requirements of sonship. We cannot live just any kind of a life if we

87. Emily May Grimes Crawford, "Upheld by Hope," 1902.
88. Cecil F. Alexander, "The Roseate Hues of Early Dawn," 1853.

truly believe that our holy Lord may return at any moment. The phrase *"purifieth himself"* (1 John 3:3) is in the present tense, implying that He is constantly purifying Himself. It is the same thought the apostle has when he tells us that *"the blood of Jesus Christ his Son cleanseth* [keeps on cleansing] *us from all sin"* (1 John 1:7). As when our spiritual light increases we discover more in our lives that is alien to His holy mind and will, so will the experience of this continual cleansing become deeper.

> With such a blessed hope in view,
> We would more holy be,
> More like our risen, glorious Lord,
> Whose face we soon shall see.[89]

SERVICE REWARDED AT THE RAPTURE

Coming to John's second epistle, we find that the key word is *truth*, that is, the whole body of revealed truth as found in Scripture. The apostle makes it clear that this is our sole authority for doctrine and life, as well as our unfailing resource in our age of spiritual declension and apostasy. Fidelity to doctrine is not only a test of whether we are in reality sons of God, but also an evidence of our readiness for Christ's return. (See 2 John 1:7–10.)

"Look to yourselves" (2 John 1:8), or "Take care of yourselves," is a call to self-examination, to discover whether we are abiding in the doctrine of Christ. If we are not, then we are not of Him. (See 2 John 1:9.)

"Lose not those things which we have wrought" (2 John 1:8). We must be careful not to throw away all the labor that has been spent on us. Paul was always cautious, lest, after having preached to others, he should become a castaway, or disapproved, or thrown to one side. If we are truly sons, we must lose many things, but we cannot lose Christ. It is possible (how sad if such should happen!) to lose the graces of the Christian life that recommend Christ to others.

"But...we receive a full reward" (2 John 1:8). We are to live and labor, not for *a* reward, but for the *"full reward"*—*"full"* implying here "completeness"

---

89. Robert Boswell, "Behold What Love," 1879.

or "the utmost," as "full corn in the ear," not able to hold any more. Ellicott comments, "The diminution of the reward would be in proportion to the gravity of the error. The reward would be the peace of God which passeth all understanding, the blessed stability, firmness, and joy which truth and love communicate."[90] (See Galatians 4:2; Colossians 3:24.)

Are we to receive the *full* reward that loyalty to Christ, His truth, and His cause merit? A reward, let us remember, must be earned. We do not work for a "gift." It would not be a gift if we had to labor for it. But the degree of our reward at the judgment seat of Christ depends upon our love and loyalty to Him. (See 1 Corinthians 3:12–15; Matthew 25:14–30.) If we are unfaithful to the Lord and His Word, we do not lose our souls, but we do lose our rewards. The tragedy is that many of us will stand before Christ on that day with a saved soul but a lost life— nothing to our credit. We will be saved—yet so as by fire. May grace be ours to labor for the highest reward the righteous Judge can bestow!

We close with John's appeal, *"Little children, it is the last time"* (1 John 2:18). As we are living in the period just before the close of this age of grace, it is imperative to make the apostle's three safeguards our very own—

1. The Lord above, as our advocate (See 1 John 2:1.)

2. The Spirit within, as the unction (See 1 John 2:20.)

3. The Word in hand and in heart (See 1 John 2:14.)

The recognition and realization of these facts make us more than conquerors, and by knowing and doing the will of God, we learn the secret of living forever. (See 1 John 2:17.)

> Toil, workman, toil; thy gracious Lord
> Will give thee soon a full reward;
> Then toil, obedient to His Word,
> Until He come.[91]

90. *A New Testament Commentary for English Readers by Various Writers*, vol. 3, 498.
91. Mildred Cable, *The Fulfilment of a Dream of Pastor Hsi's: The Story of the Work of Hwochow*, 1917.

THEME 18

JUDE: THE APOSTASY

In these days of deepening apostasy, we need to live in the priceless letter of Jude. He was no middle-of-the-roader. Conspicuous for his spiritual discernment, Jude exposed the apostates of his day in no uncertain terms.

Made up of only twenty-five verses, a distinction the epistle shares with the book of Philemon, this closing epistle of the Bible depicts the hopeless prospect of all those who abandon a God-given faith, and, on the other hand, the blessedness of those who abide faithful to the Lord and His Word. As the last epistle, it has a pertinent message for these last days. C. J. Rolls summarizes this letter in his masterly synoptical study of Jude as "the Peril of Apostasy and the Profit of Faith." S. Maxwell Coder calls his studies of this epistle *The Acts of the Apostates*. Without doubt, Jude condenses for us the truth of the previous twenty-five books of the New Testament and introduces us to the book of Revelation. Here we have *multum in parvo* (much in little), which led Origen, one of the early fathers, to say of Jude, "[It is] an Epistle of few lines, but one filled full of the strong words of heavenly grace."

My own study of Jude brought to light the interesting fact that its writer built his brief message on triads. Believing with Solomon that a threefold cord is not quickly broken, Jude groups truths together in trinities. Let us now trace some of them.

A THREEFOLD RELATIONSHIP

The epistle opens with a suggestive trinity of facts: *"Jude the servant of Jesus Christ, and brother of James"* (Jude 1:1).

1. A National Relationship

The name "Jude" not only relates him to his matchless letter, stamping him as the writer of it, but also relates him to the Jewish people. "Jude" or "Juda" is related to "Judah," meaning "praise" or "praise the Lord." It is quite possible that he was a descendant of the tribe of Judah, like the Master Himself.

2. A Spiritual Relationship

With due humility, Jude speaks of himself as *"the servant of Jesus Christ"* (Jude 1:1). He could have called himself "the brother of Jesus Christ," because this was his relationship. From Matthew 13:55–56 and Mark 6:3, we discover that, after the marriage of Joseph and Mary, several sons and daughters entered their home in a natural way. The Roman Catholic Church erroneously teaches that Mary never had other children but was a perpetual virgin. The lists confirm that Jude, or Judas (not Iscariot), was the fourth son born to Mary after the birth of Christ.

Jude, however, places the spiritual above the natural, even as the Lord Jesus, his half-brother, had taught. *"Whosoever shall do the will of my Father which is in heaven, the same is my brother, and sister, and mother"* (Matthew 12:50). Being a servant of Christ, then, was much more important to Jude than being bound to Him by human ties. The lowliest Christian is nearer kin to Christ than those of closest earthly bonds.

3. A Natural Relationship

Jude and James were full brothers in that they came from the same parents. Mary was the mother also of Jesus, but He had no earthly father: *"That which is conceived in [Mary] is of the Holy Ghost"* (Matthew 1:20). Much discussion centers around the identity of James. But this we know, Jude must have meant the one mentioned among the brothers and sisters of Christ.

A THREEFOLD POSITION

Jude gives us a threefold portrayal of those to whom he addressed his epistle: They were sanctified, preserved, and called. Some scholars reverse the order of the first verse and make it read, "The called ones, beloved in God the Father, and preserved in Jesus Christ"; and, in grace, this is the right order.

1. Called Ones

As the result of the Spirit's ministry, a believer is a "called one." After hearing the divine call, he called upon the name of the Lord and was saved. Alas, *"many are called, but few are chosen"* (Matthew 22:14). Our churches possess many who are *cold*, and some who are *frozen*.

2. Beloved in God the Father

While some of the oldest manuscripts read *"beloved in God"* (RSV) instead of *"sanctified by God"* (Jude 1:1), both designations are true. As the beloved in God, we are set apart from sin unto God. As the objects and recipients of His love, we likewise share His holiness. All His called ones are saints. Some, however, are more saintly than others.

3. Preserved in Jesus Christ

Whether we accept *"kept for Jesus Christ"* (Jude 1:1 RSV) or *"preserved in Jesus Christ"* (verse 1), the thought is the same. We are kept *by* and *for* Him. Preservation is what our Lord prayed for on behalf of His own. (See John 17:11.) As we will see, *kept* is one of the key words of Jude. How privileged we are to be included among those the Lord preserves!

A THREEFOLD SALUTATION

The triad is characteristic of salutations in most of the epistles. Paul expressed himself in similar fashion. (See Titus 1:4.)

1. Mercy

This attribute has reference to the past, in spite of all its record of weakness and failure. We would never have become "called ones" had it not been for divine mercy. And until our last breath, all of us will be deep in debt to such mercy.

2. Peace

This is our Lord's legacy to His beloved ones. He said, *"My peace I give unto you"* (John 14:27). Having thus peace *with* God through Christ, we have peace *from* God amid all the vexations of life.

3. Love

What preserving love is His! As abiding love, it assures our future both here and hereafter. These three qualities are to be multiplied unto us. We are not to have barely enough to get along with. God is never stingy in His giving. As Dr. Rolls expresses it, "There is an abundance of all three, namely, lots of mercy to keep our endangered feet, leagues of peace to garrison our enraptured hearts, and loads of love to constrain our ennobled wills."

A THREEFOLD PURPOSE

In verses 3 and 4, Jude tells us how he came to write his epistle. He commences this portion with the title *"Beloved,"* an endearing term that he uses three times. (See verses 3, 17, 20.) He then states that, with all diligence, he set out to write of three things: the common salvation, the faith delivered unto the saints, and certain apostates who had wormed their way into the church.

1. "To write unto you of the common salvation" (Jude 1:3)

It would seem as if this was the initial purpose of Jude as he took up his pen, and what a message on salvation he could have written! The word *"common"* has a twofold meaning: first, it means "something cheap, inexpensive"; second, "something universal, for all." It could not be the first meaning that Jude intended, for there is nothing cheap about our salvation! It cost Jesus Christ His ruby blood to redeem us. No, it was the second thought that Jude had in mind, a salvation for all.

2. "To write unto you, and exhort you that ye should earnestly contend for the faith" *(Jude 1:3)*

The general theme of Jude is the defense of the faith in an age of apostasy. The word Jude uses for *"contend"* is more accurately translated "agonize." It is the same word we find in Luke 13:24: *"Strive to enter in."* Too many are hesitant and weak-kneed when it comes to the defense of the faith. Others contend, all right, but are so contentious, so hard, and so loveless. The truth must be defended in love. By *"the faith,"* we understand Jude to mean the whole body of revealed truth, and this faith has been delivered once for all to the saints. Therefore, *"the faith"* is unchangeable and irrevocable, and no man dare tamper with it. If he does, dread judgment will overtake him.

3. "There are certain men crept in unawares" *(Jude 1:4)*

In this solemn warning, Jude describes the apostates in no uncertain terms. Three traits distinguish them: they creep in unawares, they turn the grace of God into lasciviousness, and they deny the only Lord God.

These *"certain men"* are ungodly men. Six times over, a double triad, Jude uses the term *"ungodly."* *"Crept"* means "to enter by stealth." In a crafty, unnoticed way, the modernist steals into the life of the church. How suave and subtle he is, but how dangerous is his work! How tragic it is that destroyers of the faith have crept into some of our seminaries, colleges, and churches! They are traitors to a sacred trust.

Wrong thinking leads to wrong living; liberty leads to license. The grace of God is turned into lasciviousness. What matters, they seem to think—whether one is as cruel as Nero, as greedy as Judas, or as worldly as Demas—is that *"God is love"* (1 John 4:8). So, why worry? How deceptive it is to trade upon the love of God, forgetting His hatred for anything alien to His holy mind and will.

The lowest step on the ladder of apostasy is now reached: *"Certain men…denying the only Lord God, and our Lord Jesus Christ"* (Jude 1:4). (It can also be rendered, *"Our only Master and Lord, Jesus Christ"* [ASV].) Jude uses the Greek word *despotes*, from which we have the English word *despot*, meaning "sovereign master." Thus, "Modernism, pressed to its logical conclusion, is the denial of Christ's sovereignty. The critics of the Word soon become the critics of the Christ, who kept that Word inviolate and constantly upheld its complete authority." Jude says of these apostates that they were ordained to condemnation. What else can they expect but the severest condemnation in the face of their initially secret and subtle (and then open and blatant) destruction of the faith?

A THREEFOLD HISTORICAL APOSTATE REFERENCE

As a Jew, Jude was familiar with Old Testament history and, in verses 5–7, he uses his knowledge with telling effect. By the Spirit's unction, Jude discerns how wonderfully the Lord has acted in the past with people, angels, and cities, and he skillfully uses Scripture examples of apostasy as a warning to other apostates. We have in order, as Dr. Rolls expresses it, "Israel's infidels (see verse 5), angelic anarchy (see verse 6), and Sodom's sensuality (see verse 7)."

1. The Unbelief of Israel (See Jude 1:5.)

Although Israel was a highly privileged nation, signally blessed of God, there were those within it who were guilty of hardening their hearts against the Lord. Their inward state did not correspond to their outward standing. Guilty of perversity and disobedience, they perished in the wilderness.

2. The Fallen Angels (See Jude 1:6.)

Are we not warranted in linking this declension of the angels to Genesis 6? Is there not a connection between the angels leaving their first estate, their original abode and function, and cohabiting with the daughters of men?[92] For their terrible apostasy, these angels are reserved unto the appropriate time of their punishment, perhaps at the great white throne. (See 2 Peter 2:4.) The same bonds of darkness await all present-day apostates.

3. Sodom and Gomorrha (See Jude 1:7.)

This verse should challenge all who deny the faith and the Lord who bought them, seeing as the destroyed, sensuous cities are *"set forth for an example"* (Jude 1:7). Whereas the evil inhabitants of Sodom and Gomorrha were consumed by material fire, the judgment of *eternal* fire awaits those who deny the faith. Our Lord, you will remember, declared that those rejecters around Him would suffer a more fearful catastrophe: *"It shall be more tolerable for the land of Sodom in the day of judgment, than for thee"* (Matthew 11:24).

One expositor of Jude says of these three warnings: "The first is the *worldly*; the second, the *satanic*; and the third, the *fleshly* opposition to the divine will."

A THREEFOLD APOSTATE SIGN (SEE JUDE 1:8–10.)

A comparison of Jude with 2 Peter 2 reveals a remarkable similarity of language describing the work and ways of apostates. The one portion, however, is independent of the other. Think of this unholy trinity: filthy dreamers who defile the flesh, despise dominions, and speak evil of dignities!

1. Defile the Flesh

Man's heart is naturally defiled. It is desperately wicked. But what a designation to use of religious professors! Their dreamings defile the flesh. Distorted visions, couched in the very language of Christianity, are common to Modernism. Apostates are those who reject the faith yet retain its outward form. (See 2 Timothy 3:5; 4:3–4.)

---

92. For more on this, see Herbert Lockyer's booklet "Are These the Last Days?"

2. Despise Dominions

What is known as destructive criticism, or liberalism, is actually spiritual lawlessness. Christ's authority is discredited and denied. The question it is not "What saith the Lord?" but "What saith our own rational minds?"

3. Speak Evil of Dignities

In Jude 1:9–10, Jude gives us an illustration of treating with contempt those who are vested with authority. Michael, in spite of his high angelic rank, would not dare rebuke the devil. Today, however, there is revolt against all authority. It is an age of lawlessness. The Modernist rebels against the authority of Christ and the Word that reveals Him.

A THREEFOLD APOSTATE CORRUPTION

In verse 11, Jude gives us a trinity of men whose names stand out as revolters against God and His authority, and upon whom divine judgment fell. Cain, Balaam, and Korah were brought out of the dim past to warn all those of the church age that God's attitude toward rebellion against His authority had not changed.

1. The Way of Cain (See Genesis 4.)

The son of Adam preferred to offer the fruit of his own labor rather than a sacrificial victim as an offering to God. C. I. Scofield says, "[Cain is a] type of the religious man, who believes in God, and 'religion,' but after his own will, and who rejects redemption by blood. Compelled as a teacher of religion to explain the atonement, the apostate teacher explains it away." Modernism, the religion of Cain, is *fleshly confidence*.

2. The Error of Balaam (See Numbers 22:25; 31:16.)

We must distinguish between the *error* of Balaam (see Numbers 22:11), the *way* of Balaam (see 2 Peter 2:15), and the *doctrine* of Balaam (see Revelation 2:14). Balaam's error was a greedy grasping for material reward. He tried to serve God and mammon. He was a two-faced prophet. Balaam "stood undecided at the crossroads facing the appeal and aspiration for righteousness, and the lure and lust for material renown, and there perished," says Dr. Rolls. Monetary advantages, popularity, and men's praise and approval form a snare. Balaam's error was love of present gain.

3. The Gainsaying of Korah (See Numbers 16.)

Korah perished because of his usurpation of spiritual privileges. He sought to rebel against Moses and Aaron, God's representatives. He wanted equality with them. He tried to bring them down to his level. Terrible judgment overtook him for his arrogance. Today, the Modernist endeavors to bring Christ down to the level of his own humanity. Christ and God are one; Christ is equal with God and *must* receive equal respect, honor, and dignity.

These three Old Testament characters of ill repute, then, fittingly describe the progressive apostasy of our own day. Would that all who deny the faith be warned by such a trinity of apostasy!

A THREEFOLD GROUP OF APOSTATE TRAITS

From verses 12–19, Jude gives us a threefold setting forth of the characteristic features of apostates. His vivid, dramatic, and most expressive appellations fall into three groups, with each group commencing with the expression, "*these are*" (see Jude 1:12, 16, see also verse 19).

1. The First Group (See Jude 1:12–15.)

At least five traits are discernible in this first set. Apostates are "hidden rocks." In verse 4, we read of how "*certain men crept in*[to assemblies] *unawares*" for the purpose of wrecking the faith of the members. The same stealth is emphasized again by Jude. Treacherously, apostates entered the love feasts under false pretense, feasting with others as if they were of them. They are described as "*feeding themselves without fear*" (Jude 1:12) of judgment falling upon them for their hypocrisy. How many there are today who are apostates in heart but who persist in wearing Christian garments! May God expose these wolves in sheep's clothing!

1. *They are "clouds without water."* (See Jude 1:12.) This simile of
    waterless clouds carried along by winds is most descriptive.
    Clouds with the appearance of holding refreshing rain for the
    dry, barren ground, yet empty of water and easily blown away
    by winds, portray the hypocrisy of those who promise what
    they cannot perform. (See Proverbs 25:14.) Too many are
    carried about with the changing winds of religious cults. (See
    Ephesians 4:14.) They are not stable but shifty. They have no
    steadfast convictions. Modernists are empty clouds. Thirsty
    souls approach them eagerly but go away unrefreshed.

2. *They are autumn trees without fruit.* (See Jude 1:2.) Religious
    professors who deny the faith may be trees, but they are
    fruitless, twice dead, uprooted. (See verse 2.) Israel, though
    a well-tended vine, brought forth wild grapes (see Isaiah
    5) and eventually became an empty vine (see Hosea 10:1).
    Modernism is barren of spiritual results, and twice dead—
    dead spiritually within, dead or destitute to influence those
    without. It is also rootless. Believers are so different; they are
    ever fruitful, because they are rooted in God. (See Psalm 1.)

3. *They are "raging waves"* (Jude 1:13). Here we have a figure of
    the ferocity of those who will not brook any opposition to
    their wills, ideas, and interpretations. Unbelief can become
    very loud, boisterous, and insistent when foisting itself upon
    those who love the truth. Then, when fully encountered,
    unbelief foams out its shame.

4. *They are "wandering stars"* (Jude 1:13). Apostates are not like
    those planets moving in their "regular orbits with mathemati-
    cal precision and order, subservient to the laws of their Creator,
    but are like erratic meteors or comets that flash in the heavens
    for a short time and disappear in darkness forever," as Robert
    Evans states in his valuable booklet on Jude. The blackness of
    darkness forever is the inevitable end of apostates.

Jude calls Enoch the prophet as a witness to the judgment that will
overtake all those who depart from and deny the faith. Four times in

verse 15, Jude calls apostates *"ungodly."* While Enoch's prophecy may be directly associated with the flood, it covers all those who ignore the authoritative revelation of God.

2. *The Second Group (See Jude 1:16–18.)*

Six further distinguishing features of apostates are given by Jude in this second section.

1. *They are murmurers.* (See verse 16.) Israel of old was guilty of the sin of murmuring, earning thereby the judgment of God. When a person murmurs, he is not resigned to, or willing to rejoice in, the will of God. Murmuring inevitably leads to open rebellion against God.

2. *They are complainers.* (See verse 16.) Finding fault with one's fellow man is all too common today. Malcontents are a plague to society.

3. *They "walk after their own lusts."* (See verse 16.) Whether the lusts belong to the "good" self or the "bad" self, the thought is the same—namely, the seeking of one's own will. These first three traits are in direct opposition to the requirements of grace, which calls us to live *"soberly"* (toward *self*), *"righteously"* (toward *men*), and *"godly"* (toward *God*) (Titus 2:12).

4. *They speak* "great swelling words" (verse 16). We can translate this phrase "loudmouthed boasters." Modernism is guilty of loud boasting. In this connection, one remembers the rebellious mouth of the little horn. (See Daniel 7:8.)

5. *They flatter others for their own benefit.* (See verse 16.) It is an abominable thing to flatter a denomination leader, for example, in order to gain an advantage! It is possible to have rebellious eyes as well as a rebellious mouth. (See John 5:44.)

6. *They are mockers.* (See verse 18.) Peter has a word about this conspicuous feature of the last days. When scoffers are numerous, the judgments of God are about to fall. (See 2 Peter 3:3.) It was so in the days of Noah. Today, many religious leaders

openly mock the return of Christ and kindred truths. Divine teachings are scoffed at and discarded as antiquated and useless. As these traits multiply, we realize how near we are to the last times.

3. Third Group (See Jude 1:19.)

Jude gives us a further trinity in the distinguishing marks of the apostate in this verse.

1. *They are divisive.* Assuming superiority of attainment over others, an unscriptural separation follows. The Pharisees, or the "separated ones," stood aloof from the rank and file of Jews around. Modernism has developed an exclusive coterie.

2. *They are sensual.* Those who fail to discern the deep things of God act upon the impulses of the natural mind. (See 1 Corinthians 2:14). Dependence is upon the senses and not upon the Spirit. Sensual wisdom ends by becoming devilish. (See James 3:15.)

3. *They do not have the Spirit.* Blind leaders of the blind are devoid of the Spirit. No matter how cultured, gifted, and religious a person may be, if his heart is destitute of the Spirit, he does not belong to God. (See Romans 8:11; Ephesians 1:13.)

A THREEFOLD APPEAL

While the short epistle of Jude begins like a bright morning, a dark cloud quickly comes over the scene. As we have pointed out, false teachers and spiritual apostasy are mercilessly exposed. Wreckers of the church are fully and faithfully portrayed by Jude. Modernism tries to destroy the body of truth. But as the liberals try to pull down, we ourselves are to increase our activity and keep on building ourselves up in our most holy faith. We cannot build the faith, but we can build our lives and witness *upon* it. Jude goes on to describe how, in a threefold way, we can build effectively.

1. We Must Pray in the Holy Spirit (See Jude 1:20.)

There is a vast difference between saying prayers and praying with all supplication in the Spirit. (See Ephesians 6:18.) Prayer in the Spirit is prayer of the highest order and from the deepest impulse. It is the form of prayer rooted in regeneration and constantly inspired by the Spirit. Such prayer brings us into harmony with our interceding Lord in heaven. Not knowing how to pray as we ought, the Spirit helps us in this infirmity. (See Romans 8:26–27.) As we build ourselves up in the faith, the heart responds to the study of the Word and finds expression in prayer.

2. We Must Keep Ourselves in God's Love (See Jude 1:21.)

The key word *"keep"* appears six times in the book of Jude. It is as we are kept from falling that we are enabled to keep ourselves in the love of God. (See Jude 1:24.) Jude does not contemplate the possibility of the believer getting outside the sphere of God's love. That is impossible. The writer is warning us not to lose the enjoyment of that love by waywardness and worldliness.

3. We Must Look for the Mercy of Christ (See Jude 1:21.)

Apostates do not have the forward look, for Bible prophecy is discredited. But all who earnestly contend for faith know that a part of that faith is a genuine expectation of the Lord's return for His own, a return completing His mercy toward us. Since we are preserved in Christ Jesus, He must return to possess us fully.

A THREEFOLD OBLIGATION

Building, praying, keeping, and looking result in sanctified activity. Those who fail to cultivate all that belongs to the faith separate themselves from others. (See Jude 1:19.) With those who love and look for the Lord, it is different. They go out to "rescue the perishing, care for the dying."[93]

---

93. Fanny Crosby, "Rescue the Perishing," 1869.

1. We Must Have Compassion on Some (See Jude 1:22.)

Remembering that Jude is dealing with apostates, we must use every legitimate effort to reclaim them. The margin reads, "convince some, who doubt," or, "on some have mercy, who are in doubt: while they dispute with you." God grant us compassionate hearts, even for those who blatantly deny our precious faith!

2. We Must Save Others with Holy Fear (See Jude 1:23.)

Fiery judgment awaits all who die out of Christ, whether they are religious sinners or conspicuously ungodly. Anyone who rejects the testimony of the Word is lost, no matter how educated he may be. With all godly fear, we must warn apostates of their dreadful end.

3. We Must Hate the Garment Corrupted by the Flesh (See Jude 1:23.)

Sin defiles everything it touches. Christ, however, could touch the leper and yet remain undefiled. We are to love the sinner but hate his sin; but our witness can be effective only as our garments remain unspotted by the world.

A THREEFOLD BENEDICTION

How fittingly Jude concludes his brief but wonderful epistle! In the midst of apostasy, as we reprove error and contend for the faith, victory is ours as we rest on God's ability. We can introduce a sublime doxology with the phrase "him [Christ] that is able" (Jude 1:24).

1. He Is "able to keep you from falling" (Jude 1:24).

God is able to guard His own from the satanic subtleties of apostates in these last days. He can grant us spiritual perception whereby we can detect the slightest deflection from His Word.

2. He Is Able to Present You Without Blemish (See Jude 1:24.)

What a day it will be when, in the presence of His glory, we will be as holy as the Lord! Exceeding joy will flood our glorified hearts.

3. He Is "the only wise God, our Saviour" *(Jude 1:25)*.

He is worthy of the superlative praise of His people. *"The only wise God"* (verse 15). Man's exalted wisdom is paltry alongside God's infinite wisdom! The margin adds the phrase "Through Jesus Christ our Lord." All external wisdom, glory, majesty, dominion, and power are God's through Christ.

Thus, this epistle, which describes a ceaseless struggle against apostate forces, ends with the eternal blessedness of those who are presented faultless before Him. What exceeding joy awaits the saints who remain loyal to the Lord and to His Word!

THEME 19

REVELATION: THE LAMB

The evolution of the lamb in Scripture forms a most profitable meditation. The Levitical and typical significance of the lamb dominates the Bible. Lambs were an integral part of almost every Jewish sacrifice. While the first mention of lambs is in Genesis 21:28—*"Abraham set seven ewe lambs of the flock by themselves"*—it is taken for granted that the firstling of the flock that Abel presented to God was a lamb. His was a more excellent sacrifice than Cain's, seeing that it represented the shedding of innocent blood. (See Hebrews 11:4.) But Christ's offering resulted in better things than that of Abel. (See Hebrews 12:24.)

Lambs chosen for an offering had to be faultless males and in keeping with the established estimate of animal perfection. They had to be under one year old, meek, gentle, and have a tractable nature. (See Malachi 1:14.) Lambs for sacrifice had to be kept whole—*"A bone of him shall not be broken"* (John 19:36; see also Exodus 12:46; Psalm 34:20)— and must be roasted. The lamb was the symbol of unity: the unity of the family, the unity of the nation, and the unity of God with His people, whom He had taken into covenant relationship with Himself.

The typical significance of the lamb is not hard to trace. It typifies:

1. Christ, the Paschal Lamb, who became a sacrifice for our sins (See John 1:29; Revelation 5:6, 8.)

2. True believers, manifesting the lamblike qualities of humility and meekness (See Isaiah 11:6; Luke 10:3; John 21:15.)

3. Beneficent teachers, who are not guilty of cruelty or barbarity (See Jeremiah 11:19.)

4. Innocence, as personified by a wife (See 2 Samuel 12:3–4.)

5. The Antichrist, who will ape the power and prerogatives of Christ as the Lamb (See Revelation 13:11.)

The offering of lambs by sinning Israelites could never grant them redemption from sin. They were accepted by God in virtue of the sacrifice of His Lamb, the Lord Jesus Christ. The question asked by Isaac as he accompanied his father up Mount Moriah—*"Where is the lamb for a burnt offering?"* (Genesis 22:7)—is unanswered all through the Old Testament. Multitudinous lambs had been placed upon blood-stained altars, but the cry for *the* Lamb was not answered until John's declaration, *"Behold the Lamb of God, which taketh away the sin of the world"* (John 1:29).

Abraham's reply to Isaac's question is significant: *"God will provide himself a lamb"* (Genesis 22:8). In His love and mercy, God did provide Himself as the Lamb. His Son, who was "very God of very God," became the Lamb through whose stripes we are healed.

> Not all the blood of beasts
> On Jewish altars slain
> Could give the guilty conscience peace
> Or wash away the stain.
>
> But Christ the heavenly Lamb,
> Takes all our sins away;
> A sacrifice of nobler name,
> And richer blood than they.[94]

Prophets and apostles loved to think of Christ as the sacrificial Lamb. Isaiah wrote of Him as the Lamb led out to slaughter. (See Isaiah 53:7; Acts 8:32.) John the Baptist had the distinction of being the

---

94. Isaac Watts, "Not All the Blood of Beasts," 1709.

forerunner of Christ, the Lamb. (See John 1:29.) John Wesley said that his whole business here was to cry, "Behold the Lamb." It is our solemn business to reecho that cry. Peter extolled the preciousness of Christ's blood, the blood of the One who died as a Lamb without blemish or spot. (See 1 Peter 1:19.) The apostle John was also lost in contemplation of Christ as the Lamb, as the last book of the Bible clearly proves.

Let us meditate upon this unique figure of the Lamb, describing as it does the person and plan of Christ.

Think of His Nature

John tells us that Christ is *the* Lamb. All the lambs of the Old Testament upon Jewish altars slain, merely typified the offering up of this perfect Paschal Lamb. The Lord Jesus is the great and only Lamb whose sacrifice is efficacious to redeem and save lost sinners. Yes, the Lamb was a fitting figure to use, seeing that Christ completes all the hopes enshrined in the sacrifices, rites, and symbols of Jewish ritual.

Think of His Innocence

A child untried and ignorant of the great and gross sins of life is spoken of as an innocent child. But Christ's innocence was greater. His was innocent holiness, an innocence tested but never lost. His life remained unsoiled. As sunbeams never contract the filth they shine through, so our blessed Lord remained holy, harmless, and undefiled. True, He became sin (see 1 Corinthians 5:21), but never a sinner. Had He sinned, He would have forfeited the right to be our Savior; but being sinless, He can save.

Old Testament lambs remained innocent simply because they had no consciousness or knowledge of evil, but God's Lamb was holy. He had a very intimate acquaintance with evil, yet He refused its seductive charms. He was tested as we are, yet He remained victorious.

Think of His Gentleness

Meekness is associated with a lamb, but in God's Lamb, meekness was not weakness. A lamb is a docile animal. How astonishing it is, therefore, to read of *"the wrath of the Lamb"* (Revelation 6:16)! God's Lamb was silent amid suffering, but His very gentleness makes Him great. The meek inherit the earth, said He, and as God's meek Lamb, He will yet see the whole earth filled with His glory.

Think of His Submission

A lamb does not complain when it is slain since it is destitute of the elements of personality. Old Testament lambs were dragged to the altar. Christ, however, was not an unwilling victim. He gave Himself as our ransom. The world has witnessed many kinds of death, as, for example, of covenanter, hero, and martyr; but these men were liable to die. Our Lord Jesus Christ, on the other hand, chose death. Death did not claim Him. He was born in order that He might die. We often say that if we had known what would face us, we could never have lived, but the Lord Jesus knew every step of the blood-red way and walked the whole road with bleeding feet until He reached the cross. His whole life was one of voluntary sacrifices. Sacrifice, for Him, commenced at His incarnation and culminated at Calvary.

Just as a lamb exists for others, so the whole of Christ and His work are for us. A lamb gives its wool, that we may have clothing, and it gives its flesh, that we may have sustenance. From God's Lamb, likewise, we receive both covering and food.

Think of His Deity

Our Lord was no ordinary man. The Jews could bring any lamb to the altar, providing it fulfilled certain conditions. With God's Lamb, it was different. There was none other who could die for man's sin. "There was no other good enough to pay the price of sin."[95] He who was good enough gave virtue to what He did. The blood He shed was the blood of God as well as the blood of man. (See Acts 20:28.) Since Christ was the God-man, His sacrifice was efficacious, seeing that deity was joined to humanity. The blood has transcendent power owing to its unique character. The Lamb was God and of God. And it is just here that we

---

95. Cecil F. Alexander, "There Is a Green Hill Far Away," 1847.

can mark the difference between Christianity and other religions of the world. In pagan religions, man provides a sacrifice for his god. In Christianity, God provides a sacrifice for man; and the mystery of mysteries is that God gave Himself! God is the source of our salvation. It was *He* who loved the world and, in His beloved Son, died to reconcile it to Himself.

Revelation is essentially "the Book of the Lamb." Within it, Christ is only once referred to as a Lion, but twenty-eight times as the Lamb. While there are various ways of approaching the book of Revelation, the most dramatic of the Bible, it is conspicuous as the Lamb-honoring book. The Greek word used for "lamb" in the Apocalypse is *arnion*, meaning "the little lamb," not *amnos*, as in John 1:29. Over against the arrogance and wickedness of the Beast, the false lamb, John placed the meekness and innocence of Christ, the little Lamb. Such a title combines the almightiness and invincibility necessary for the full and final subjugation of all evil forces.

The entire book of Revelation revolves around the Lamb. He is the center and circumference of this mystic and glowing book. It is also to be noted that Christ is always presented as the Lamb that was *slain*. The scepter of universal sovereignty will rest in His pierced hand. His cross wins Him the crown. Government is founded upon His grief. His reign, as the Sovereign over all, is one of His redemptive rights. His wounds, evidence of His past sufferings and a token of our present unworthiness, are also precious in that they forecast His vengeance upon His foes. His Calvary marks form the grounds for the coming judgment. His pierced hands and feet are a source of comfort for His own (see John 20:20) but will strike terror in the hearts of His enemies. Those sacrificial scars, declaring Christ's willingness to be slain rather than submit to sin, cannot possibly compromise with iniquity, and are, therefore, alone worthy to dispense righteous judgment.

There are many serviceable outlines of Revelation, but, because of the way in which the Lamb dominates the book, we can organize its chapters in the following way:

1. The vision of the Lamb (See Revelation 1.)

2. The church of the Lamb (See Revelation 2–3.)

3. The adoration of the Lamb (See Revelation 4–5.)

4. The wrath of the Lamb (See Revelation 6–19:6.)

5. The marriage of the Lamb (See Revelation 19:7–10.)

6. The reign of the Lamb (See Revelation 19:11–22.)

As we look at John's references to Christ as the Lamb, we notice these recurring themes:

THE LAMB AND HIS ETERNAL WOUNDS

Two pregnant phrases call for attention: *"A Lamb as it had been slain"* (Revelation 5:6) and *"the blood of the Lamb"* (Revelation 7:14). Here we have reminiscences of His "blood, sweat, and tears" on our behalf. When Winston Churchill promised the British people this trinity of anguish, did he recall Byron's use of it in the memorable lines:

> Year after year they voted cent for cent,
> Blood, sweat, and tear-wrung millions—why? for rent!

It is interesting to note that for the word translated *"slain"* (Revelation 5:6), John uses a word that means "newly or freshly slain." Further, Christ as the slain Lamb implies that He carries the scars of sacrifice. In heaven, those "rich wounds, yet visible above"[96] eternally remind the saints of all that they owe to Christ, who became both victim and victor. Faith has no difficulty in believing that the glorified body of Christ bears the indelible scars of the cross. (See John 20:20–27.) Memories of Calvary are treasured in heaven. On earth, we see the Lamb wounded and slain; in heaven, He is the center of power and glory.

John turned to see a lion but beheld a lamb. Christ is both. Majesty and mercy are combined in Him. But the Lamb that John saw was not nailed to a cross or even sitting, but "standing" between the throne and the elders. (See Revelation 14:1.) He is about to assume His redemption and inheritance. Now He is seated at the Father's right hand (see Hebrews 1:3; Revelation 3:21; Psalm 110:1), but His patience will soon

---

96. Matthew Bridges, "Crown Him with Many Crowns," 1851.

ended. The Lamb will vacate the throne to take unto Himself His power and reign. "Sitting" is a state of rest; "standing" bespeaks readiness for action. How we love the sight of the scarred, standing Lamb.

> Dear suffering Lamb, Thy bleeding wounds,
> With cords of love divine,
> Have drawn our willing hearts to Thee,
> And linked our life with Thine.[97]

We are thrice blessed if we have the mystic robes made white by the blood of the Lamb. His scars are our only right of access into the holiest of all. The blood alone can make saints, whether they are of this present age or of the tribulation. Trials and tribulation make sacrificial sufferers of saints.

THE LAMB AND HIS WORSHIP

All within creation are stirred to the depths as they come to worship the Lamb. Angels adore the Lamb, yet they cannot praise Him as the redeemed of earth love to do, for the saints alone can sing the new song.

> They sing the Lamb of God
> Once slain on earth for them;
> The Lamb, thro' whose atoning blood
> Each wears his diadem.[98]

The Lamb, the bleeding Lamb, is the theme of the new song, which is the only theme worth singing about. The cross is the grandest fact of all time. Without it, Christ would have been in glory alone and sinners would have had no deliverance from the guilt and government of sin. But the suffering, conquering Lamb of God has all intelligences ascribing praise and honor to His name. (See Revelation 5:8–14.)

While He was on earth, God's Lamb was silent before His shearers. No word of rebuke or reproach fell from His lips as He willingly endured all the contradictions of sinners against Himself. He never exercised His inherent power to save Himself from all who put Him to

---

97. Edward Denny, "To Calvary, Lord, in Spirit Now," 1839.
98. T. J. Judkin, "Enthroned Is Jesus Now," 1849.

shame. Now all is changed. He no longer stands amid the godless horde, silent and alone in His holiness, in His calm dignity, with spittle and blood covering His face. Universal adoration is His. He is acclaimed as the object of heaven's worship. Once patient in His agony, this is now the Lamb's supreme moment, when all are prostrate before Him.

Around the throne we have the redeemed of all ages, with angels forming the outer circle. Having taken the seven-sealed book, thus accepting authority and government, the Lamb is now worthy to receive every mark of distinction that it is possible to confer upon Him. He is praised for the perfection of attributes He can now manifest. (See Revelation 5:12; 7:12.)

1. *Power*: This is first named, for the Lamb is about to exercise power in its widest, most comprehensive character.

2. *Riches*: All wealth, whether material, moral, or physical, is His due. As the Lamb who gave His all, He claims our best.

3. *Wisdom*: This comes as the personification of divine wisdom, and, being made unto us wisdom, He will manifest highest wisdom when He comes to reign.

4. *Strength*: Here we have the quality that enables Him to carry out all He determines to do for His own and for the earth as He comes to reign.

5. *Honor*: As the Lamb, He died dishonored. Religious leaders caused Him to die as a felon on a wooden gibbet. Now deserved recognition is His.

6. *Glory*: He is also worthy to receive all public glory. Now the Lamb can be glorified with the glory He had with the Father in the dateless past.

7. *Blessing*: All forms and characteristics of blessedness or happiness are to be His. Full contentment will be the Lamb's.

What exaltation is His! The tide of praise gathers force and volume until the whole universe ascribes honor to the Lamb.

The Lamb is all the glory of Immanuel's land.[99]

---

99. Anne R. Cousin, "The Sands of Time Are Sinking," 1857.

THE LAMB AND HIS WRATH

John writes as an eyewitness of the act of the Lamb opening the seals containing the sore judgments of heaven for earth. The Lamb is related to the seals; the angels to the trumpets; and God to the bowls. In his gospel, John reminds us that God has given His Son the necessary authority to execute judgment (see John 5:27), and now in the Apocalypse, John depicts Christ as the Lamb about to exercise all governmental and civil authority. All must bow to Him when the great day of His wrath is come. (See Revelation 6:17.)

What a vivid emblem of terror the last section of chapter 6 presents! How staggering it is to read about *the wrath of the Lamb*" (Revelation 6:16). The Lamb! The One who is noted for meekness, gentleness, and patience now is swept along by a fearsome, righteous indignation. It is very seldom that a lamb gives way to anger or disturbed feelings. When it does, we are told it can become most ferocious. Thus will it be when the Lamb of God comes to execute judgment upon the godless of the earth. The outburst of His concentrated anger will be terrible in the extreme, causing the rebellious to seek shelter in caves. How grateful we should be that, because of the cleansing blood of the Lamb, we never need to bear the wrath of the Lamb!

Divine and satanic anger form another profitable study of Revelation. Not only does John speak of *the wrath of the Lamb*" (Revelation 6:16), but many times over we read of *the wrath of God*" (Revelation 14:10, 19; 15:1, 7; 16:1). God and Christ are one in their determination to rid the earth of all Beast worshipers. Such a scene, depicted in the fall of Babylon, fulfills the prophecies about *the day of vengeance*" (Isaiah 63:4; see also Matthew 25:31–46).

Then there is the great wrath of Satan. (See Revelation 12:12.) Exiled from his domain in the heavenlies, he realizes that his time is short and indulges in one final outburst of rage and destruction. That these will be terrible days when Satan is here in person can be gathered from John's warning *Woe to the inhabiters of the earth and of the sea*" (Revelation 12:12). Deposed as the prince of the power of the air, after his war with Michael and his angels, the devil will be more diabolical than ever.

THE LAMB AND HIS SOVEREIGNTY

Christ, as the Lamb, is often associated with a throne in this climactic book of the Bible. He is on a throne and also in the midst of a throne. (See Revelation 7:10, 17; 22:1.) The sacred head once crowned with sharp cactus thorns is to bear many a diadem. Rejected by earth, Christ is to rule over it. Regal glory is to be His. With all His sorrows and sacrifices past, the strength and security of the throne are the Lamb's.

Exercising all dominion and power from the midst of a throne, He is able to meet every need of His own, conquer all His foes, and dispense salvation in its most comprehensive sense to Jews and Gentiles alike. This is why the throne is the prominent object in the last part of the vision granted to John. The saints also are to reign with Him. They are to be sharers of His royalty.

It must not be forgotten that it is as the Lamb that Jesus Christ is to reign. Thus, when He climbed those bloody slopes leading to His cross, He secured more than deliverance from the penalty and power of sin. Certainly He died as the sinless substitute for sinners. But more than salvation was provided by His death. With it came His sovereign rights as the King of Kings. In a Messianic psalm, we read, *"Say among the nations, 'The LORD reigns'"* (Psalm 96:10 RSV). Some of the old versions of the Bible include an addition to this verse: "The Lord reigns *from the tree.*" From the tree! Ah, yes, those scars of the Lamb mean sovereignty as well as salvation. The Redeemer is to reign. In virtue of His cross, the slain Lamb will exercise His kingly prerogatives. Because of the tree, He is to have a throne. The royal diadem is to adorn the brow that cruel men crowned with thorns. Instead of a mock coronation, unsurpassed majesty will be His when, from *"the throne of God and of the Lamb"* (Revelation 22:3). He reigns in righteousness.

THE LAMB AND HIS REGISTER

While various registers are mentioned in Revelation, there are two specific references to the Lamb's roll call: *"The book of life of the Lamb"* (Revelation 13:8) and *"The Lamb's book of life"* (Revelation 21:27). This register contains the names of those who have been washed in the blood of the Lamb and inscribed in the sacred volume before the foundation of the world. (See Ephesians 1:4–5.) None of these names will ever be erased. Once we become the Lord's, we are His forevermore. "What God doeth is forever." It is different with the book about which we read in a previous chapter, *"I will not blot out his name out of the book of life"* (Revelation 3:5). This is a record of professors and possessors. All who make a Christian profession, true and false, make up this register. The true are those who have had their names written in the Book of Life from the foundation of the world. (See Revelation 17:8.) But in this particular register, the names of the unsaved do not appear, for this is the book of the redeemed. *"Whosoever was not found written in the book of life was cast into the lake of fire"* (Revelation 20:15). Only those whose names are written in the Lamb's Book of Life (see Revelation 21:27) are delivered from eternal separation from the Lamb, and enter into the eternal blessedness of the Holy City. Thus the question of paramount importance for each of us to face as we think of the Lamb's register is, Is my name written there?

Commenting on the solemn declaration of John, *"Whosoever was not found written in the book of life was cast into the lake of fire"* (Revelation 20:15), William R. Newell says:

Let us mark certain facts here:

1. It is not the absence of good works in the book that dooms a person. It is the absence of his *name*. Only names, not works, are in that book!

2. It is not the fact of evil works. Many of earth's greatest sinners have their names in the Book of Life.

3. All whose names do not appear in the Book, are cast into the lake of fire.

4. All names there found in that day, will have been written before that day. There is no record of anyone's name being written into the Book of Life upon that day, but rather the opposite: "If any was not found written." How overwhelmingly solemn is this![100]

100. William R. Newell, *Revelation Chapter-by-Chapter: A Classic Evangelical Commentary* (Grand Rapids, MI: Kregel Publications, 1994), 334.

THE LAMB AND HIS FIRSTFRUITS

Chapter 13 presents the false lamb and his followers, for whom there is nothing but doom. In chapter 14, John brings us to the true Lamb and His followers. By the mention of the number 144,000, we understand John to mean the spared Jewish remnant, the tribe particularized in chapter 7. These Israelites are loyal in their witness to God and the Lamb and are now publicly owned by heaven. Many of these Jews are depicted as sealing their testimony with their blood. Others are spared through the sorrows of the tribulation and share the seat of royalty. They pass from tyranny under the Beast to triumph with God. From the scene of suffering they go to the seat of sovereignty.

The divine estimate of these faithful followers of the Lamb is full of spiritual instruction for our own hearts. Apart from participation in the new song, they are described as walking in virgin purity. They were also obedient to the Lamb, following Him wherever He went, and that in spite of surrounding idolatry. Multitudes were giving their loyalty to the Beast, but this godly remnant gave the Lamb undivided heart affection. Theirs was a "magnificent obsession." We are also told that no guile was in their mouths, and that they were without fault before the divine tribunal. (See Revelation 14:6–8.) What a reputation to have! Beast worshipers, deluded by his false claims, believed a lie; but no lie was found in any mouth of this godly company. They acknowledged the Messiah to be the true Lamb, refusing to conform to the blasphemous edicts of the Beast.

No wonder these redeemed ones are spoken of as being *"the firstfruits unto God and to the Lamb"* (Revelation 14:4). Priority in time and blessing is theirs, and they form the earnest of a more glorious harvest. William R. Newell says of them:

> They are the "firstfruits" of the millennial reign. They connect the *dispensations*—somewhat as Noah did, who passed through the judgment of the flood into a new order of things. Therefore, the Lamb is seen standing on Mount Zion (*before He actually comes there*, as in Revelation 19 and Psalm 2), that with Him

may be seen this overcoming host, who will very shortly share His actual reign there.[101]

THE LAMB AND HIS VICTORY

What jubilant overcomers are before us in the issue of the war in heaven: "*They overcame him by the blood of the Lamb*" (Revelation 12:11)! Satan, as the prince of this world, heads up imperial powers on earth, just as he controls all evil spiritual powers as the prince of the power of the air. All saints, however, are victorious as they seek the shelter of the blood, representing as it does the empowering virtue of Christ's death and resurrection. The cross was Satan's Waterloo. Pleading that cross, we conquer him. We often sing about marching on to victory. Is it not true that we are marching on *from* victory, even the victory of Calvary? Deliverance from all diabolical machinations will be experienced by the devil-driven Jews as they plead the abiding efficacy of the blood. Along with this evidence of victory, we also see prophetic witness and willing martyrdom. Released from satanic oppression, the accused brethren rejoice. Are we among the singing victors?

Later on in Revelation, we see the victorious Lamb Himself: "*These shall make war with the Lamb, and the Lamb shall overcome them*" (Revelation 17:14). This conquest brings us to the final act of the Beast and his allies. The conflict between the Lamb and these satanically inspired forces is more fully described in chapter 19. But here, in chapter 17, the war is anticipated, and the victory is assured. The Lamb is the mighty conqueror, exercising all vested authority. As the Lion and the Lamb, He is to reign, combining tenderness and power. (See Revelation 5:5–6.) The victor of Calvary is to take the throne, and, when He does, earth's sin, sighs, sobs, and sorrows will cease. "*The LORD shall be king over all the earth*" (Zechariah 14:9). Inflexible righteousness will characterize His reign. There will be no more contention between right and wrong, truth and error, peace and war. "*He shall be a priest upon his throne*" (Zechariah 6:13). How glorious will be His reign as He manifests priestly grace and kingly authority! What ultimate triumph will be

---

101. *Revelation Chapter-by-Chapter: A Classic Evangelical Commentary.*

His! All His enemies will be routed, and His church will be entirely free from all blemish and the antagonism of sin and salvation.

THE LAMB AND HIS BRIDE

As we have several glimpses of the church under the figure of the bride, it may prove profitable to gather them together under this section. There are some who affirm that Israel, and not the church, is the bride. The Scriptures, however, are explicit in that Israel is the adulterous wife of Jehovah. Those who reject the church as the bride affirm that she cannot be the bride and the body at the same time. But why not? It is no more incongruous to think of the church as a bride and a body than it is to speak of Christ as the Priest and the Lamb. Yet He is both, is He not?

First of all, we have the marriage of the Lamb, which takes place in heaven amidst rapturous scenes of joy. (See Revelation 19:7, 9.) Here the bride is spoken of as the wife for the simple reason that as soon as a marriage is completed, the bride becomes the wife. "The 'bride' speaks of her deep place in the affection of the Bridegroom," says Walter Scott. "The 'wife' intimates the established relationship existing between the Bridegroom and the bride."

This celestial marriage precedes the assumption of the kingdom by the Lord. Because of the relationship existing between the Bridegroom and the bride, the latter is to share the former's glory and reign with Him while occupying her special place in His heart's deep love. In Revelation 21:9, the bride, as a city, is shown to Israel in her millennial glory. The church is the city of millennial and eternal days. A city represents an organized system of social life, united interests, and activity of government, all of which the church will experience.

The bridal robes of the wife (see Revelation 19:8) are in sharp contrast to the gorgeous attire of the harlot (see Revelation 17:4). The glorious clothes of the bride speak of character, of a righteousness provided and practiced. The deeds of the bride are appraised at their true value in heaven. The bride, clothed in pure white linen, as beautiful as her trousseau will be, will not eye her garments but "her dear Bridegroom's face."[102]

---

102. "The Sands of Time Are Sinking."

The guests are distinguished as friends of the Bridegroom (see Revelation 19:9), of whom John the Baptist will be the most honored one (see John 3:29). All saints not incorporated within the church will be among the invited guests to the marriage of the Lamb.

Presently, the Spirit and the bride are united in their desire for the Lamb to return. (See Revelation 22:17.) It is not merely the Spirit *in* the bride crying, "Come!" Both cry as one. The Lamb will appear as the Bright and Morning Star when He comes to claim His bride. For Israel, He will appear as the Sun of Righteousness in all His noonday splendor. No one can meditate upon the revelation granted to John without realizing something of the glorious heritage awaiting both the church and Israel.

THE LAMB AND HIS SONG

Two songs are united since they both celebrate redemption—one, redemption by power; the other, by blood. *"They sing the song of Moses the servant of God, and the song of the Lamb"* (Revelation 15:3). The first song celebrates the marvelous deliverance that God gave to Israel at the Red Sea. The second song magnifies the Lamb for the redemption that He provided from sin's guilt and government. The one was an earthly redemption; the other is a spiritual redemption. The song of Moses speaks of triumph over the power of evil by divine judgment. The song of the Lamb is taken up with the exaltation of the rejected Messiah. It is the song of the faithful remnant, sung in the midst of the unfaithful, apostate Israel; it is the song of martyred victors.

The theme of the song is the Holy One of Israel. What a tower of strength we have in the combination of titles given. (See Revelation 15:3–4.) He is great and marvelous; just and true and holy. He is the King not only of the saints but of the nations. When the Lamb appears on the earth, it will be as the Sovereign of His redeemed ones of Israel and of all the nations of the earth.

> *Who would not fear thee, O King of nations? for to thee doth it appertain: forasmuch as among all the wise men of the nations, and in all their kingdoms, there is none like unto thee.* (Jeremiah 10:7)

What a day that will be when the Lamb is lauded as the world emperor! What a relief for our blood-soaked earth it will be when, with Satan imprisoned in the pit, Christ takes the throne as King of the nations! Are you not grateful that, having the assurance of having been washed in the blood of the Lamb, yours will be the joyful privilege of joining in the glorious "Hallelujah Song" as Christ takes the throne?

The last reference to the Lamb in the Lamb-exalting book of Revelation is in its concluding chapter, which says that the servants of the Lamb will serve Him. (See Revelation 22:3.) Note what all lovers of the Lamb are found doing:

+ *They serve Him.* (See Revelation 22:3.) We are not to idle eternity away playing harps. Highest and holiest service will be ours.

+ *They see Him.* (See Revelation 22:4.) What soul-thrilling rapture will be ours we we see His face and eternally to behold it!

+ *They bear His name.* (See Revelation 22:4.) This means that we are to reflect His character. *"In their foreheads"* implies in the place easily seen.

+ *They bask in His light.* (See Revelation 22:5.) Natural and artificial illumination will no longer be necessary. The Lamb will be the Light of our world.

+ *They have His eternal provision and guardianship.* (See Revelation 7:16–17.) The enthroned Lamb is to feed and lead His own forever. Through all eternity, He will shepherd and protect His followers.

Through the ageless future, we will not be able to repay Him. We will be the Lamb's dear debtors forever. He will be our Guide and glory in Immanuel's land.

ABOUT THE AUTHOR

When Dr. Herbert Lockyer (1886–1984) was first deciding on a career, he considered becoming an actor. Tall and well-spoken, he seemed a natural for the theater. But the Lord had something better in mind. Instead of the stage, God called Herbert to the pulpit, where, as a pastor, a Bible teacher, and the author of more than fifty books, he touched the hearts and lives of millions of people.

Dr. Lockyer held pastorates in Scotland and England for twenty-five years. As pastor of Leeds Road Baptist Church in Bradford, England, he became a leader in the Keswick Higher Life Movement, which emphasized the significance of living in the fullness of the Holy Spirit. This led to an invitation to speak at the Moody Bible Institute's fiftieth anniversary in 1936. His warm reception at that event led to his ministry in the United States. He received honorary degrees from both the Northwestern Evangelical Seminary and the International Academy of London.

In 1955, he returned to England, where he lived for many years. He then returned to the United States, where he spent the final years of his life in Colorado Springs, Colorado, with his son, the Rev. Herbert Lockyer Jr., a Presbyterian minister who eventually became his editor.